Single Set of Bootprints

A story of a God-made *Green Beret*

John & Julie,

    God bless you both. You have been such a blessing to our family.

Kirby Calhoun

K. ⎯

De Oppresso Liber

ISBN 978-1-64349-083-0 (paperback)
ISBN 978-1-64349-084-7 (digital)

Christian Faith Publishing, Inc.
832 Park Avenue
Meadville, PA 16335
www.christianfaithpublishing.com

Printed in the United States of America

Contents

Introduction..7

Childhood..11

    Retrospective...24

Seeing Ghosts...28

    Retrospective...29

Enlisting in the Army...31

    Retrospective...33

Basic Training..35

    Retrospective...39

Advanced Individual Training—Human Intelligence Collector 42

    Retrospective...47

Third Infantry Division...49

    Retrospective...54

Kuwait 57

    Retrospective...59

Iraq 61

    Retrospective...80

WLC/Air Assault School 84

    Retrospective...88

Before Selection..90

    Retrospective...94

Special Forces Assessment and Selection 96

    Retrospective...110

After Selection...113

    Retrospective...116

Airborne School 118

    Retrospective...122

WLC/BLC 124

    Retrospective...131

Language Training..134

    Retrospective...138

The Gates...141

    Retrospective...146

Second Chance at Land Navigation..............................149

    Retrospective...155

Small-Unit Tactics—Squad-Level Training 167

    Retrospective...179

Small-Unit Tactics—Platoon-Level Training................182

    Retrospective...197

SERE School with Retrospective 201

Communications Training..204

    Retrospective...208

Robin Sage 209

    Retrospective...214

Graduation and Language Training 217

    Retrospective...222

First Impressions 225

    Retrospective...234

Afghanistan 236

    Retrospective...252

Pre-Scuba 256

    Retrospective...265

ODA 7112..267

    Retrospective...272

Team Training 274

    Retrospective...279

Colombia 283

    Retrospective...290

Getting Out 292

    Retrospective...296

Turning Point..300

    Retrospective...307

Conclusion..311

Introduction

"Do you not know? Have you not heard? The
everlasting God, the Lord, the Creator of the ends
of the earth does not become weary or tired. His
understanding is inscrutable. He gives strength
to the weary, and to him who lacks might He
increases power. Though youths grow weary and
tired, and vigorous young men stumble badly,
yet those who wait for the Lord will gain new
strength; they will mount up with wings like
eagles, they will run and not get tired, they will
not walk and not become weary."
—Isaiah 40:28–31

This book is structured with main chapters followed by mini retrospective chapters. When I wrote this book, I wrote the entire book's
main chapters first. I tried to capture, to the best of my ability, how
I felt and thought during each time frame I was writing about, first.
Then, once I completed the main chapters, I went back through
and wrote the retrospective chapters based on how I view my life
after having read the Bible. In the main chapters, you will see that I
credited my successes to luck and my own abilities. The truth, within
the retrospective chapters, is that everything I was able to accomplish
and endure was in spite of my inabilities, and all thanks to God
alone. Once I knew God was real, I looked back at my life to understand where God had been all along. I found that He was always with
me, and this book illustrates how I connected the dots of God's work
in my life. Throughout my life, I reached the end of my capabilities,

over and over again; but when I would reach the end of myself without giving up, Jesus would carry me the rest of the way.

I have come to learn that God does not make mistakes, but we do. God is always in control, even and especially when we aren't aware of His plan. Rarely can I see and understand the possible "why" behind events that take place while they are happening. Once I am far enough removed from the emotional clouding that I experience in the moment, I find that I can more easily see God's blessings in my life.

I have also come to learn that there are forces in this world that do not want us to fulfill the purposes that God has called us for. I now know that the battles and difficult situations we face in our lives can be directly related to the battles being fought in the heavenly realm. If we will just keep walking in faith and not quit when times are hard, good will prevail and God's blessings will be poured out on us.

I am just a normal guy who has endured some extreme circumstances. This book is, mostly, a chronological account of the events that took place throughout my life. I have faced many attacks from the devil. This book will give you a glimpse into some of the attacks I have endured and how God ultimately protected me from or helped me to overcome those attacks.

I felt called to write this book, and I believe it's because there is at least one person who needs to hear a story like mine. I pray that me finding God's thread in my own life will help someone else to identify the thread of God's work in his or her own life.

I humbly ask one favor of you, the reader, as you read this book. If you become overwhelmed with emotion—whether on behalf of someone in my story, or because my story hits a sore spot deep within your soul—that you pray to God before continuing. We should always take a minute to embrace the feelings of sadness and loss in the world, because wherever there is sadness and loss, there is room for Jesus. Prayer is how we communicate with our Lord, and if you feel saddened or angered by any story of mine, pray to God, for He is the only true Healer.

Many of the men mentioned in this book are actively still fighting terrorism and placing themselves in harm's way so that we can enjoy our American way of life. I am intentionally only using first names or nicknames for all personnel still working on behalf of American interests for their own safety and privacy. MSG George Vera, you have been and will always be an inspiration to me; your sacrifice for our country will never be forgotten. I am honored to know an American hero like you. There are a few who have passed on into God's presence. 1SG Andrew McKenna, you will never be forgotten and your story will inspire future Green Berets for decades. SSG Raul Guerra, SGT Clint Loughmiller, and SFC Wil Cumbie, your stories will forever live on in my memory.

I want to inform you that this entire book was written from memory. I had no intention of writing a book when I was going through these events, and therefore there may be minor details or time sequences that are slightly off because of the time that has passed since the events. These stories and how they affected me are my best attempt at laying my soul out for all to see, so that Jesus may receive all the glory for what He did in my life.

Lastly, I want to thank and dedicate this book to the three most important women in my life. My grandmother, my mother, and my wife have been the foundation for my success. I know it was only the intercessory prayers my grandmother, mother, and Holy Spirit prayed on my behalf that enabled me to survive and write this book. My wife has been the best partner a man could ask for, and nothing in this book would have been possible without her in my life.

Childhood

In September of 1999, my family was driving home from a shopping trip in Germany and we were involved in a horrific car accident. We were a military family stationed in Germany. I was young at the time, and even though I have a vague recollection of what happened, I asked my dad to send me a synopsis of the events that transpired, and this is what he sent me.

> Kirby,
>
> I remember the crash very clearly—and not for good reasons. It was raining and cold as the weather often is during September (I know it was September because the Octoberfest was starting). It was a Saturday, and we decided to drive to Garmisch, Germany, to go to the PX (Post Exchange) and their commissary. We spent a few hours and began the drive back. The roads were narrow and wet—and it was slightly foggy. We were near a town called Mirnau, a very beautiful and old town. You boys were reading or playing with your Gameboys. Your mom was reading for the most part. But at some point we began talking about money. She mentioned that she wanted me to apply for Warrant Officer School and I told her that I wanted no part of it. She reminded me that the money would be better (which it would have been). Shortly after this conversation, a panel van coming from the opposite direction swerved directly in front of us. An

Italian citizen drove the van. We were driving approximately 60 miles per hour; he was driving a little slower due to traffic. He had fallen asleep. There was no time for me to react because it happened within a second or two. We hit him directly head-on. The force of the impact drove our engine under our car. We had front bucket seats. My seat completely ripped out because I had my leg and foot straight out in front of me on the break. It twisted your mom's seat around 45 degrees. The car behind us hit us so hard that it set off the road flare we had in the trunk. The impact was so great that it dented the cans of food we had bought from the commissary that were in the trunk. I still remember my very first thought after the impact. I said to myself: "That wasn't so bad." I don't know why I thought that because it was actually quite horrible. I looked around, and your mom was pretty much unconscious. I didn't see any blood, but I realized she was hurt really badly. My first act was to crawl out the window. Before I jumped down, I didn't know that I'd broken a small bone in my ankle. When I landed, I fell down. I got up, and people were standing all around. I looked in the back seat at you boys, and you were completely ashen—you were both in shock. I still remember that most people stood around very quietly, but a man came to assist—he was German, and a doctor. He, a few others, and I helped get you boys and your mom out of the car. It got kind of blurry after that—I think I went into shock. I think there were two ambulances—they took your mom first. They took the three of us together. You guys had severe bruises from the seat belts. Your mom had a burst gallbladder, and every one of her ribs had been broken. She spent a lot of time in intensive care. The three of us stayed in a room together for a day or two. I think I called Roger Bauer and/or Kelly Denton. They were down there within a few hours. I can't remember how long your mom was in the hospital, but it was awhile. You boys seemed to have handled it pretty well—I think because the people at the hospital were very nice. I do remember one other thing: one of the ambulance drivers stopped by to see us. He said he couldn't believe that we survived the crash. He said the first thing he was told was not to expect survivors. So some could say that we had a very bad day. Others would say that it was a miracle because we all survived.

—Dad

When I asked my mom for her version of the story, she told me the same things, minus a few details because of her medical state at the time. She remembers me throwing up red vomit and seeing the doctors become alarmed, because they didn't know I had been drinking a red slushy when the accident occurred. It was only after a few brief moments of panic that the doctors were informed by one of the bilingual nurses at that hospital why my vomit was red.

I remember a few things definitively, working backwards. The first was while we were in the hospital room. One of the doctors came to tell my dad that less than an hour prior to our accident an eerily similar accident had occurred in an area very near where ours did. In that accident, the single driver of another van and an entire family, just like ours, in the other vehicle—collided, and all five were killed on impact. The second memory was that we had Twinkies in the trunk of the car. I remember thinking to myself while I was in the hospital that we should go get the Twinkies; so my brother and I could have some good American junk food. The third thing I remember seeing, at the scene of the accident, was the paramedics ripping my mom's shirt open from the front and watching them give her CPR. Watching that led me to believe she had died. The last thing I remember was that my little brother's crying brought me back to consciousness while in the back seat of the car. When I opened my eyes, the first thing I saw was a strange German man clearing out the broken glass from my window to help get me out of the car. As he pulled me out, I noticed how high up the hilly terrain was that we were on. We weren't far from the cliff's edge, after all of the vehicle collisions had ceased. It wasn't until years later that I began to comprehend how close we had all come to dying, and how blessed my entire family was to have been protected by God in that accident-prone section of mountains.

Unfortunately, the car accident wasn't the first time I came under physical and spiritual attack. It was only four years earlier, in 1995, when the first tragedy struck. I was only nine years old, and we were visiting my dad's family in a country town in deep Georgia. Everyone was out on the porch drinking iced tea, except my uncle and me. I had only met him once or twice, I believe, at that time. He was a teenager, and I thought he was "cool" because his behavior mimicked a child. I wanted to play with his video games, and for a few hours we spent time like any ideal uncle-nephew combo. But when the whole family went outside to sit on the porch, he and I did remain inside. After a few moments of silence in the house, he told me that I could play all the video games I wanted if I would play a game with him, which I had to keep secret. By this time, I trusted him completely, and because of that trust, he bent me over a bed in one of the rooms in my grandparents' house and sexually molested me. The next thing I know, he was pulling his pants up and he was telling me not to tell anyone before walking away. I remember feeling numb during the penetration, almost like I was somewhere else while it was happening. I don't remember much of the actual act—thanks be to God, because I don't think my childish brain was meant to handle that type of sin.

While I was a kid I would never have admitted that this event affected me at all. I will confess that I thought about it often, and it scarred me. I only feel it necessary to give you a little insight so that you can understand how drastically different I would become, and how I came to view the world in the way that I did. To be honest, I can say that I put the molestation out of my mind as a coping mechanism. I remember the visit correlating with us getting military orders back to Germany where I would attend elementary school. We were at my grandparents' house trying to visit family before we left.

One night, maybe two or three months later, I was unable to control my thoughts and was forced to relive the moment more vividly. I realized then that my uncle wasn't like normal people. I remember coming out of my bedroom that night, in our three-bedroom apartment in military housing in Augsburg, Germany. I sat my parents down at the table and told them the entire story, sobbing uncontrollably the entire time. I knew that my telling them wouldn't change what happened, but I was not able to be silent anymore. Now, as a kid, it's hard to understand why parents do the things they do; and even though I had established a pattern of lying, fibbing, and bending the truth (as most kids do), I expected them to believe this story of mine. I found out years later that my mom wrote him a letter, letting him know what I accused him of and that she hoped it wasn't true. He never responded. When being stationed overseas, it was a much longer process to communicate with family because the Internet was slowly being established but mail was still the main means of communication. My viewpoint on family relationships changed after that as did my willingness to rely on family to help deal with trauma and stress.

I never again allowed that memory to come into focus and would do everything and anything to make sure it stayed gone. Fast-forward almost twenty years, and there I was getting my post-military psychological evaluation. Here was this balding, short man with glasses asking me about my service in Iraq, Afghanistan, and Colombia. Then suddenly, out of left field, he asked me if I had ever been the victim of a sexual assault. I wanted so badly to lie and to tell this grown man that I, me, a Green Beret, would never allow something like that to happen, but I couldn't. Instead I bowed my head in shame and cried, telling this stranger something that I hadn't talked about in almost two decades. I understood he was evaluating my mental stability and my ability to fit in with normal people. Even now I wonder if and how my life changed because I couldn't self-diagnose the issues I had.

Back to 2001, I remember it like it was yesterday, less than two years after the car accident. I was fourteen years old and a thriving teenager. Maybe two weeks prior to the 9/11 radical Islamic terrorist attacks on the twin towers, the Pentagon, and a thwarted attempt to target the white house, I was uprooting my life because my parents were getting a divorce. I was living in Darmstadt, Germany, at that time on a military housing installation, alongside many other children fortunate enough to have grown up experiencing the world from a unique perspective: one of a military dependent. I hated traveling as a kid. I didn't care about the Eiffel Tower, the Leaning Tower of Pisa, or any other famous architecture or piece of art.

I once walked under the Arc de Triumph with no feeling of grandeur or historical bond. I was just a kid seeing things without any understanding of their significance. I was too attached to my Game Boy and Cassette Walkman to care about the Coliseum in Rome. I did not grasp that I was looking at an arena that defied its time with popularity. The history and death related to that arena is something many have been entertained by, thanks to Hollywood. In reality, nobody can truly appreciate the horrific nature of that time period. It is nearly impossible for us to imagine being thrown into a kill or be killed environment, for sport and against our will.

While I didn't appreciate traveling as a kid, I am now very grateful for those experiences—all thanks to my mom. My mom is one of the best people I have ever had the privilege of knowing. She used to drag me (and when I was older, my younger brothers as well) all over Europe to see the gorgeous scenery and take in the history.

During some of our trips, we visited different concentration camps throughout Europe. I can still remember in vivid detail the Dachau Camp. I remember seeing the ovens—directly outside of a shower room—where Jews were forced in naked, gassed to death, and then burned. The ash is said to have been so thick at times, with Jewish bodies, that the ash was often mistaken for snow by new detainees in the camps. The walls in the showers were made of cement bricks and had scratch marks in them from human hands.

As people were dying, they literally lost fingernails trying to claw through the walls before succumbing to their deaths. The image of these showers, and the feeling that I got while walking on the ground where millions were forced to die atrocious deaths, remains with me to this very day. At the time, though, I was still just a kid. I didn't really have any knowledge or perspective for the things I was seeing and feeling.

During my freshman year of high school in Wiesbaden, Germany, my mom surprised me in the worst of ways by telling me that I would be flying to Wisconsin within a week. I would be living with my grandparents until my mom and brothers could join me there. She wanted to make sure that I started school on time. I had attitude and discipline problems as a child, so my mom was willing to work three jobs to put me into a Catholic private school that put God first and foremost. I would be attending Pacelli, in Stevens Point, Wisconsin. My mother knew it was a great school, being an alumna of theirs, and she told me I would do just fine until she got there.

Now, up until this point, I had not seen my grandparents very much, and the idea was both exciting and extremely hurtful. I felt at that time like I was the only one who was suffering from this divorce, because I was the only one on a plane. I remember thinking particularly about a girl who had just moved into our neighborhood and whom I was really into before having to tell her goodbye. I was so upset that it was my life being destroyed and (from my view) nobody else's was. That plane ride to the United States was extremely long and stressful, because I was full of anger and contempt and I wanted to lash out at the entire world.

A couple of weeks after school started, on September 11, 2001, I remember eating breakfast and watching the news before heading to school. On the news I saw that a plane had smashed into the World Trade Center. While I had no clue what the importance of that building was, I knew those were Americans who were dying. Shortly after, a second plane struck the second tower. That time I knew we had been attacked. I walked to school that morning feeling numb. I didn't know why I was feeling the way I was, but I felt as if something that I loved had just been hurt or broken. Of course, as we all know, more attacks took place and too many innocent people were killed in those cowardly attacks conducted by evil men.

During these high school years of my life, I have to admit, much of it is fuzzy because I was high and drunk often. I wasn't the best kid in any aspect or way. I used to make up ingenious methods of vandalizing Pacelli and breaking their rules. I used to take ketchup packets and throw them at hard-to-reach surface areas in the school hallways, just so that it would be difficult to clean. I was a little punk with no respect for others. One time I took my belt off and whipped a kid one year younger than me for being a little punk, right in front of the security cameras near the main gymnasium doors. I drove my car on their softball fields, and I argued religion with Catholic priests in class so argumentatively I would oftentimes be asked to leave the classroom. I quite literally had a desk in the front office. That desk was so frequently visited by me that I had etched my name into it, and until the day I left that school I never once saw anyone else ever sit in it.

I played in the band in middle school, while I was in Germany. I liked band, and it was because of this that I signed up for band while attending Pacelli. I only went to Pacelli for approximately two years, but it was during my sophomore year that my life would change. During that year our band class was going to New York City to participate in a music symposium with other high school bands from across the country. While we were in New York, we all ate delicious New York–style pizzas, which are still among the best I've eaten. Although the Statue of Liberty is a sight that one simply can't forget, I distinctly remember going there because I haggled with a street vendor in the courtyard adjacent to the ferryboat lines over fake Oakley sunglasses and fake Rolex watches. For what it is worth, I definitely won the negotiation and saved an additional five dollars on what I was told was an original Rolex watch.

The hall where the different high school bands gathered was crowded with fold-up chairs and tables, as we all rotated through our routines. It was after this that we drove to a parking location, dismounted our bus, and walked to Ground Zero. I remember feeling emotions that as a child I wasn't familiar with and was extremely saddened by. The two towers used to stand merely two hundred meters from where I was standing. I was trying to peer through a privatized chain-link fence among the twenty or so Americans standing around the memorial wall, in a vain attempt to see what the ground looked like and how bad the damage was. I remember seeing smoke rising from the ground, more than a year after the attacks.

I would be lying if I told you I understood what happened to me at that site when it happened. I knew that my life would be different after I left there. I knew in that moment that good people were meant to stand in the way of evil. At that time I weighed no more than 120 pounds. I would not have believed that I would have anything to do with America's response to 9/11, but I think my sense of patriotism firmly rooted itself while I was at Ground Zero. I would like to note that for no particular reason known to me, my desire to remain in band was gone after this trip.

Unfortunately for my mother and me, my behavioral issues progressed until eventually I was no longer welcome at Pacelli, and my mother withdrew me from the school before they were able to expel me. I then transitioned to, Stevens Point Area Senior High School (SPASH), the nearest public school. My disciplinary issues got even worse while I was in public school. I had such bottled-up anger and hate for the world, but I loved anything that could get my adrenaline pumping. Fighting, racing cars, using drugs, and drinking alcohol—those were the things I did to fill the void in my life.

Most of my friends during that time attended Pacelli, but I did have a few friends that attended SPASH. Kevin attended SPASH with me, but I knew him through mutual friends while I was still going to Pacelli. I remember when Kevin and I started hanging out together. We liked the same stuff, were down for whatever, and always had each other's backs. Kevin and I used to smoke weed all the time, because when we did that we didn't feel the need to go out and get wild. We just wanted a place that was clean and safe to hang with friends—a place where we could smoke and watch TV or play Halo on Xbox.

I used to try hiding the weed-smoking from my grandparents and my mom, but I always knew that they knew. I just didn't care and worried about the one and only me. I used to listen to Eminem and would often freestyle while enjoying a smoke session with my boys. My favorite music group was always D12. I used to listen to D12 every day on the way in to school, just to prime up for the day, never knowing what was going to happen. Music was a huge coping mechanism for me, but it did me zero favors when I needed help addressing the real issues at hand.

The day that my poor choices finally caught up to me was a cold and rainy night. Kevin and I had just picked up some alcohol and were headed back to my house to drink. I'll never forget that the speed limit on the road we were driving on was forty-five miles per hour and we were making a very sharp left-hand turn. We had slowed down to around thirty miles per hour to make that sharp turn. A very "cheery" police officer saw us making the turn just as the light turned yellow, a fact that would end up being very important. He flipped his lights on and got behind us. I remember seething, because I knew we had not violated any traffic laws that would warrant his pulling us over.

He pulled us out of the car and found liquor, weed, a glass pipe to smoke it out of, and a pack of cigarettes—nothing felony level, but it was enough to put us in a predicament. I remember him getting in my face—his breath reeked of coffee and made me want to gag—telling me he knew we messed up big time and that if we didn't start talking he would make us pay. It was around this time that about two or three more police cruisers showed up for the party...and the shark attacks began. I had three officers circling me, while I was in handcuffs, freezing my ass off (it was winter in Wisconsin and the sun had set). The officers were yelling at me and telling me that if I didn't tell them where we got the weed and booze, we were going to jail. I was so proud of this moment because I was truly prepared to go to jail instead of ratting; it just wasn't going to happen. At this point in my life, I was willing to take risks that I wouldn't dare take today.

I told the police officers in a very respectful voice, "We were pulled over illegally, sir. We wouldn't have had the time to stop; we were already across the line." I remember hearing a "Shut the fuck up and don't lie to me." Which I responded to by saying, "I know we were in the right. I am willing to take my chances. Either arrest and book me, or let me go, either way I'm done here."

My responses obviously didn't go over very well for me. After approximately two more minutes of the officers yelling at me, they moved on to Kevin. I don't remember being able to hear everything he said, but I distinctly remember at one time hearing Kevin say over their voices, "Everything he said goes for me too," while he was pointing his finger at me.

The officers confiscated the contraband, and we ended up with a court date. I remember praying that night to God, and asking Him to find a way to help me through this. It really affected my mother and what I felt her view of me was. I had long since been a thorn everywhere she stepped, but she never wavered in her love for me. I don't even remember her being very upset when she found out what happened. She had come to expect such shenanigans from me and was primarily concerned with how we would be able to afford another citation. Things for me changed that day. I felt different somehow. I had been forced to go to Catholic mass since I was a baby. I knew about God, but I didn't know Him. I was a kid with three or four things on the mind all the time, just like every other boy in the world, and church was never one of them.

I remember the day of my court hearing. I was in my small bedroom, living with my grandparents still. I was looking at myself in the mirror, trying to remember the proper way to put a tie on. The telephone rang, and when I answered the call my public defender asked for me by name. I identified myself, and she proceeded to tell me that they had thrown out the citation. The officer's statement, my statement, the officer's history with teenagers, and evidence brought forward about the timing of the traffic light all pointed to the con- clusion that we were wrongly pulled over. My lawyer told me to relax. My fight was over and I never even had to step foot in the courtroom.

I remember the feeling I had, the high that I felt—like getting away with something you know you were guilty of (smoking weed and drinking alcohol) unscathed. I immediately called Kevin and told him that we were okay and the case was thrown out. We cele- brated soon after that with a bowl of weed and a good laugh.

I remember going to my room and asking myself out loud, "Was this Your will, God? Did You answer my prayer?" I will never forget the peace I had that night. I woke up the next morning and just felt different from the day before. I quit smoking cigarettes cold turkey that day, and I quit smoking weed shortly after. My grades came up when I stopped skipping class, and I actually began to appreciate all that I had.

Within a few months, I decided I would eventually join the military. I wanted to use my mind to fight terrorism as an intelligence collector. I felt like my moral standards had risen several levels, and I became somewhat aware of the purpose, or reason, for my existence. I started running daily. I started studying for the ASVAB (Armed Services Vocational Aptitude Battery) test, and drank cranberry juice like nobody's business, hoping to have the marijuana out of my system in time for the drug screening. I also took this time to eat as much peanut butter as you can imagine a kid eating and washing it down with malted milkshakes that my grandma always made for me. I was too skinny, during this time; I was actually five pounds under the Army minimum standard and had to intake calories nonstop to be able to enlist.

I was nearing the end of my senior year of high school, and even though I was starting to straighten out my life, I wasn't going to be able to turn everything around enough to walk for graduation. There were consequences to my actions and behavior. I skipped so many classes that I had paid two misdemeanor citations for truancy throughout that school year. I played this off with my friends at the time like it was somehow cool that I wasn't walking. In reality, it hurt and made me feel inadequate, because I failed a gym class. Yep, a gym class. No, not because I wasn't good at gym class, but because of my lack of attendance. I loved that class, until the scuba education started, where we would be learning how to use scuba gear in our school pool. I have always had a deep fear of being submerged in water, especially water that is cold or has animals that can eat me. Well, this class was the last class of the day for me, and this was Wisconsin. It was in the winter, and I walked home from school each day. I respectfully told the teacher that getting in water before walking home wasn't smart, and I wouldn't do it. She pointed to the door, and that was that. I would end up making this elective class up at summer school directly following my class's graduation, with soon-to-be sophomores trying to knock out credits early so that they could get ahead of their classmates.

Retrospective

"And we know that God causes all things to work together for good to those who love God, to those who are called to His purpose."
—Romans 8:28

I felt I was so quickly ripped from my home, family, friends, and life in Germany, without much notice. I was enrolled in a strict Catholic private school, where I rebelled in every way I could think of, before having to be withdrawn to escape expulsion. I made new friends and developed stereotypical bad teenager habits. I started smoking and drinking to cope and relax. I allowed myself to get into a situation with the law that could have taken my future out of my own hands.

That's what I could see and understand about my life at that time. Anyone can read or hear my story and come to that same understanding.

By now you may be wondering why in the world I am telling you this backstory that seemingly has no relevance to the story, right? I am trying to adequately portray the lifestyle that I was living. I want to be clear about the road I was traveling down as a teenager. By the grace of God I was able to make something out of my life, but I didn't have a stellar beginning. I don't want anyone to think that because of their past, the decisions they have made, or the situation they are in, that there is any less hope for them and their futures. It doesn't matter what our beginnings look like, God can turn anything around for our good and His Glory.

I lied to people that loved me. I stole money out of my mom's sock drawer, for weed, knowing very well that she was financially stressed. I lived with my grandparents throughout high school, which felt constricting to me at the time. I felt so bad for myself, pitiful even. I remember the few times I flirted with suicidal thoughts. The darkness that was so easily enveloping me made me feel like I was alone. I felt as though I couldn't do this anymore. I never attempted suicide. Although, I once used a grand gesture with a knife that freaked my mom and grandmother out. Other than that one incident, I mostly just had depressing thoughts that I never let settle down permanently. We can struggle, even as kids, but we can't let that define who we become. You are not alone and there is hope in Jesus!

It took years, intercessory prayers from my family and the Holy Spirit, an awakening of my spirit, reading the Word of God, and retrospectively looking back on my life, for me to see my life from any other perspective. Thanks be to God, all those things took place, and now I can tell my story differently.

While my family was under spiritual attack, I was brought back to the United States just before the September 11 attacks. When I was watching the news that morning, it was the first time I felt sorrow and a stirring in my spirit for our fallen and a deep desire to make sure nothing like this happened again. I believe it made a difference that I viewed these acts of violence against our country from our soil. I was surrounded by fellow Americans who felt the way I felt. I don't know if seeing these attacks would have hit me the same, if I were still in Germany.

Rarely is a family breaking up viewed as a positive event, and this isn't an exception to that rule; however, I was instantly put into a God-fearing home of devout believers and servants for our Lord Jesus Christ. My grandparents were gifts from God during that time in my life, even though I could not see it then. God worked this situation for my good and His glory, as He does all things. There were a few huge changes that took place within me while I lived there. Those changes might have seemed small to my family at the time or might have gone unnoticed altogether. But today, sixteen years later, those changes made every difference in the path I chose for my life.

I joined band in Pacelli because it was something familiar from my middle-school years. Joining band in Pacelli brought me to Ground Zero in New York City a year after the 9/11 attacks. Ground

Zero was where I was shaken to my core. I am not left wondering why my desire to remain in band fell away after that life-altering trip to New York. I believe my participation in band may have been just to get me on that trip.

Bad decisions, behaviors, and habits got the best of me, but even during those times, I had friends who prevented me from feeling isolated as I so easily could have. My friends might not have been trying to straighten my path, but they were exactly what I needed at that time in my life, and none of them prevented me from pursuing the next phase of my life. To this day, I don't know what I would have done without Kevin's friendship. Military brats would be the first to tell you it's hard to maintain friendships with the frequency of moving from one place to another. When I finally made a "permanent" friend, someone who was just like me, it felt great.

I am not proud of how I handled the situation with the law enforcement officers. I may not have been speeding, but I was in the wrong in so many ways. I was a punk, and my priorities were all messed up. My number one priority was not "ratting" anyone out, and I was willing to accept whatever that meant for my future. The poor decisions that I made that night could have cost me dearly. God alone got me out of the bind that I had put myself in.

My dealings with the law miraculously all worked out in my favor, and I was free to follow the purpose that God had placed in my heart. I will admit that at that time, I did not know I would be following God's call for my life. I only knew that I felt called to serve a greater purpose and to do something with this second chance I had been given.

I look back now on my time spent in summer school gym as a blessing in disguise. I was fortunate to enjoy three additional months with my grandparents, whom I had come to greatly love and appreciate the nearer to graduation I got. I will never be able to tell them how much their love meant to me in words that would properly portray the emotions. My grandfather has since gone home to be with the Lord, but to this day, my grandmother prays for me daily. I have felt her prayers since the day I left her house.

The hardest thing some of us can ever be asked to do is to forgive someone of something they did. When I was just a child and sexually molested by my uncle, I allowed myself to ignore the pain that it actually inflicted. In the ten years of my active duty military service, I even went to visit him three or four times. I never once mentioned what he did. The last time I saw him was in June or July of 2017, when I drove to his house and told him to his face that I forgave him for what he did to me. I told him that I may have to forgive him many more times before it gets any easier, but that I would always forgive him in the end. If Jesus can forgive me of my sins, who am I to judge someone else for theirs? God is the only righteous judge. Even though I have found it in my heart to forgive my uncle, I have made it quite clear that his actions have cost him a relationship with my children.

Actions have consequences, but to hold hatred within ourselves denies Jesus the proper place in our hearts. It took me two decades to learn this, but when Jesus removed this yoke from around my neck, which I had carried for twenty years, I felt truly free. It was almost like realizing I could breathe again and that I had been breathing as if I had a cloth over my face, not knowing about the cloth until I had been freed from it. I felt a weight fall from my shoulders as I forgave my uncle for sexually molesting me. I won't ever allow that sin to weigh me down again.

> "For if you forgive others for their transgressions, your heavenly Father will also forgive you. But if you do not forgive others, then your Father will not forgive your transgressions." (Matthew 6:14-15)
>
> "Do not judge, and you will not be judged; and do not condemn, and you will not be condemned; pardon, and you will be pardoned." (Luke 6:37)
>
> For we know Him who said, "VENGEANCE IS MINE, I WILL REPAY." And again, "THE LORD WILL JUDGE HIS PEOPLE." (Hebrews 10:30)

Seeing Ghosts

Now, before you move on to the next chapter, I'm going to share a story with you that again helped to shape my beliefs and thoughts toward the supernatural. I want to say that I was a sophomore in high school at the time, possibly a junior. My friend Tony and I were watching TV in my grandma's basement. We were just hanging out, when we both saw something that I can't explain to this day. I remember knowing exactly what I saw, but I wouldn't say a word until Tony told me what he saw. I turned to look in his direction, and he was white in the face with his mouth wide open.

He stayed that way for about five seconds before he asked me clear as day, "Did you just see that guy run into your wall?" The breath was sucked out of my lungs at that time, because I had in fact seen a person as real as you and me run from one side of the basement to the other side. Whatever I saw appeared to be in a full sprint—but I'm talking like a Usain Bolt kind of sprint, if you catch my drift.

To this day I can't explain it. I looked at the history of the property, and nothing crazy showed up. I knew what I'd seen, but there was no way I was going to tell anyone—anyone, that is, except my grandma. I'll never forget the stories she used to tell me about being visited by angels. She would even describe how she sometimes felt the presence of angels during or after she had been in deep prayer. Those stories were like seeds that took root in my mind.

Retrospective

The Lord said to Satan, "Where have you come from?" Then Satan answered the Lord and said, "From roaming about on the earth and walking around on it."

—Job 2:2

I come from a spiritual family. My grandmothers on both sides of my family and their relatives have had supernatural encounters with things not of this earth. They are both devout Christians, and I believe that their encounters with angels and spirits helped solidify their belief system in an afterlife.

I was shocked to see a man run through my grandmother's basement, especially once my friend testified to seeing the same thing. I had never experienced anything supernatural before. That one experience combined with the stories my grandma used to tell made it impossible for me to deny the supernatural. Once I started to read the Bible, I would read about many things that I may have found harder to believe if my mind was not already open to things that were supernatural in nature. While I was reading the Bible, I found the stories were ringing true to me and the Bible verifies and explains everything that is taking place that we cannot see.

When I think of reading the Bible, I often compare it to turning on the lights or waking up from a deep sleep. I think it is easy to not read the Bible, but I think we all stumble around needlessly when we don't. When we choose to walk around in the dark, we can run into something that may cause us great pain. It can be scary to walk in the darkness, because we don't know what we may walk into or if a cliff or hole is directly ahead of us in our path. Many of the things we struggle with or that cause us pain in life can be avoided if we could just see where we are going and walk around the things we don't need to walk through. There is evil at work in this world, and when we cannot recognize it or don't know how to overcome it then we will stumble and fall more than we should. We should all seek the light that lights up all darkness and will guide us through life and every challenge. God tells us exactly what we will face in this life, and more importantly He gives us instruction on what to do no matter what we face.

> "Do this, knowing the time, that it is already the hour for you to awaken from sleep; for now salvation is nearer to us than when we believed. The night is almost gone, and the day is near. Therefore let us lay aside the deeds of darkness and put on the armor of light." (Romans 13:11-12)

Enlisting in the Army

I was attending summer school gym class for one-hour a day, every day, for the first two months of summer. After class, on the first day of summer school, I went to the Army recruiter's office and told him I wanted to enlist. Staff Sergeant (SSG) Nelson was a good recruiter. He had seen war, and he was now enjoying his time as a recruiter.

For security purposes, I won't divulge what my father did while serving in the military. The little that I did know about his job helped me to know which MOS (Military Occupational Specialty) that I wanted to pursue. So, when I walked into the recruiting office and sat down in SSG Nelson's chair I told him that I wanted to be a Human Intelligence Collector (HUMINT). He was an infantryman himself, and he had no idea what that MOS even was.

So I signed up, passed my drug tests, took and crushed my ASVAB test, then went to Milwaukee's Military Entry Processing Services (MEPS) to get physically cleared to serve and to swear my oath to Uncle Sam. It was a life-changing day. Yet, as anyone who has been to MEPS can tell you, it's exhausting. I was so exhausted that I don't remember a whole lot from those days except one thing: when the contract-writing officer tried to tell me at the last minute that they were all out of Human Intelligence (HUMINT) slots. She told me I'd have to do something else. She just wrote it in the contract, as though we had already discussed this and I had already blessed off on it. As you can imagine, I didn't let this fly. I told her I was leaving and wouldn't sign the contract if I didn't get the slot I was promised, and I meant it. I walked out of her office, and I was headed to the exit in defiance when she came out and yelled, "CALHOUN...we found your slot, please come back."

I often wonder where I would be now, if I had just walked out of that door. More than likely, I'd have taken some college courses, but I almost certainly would have spent time in jail or prison. Thanks to God, my contract ended up reflecting everything that was originally agreed upon, and I enlisted. I returned to my hometown after leaving MEPS to wait until my Basic Training (often referred to as Basic) start date. I spent the time in between when I enlisted and my Basic start date: working out, eating a lot of food, and learning Army tasks. My goal was to get promoted before I even left for Basic, and I did get promoted from PV1 to PV2 before shipping out.

Retrospective

Then I heard the voice of the Lord, saying,
"Whom shall I send, and who will go for us?"
Then I said, "Here am I. Send me!"
—Isaiah 6:8

I had two reasons for enlisting in the Army. The first reason was to remove myself from the environment that I was in. I loved my family and friends, but I just felt compelled to get away and start over fresh. The second reason was my trip to Ground Zero. I was happy to give up the drugs and party habits if I could go fight terrorists. I had always been told that I had potential; I just didn't know what that potential could be used for. God has an amazing ability to bring good out of bad, and that is evident here in my life.

My father and I didn't have a good relationship at this point, but he still had an impact on me when it came time to choose my military path. When I learned what HUMINT was and read all the books I could on the topic, I knew that HUMINT would be my purpose in the Army. I knew I could be good at that job, but even in MEPS the devil tried to pull me off course by almost having me walk out that door when she claimed to "lose" my slot. The devil schemes against us and is a master of deceit. Fortunately for us, when God has put us on a path to do His will, the devil can't stop us if we don't let him. The deceiver has been after all of us since birth, and it is only through the grace and Word of God that we are not completely consumed by the devil's lies.

I can't express enough, how strongly I felt the need to join the Army. There was a deep burning desire to leave home and join the Army. As Isaiah was called in the Bible, I believe I was called to join the Army. It was part of God's plan for me all along. I just didn't realize it until much later on in my life. We all have to be ready for God's call. For me it was a desire to start over. That little desire is all it took to get me to join the Army. God put that desire inside of me for a purpose. God has placed a purpose in each one of us. Make yourself available for God and He will use you for His glory.

> "I will instruct you and teach you in the way which you should go; I will counsel you with My eye upon you." (Psalm 32:8)

Basic Training

I remember when I got to Fort Leonard Wood; hundreds of new recruits were being put into the Army system and into their future Basic Training classes. This was my first real look at Army life: the "hurry up and wait" lifestyle. Everyone is always in a hurry to get where they are going, even when they know they have to wait when they get there. This started from day one and followed throughout my career. I grew up talking to people however I wanted to, and I never really adhered to the rules. I wasn't even close to being a formidable fighter or opponent, but what I lacked in physical size, I made up for in my nature. I have never been a quitter when things got tough and have always been an "all in" kind of guy.

To me, rap, television, and the crowd of people I had grown up with romanticized the loyalty and brotherhood between men. So when I called someone a friend, which meant that I was willing to accept harm for him or her and was willing to inflict violence upon those that would harm them. Being a friend of mine has always had meaning and substance, because I love my friends like I love my family. I knew the Army was going to change me, but I never really thought it could truly change my heart.

My new "friends" and I had our two duffel bags full of new Army gear and a rucksack on our backs. We were standing in the back of large horse trailers that had been tailored to meet the needs of the Army—I felt like we were cattle being sent to slaughter. The doors opened after the shortest drive of my life from the in-processing center to our new barracks. We arrived at the home of Alpha Company 1-48 Infantry Regiment, and we were met at the doors by our gracious hosts: the drill sergeants. I remember taking the awkward step off of the trailer, trying to balance my bags and orient myself to my new surroundings. During this time a drill sergeant was in my ear, screaming at me to run faster, to stop looking at him, to not address him, to stop being me, period.

I looked right at him and asked, "Why are you screaming at me? I don't even know who you are!" Boy, was that the wrong thing to say. I learned how to do push-ups, flutter kicks, and pull-ups that night.

After that I was depressed for about a week, asking myself why I signed up for something like this. But I got through it. One day at a time I woke up and just did the best that I could. I went from being the weakest and slowest soldier in formation to one of the fastest. Although my strength in comparison to others was nothing to brag about, I was beginning to put up high physical fitness test scores, and to me that was a big deal. One of the days after I came out of my depressed state, I remember being in the chow hall one evening eating dinner. After an extremely quiet wait in line, we were given an entire sixty seconds to eat dinner. After the sixty seconds was up, soldiers were rushing for the exits. I never did understand why they rushed out of the dining facility or DFAC so quickly, until the day that I learned firsthand.

As I walked down the narrow corridor in the DFAC, guided by metal rails, toward the exit of the building, I heard a loud voice yell, "Hey, Private! What the fuck do you think you are doing pimp-walking in my DFAC?"

I can honestly say I still don't think I could do a "pimp walk" justice, but that drill sergeant wanted to make a martyr out of me for lollygagging (not moving with a purpose), so he did.

In front of at least 150 to 200 new recruits, he yelled at me from across the DFAC and told me to pick up a saltshaker. He instructed me to hold it up perpendicular to my body and out in front of me using only my forefingers. So with only my two fingers holding the saltshaker, and my arms outstretched, he told me to take a seat in the iron chair. I looked around for an iron chair, but didn't see any. After looking around with the "deer in the headlights" look for what felt like forever, he told me from across the chow hall to put my back up against the wall and to bend my knees until seated at a ninety-degree angle—or in other words conforming my body to look like a chair on a wall...or an iron chair.

He told me, if I dropped that saltshaker, everyone in the chow hall would be done eating and would end up right alongside me. Being so new to the military, I didn't realize this was a tactic used to develop bonds amongst recruits. All I knew is that the hungry and cranky recruits would probably kick my ass later that night if they were forced to forego chow because of my weakness. Therefore, I held my position until the drill sergeant yelled at me to get out of his DFAC and to never pimp-walk again. I never have to this day.

What does any of this have to do with my story?

Drill Sergeant Polk, the same one who yelled at me for pimp-walking, taught me something that day. He planted a seed in me that would one day flourish. I would never have been able to hold that saltshaker if it was only for my skin or gain. My legs burned within seconds (keep in mind, this is after a day's worth of training). Out of sheer fear of embarrassment and everyone looking at me, I was sweating profusely. The sweat was pouring into my eyes and burning fervently. But then something clicked. A voice in my head told me something along these lines, "If you can't do it for you, do it for them." I had no idea in November of 2005, when this event happened, that it would have such a grandeur effect on me.

I made lifelong friends in Basic Training, one of whom is among my best friends. Isaiah and I became close friends and battle buddies in Basic Training. We had many similarities and we were both go-getters. So whenever we could work together, we did, because we always knew we would both give our absolute best. I welcomed him into my life joyously because my bunkmate and battle buddy throughout Basic Training was a guy named Calvin. Calvin told me he was a Wiccan and he spent his Sunday mornings talking to trees and to the grass. All this guy did was tell me about the spirits all around us and how to communicate with them, for the purpose of becoming subservient to their awesome power. I mean, this guy literally was trying to get me involved in demonic worship, and although that's not how I saw it back then, the pit of my stomach said I had to ignore him as much as possible.

Right before Calvin quit Basic Training and was sent home, I came down with a high fever and ended up going to the hospital with a temperature of 104 degrees. I missed out on throwing live grenades because of that fever, but I was fortunate that I wasn't forced to sit in a foxhole with Calvin during that exercise. I can say that the fever was a blessing when the alternative would have been to trust my life to an emotionally erratic person. He not only talked to trees, but he told me multiple times that he had put curses on me for not respecting his religion. The Lord works in mysterious ways, but this particular blessing doesn't seem so mysterious.

Retrospective

"And everyone who has left houses or brothers or
sisters or father or mother or children or farms
for My name's sake, will receive many times as
much, and will inherit eternal life."
                                        —Matthew 19:29

Basic Training was a challenge for me because I wasn't one to adhere
to the rules, and that isn't how the Army operates. I had never lived
away from home and was living in less-than-comfortable conditions,
but I wasn't going to let hard conditions in Basic Training deter me
from achieving my goals.

The saltshaker incident was where I first learned the lesson of
putting others first. It was in that dining facility, where Drill Sergeant
Polk made me a spectacle for others to see and where the Holy Spirit
filled me with the strength to not drop that saltshaker. I was just
a scrawny kid but one that was willing to work hard to not be a
burden to others. That event was the catalyst that transformed my
internal thinking from being self-centered to considerate of the
common-good. My new priority, born that day, was for my fellow
soldiers.

I would start to learn the limits and punishments that my body
could tolerate. I would never become a professional weight lifter. I
would never be known as the strongest man. But I would come to
learn where my strengths lie, and that was in my ability to push
myself. Sometimes the greatest strength any of us can possess is the
resolution to never quit.

As a young soldier and man, I had no real sense of identity or
belonging. I knew I wanted to serve my country, but I didn't have the

slightest idea of how the world worked or what serving my country would entail.

When we arrived at Fort Leonard Wood at our barracks for Basic Training, I found out that Calvin would be my bunkmate. We were about the same size and height, but far different in every other aspect. One of the rules in Basic Training is to always have a battle buddy, no matter where you go. Calvin was assigned as my battle buddy. When I found out he was Wiccan I was apprehensive, because I'd never met a Wiccan before. But the last thing I expected, or needed, was to have a bunkmate that would often curse me and say incantations that sounded like something out of a sci-fi movie. Basic training is stressful enough; I didn't appreciate having a battle buddy that was working against me instead of with me. He began to affect my moods, and I started to become depressed and angry that I had signed up for this; that was when Isaiah walked into my life.

Isaiah introduced himself to me after a really rough day, almost as if in answer to the Holy Spirit's urging me to find a friend who would keep me strong and faithful. We have been friends ever since. I don't think he truly understands how grateful I am that he was there and accepted me as a friend. I can look back on this event and speak with great certainty that spiritual warfare was prevalent in my life back then. Basic Training is intended to be very stressful, and one of the reasons for that is to weed out anyone who can't adapt to high stress situations. Fortunately for the Army and everyone serving in the Army, Calvin didn't make it through Basic Training. I'm sure Calvin would have taken me down with him, if I hadn't of had the feeling of disassociating with him when I first met him.

I don't believe in coincidence now that I know Jesus as my personal Savior. One day in particular, I was feeling especially depressed. I had been stuck with Calvin all day on a guard shift, when one of the guys (Isaiah), who lived in the room next to mine, came up to me out of the blue and started up a conversation. There are so many people in Basic Training classes that it's hard to get to know them all, which makes Isaiah's seemingly random introduction so important to me. We came from totally different backgrounds and had nothing in common at first glance, and yet he became a place of solace for me.

I didn't feel the sense of dread I did around Calvin, and oftentimes Isaiah would remind me that Basic Training was only temporary and Calvin wouldn't be a long-term problem for me.

I can now see that Calvin was a physical manifestation of a spiritual battle that was waging above me. The devil didn't want me to get comfortable in the Army. I don't think it's a coincidence that a man with the biblical name of Isaiah walked into my life at a point when I desperately needed a break from constant spiritual attack.

To this day, Isaiah and I remain good friends, and we both remember Calvin very well. I pray that Calvin will one day open his eyes to see and his ears to hear the wonderful news of the Lord, if he hasn't already. I have since rebuked the curses he laid upon me in the name of Jesus Christ and have put on the full armor of God that the Apostle Paul speaks of in *Ephesians 6*. I pray for all the people that have helped me along the way, and that they would also find help from the Lord should they ever need it.

> "Be devoted to one another in brotherly love; give preference to one another in honor." (Romans 12:10)
>
> "Do not merely look out for your own personal interests, but also for the interests of others." (Philippians 2:4)

Advanced Individual Training— Human Intelligence Collector

Advanced Individual Training (AIT) was one of the most important years (if not the single most important year) of my life to date. Now, many of you may know that after Basic Training there comes another period of training when the soldier learns how to do their technical jobs. Some people are cooks, engineers, infantryman, administrative clerks, Special Forces candidates—to name just a few. This is where soldiers learn how to perform tasks beyond those of basic soldiering. At the completion of AIT, soldiers are supposed to be able to perform their assigned jobs.

For many military service members, this is as far as their military training will take them. After Basic Training and AIT many soldiers decide they do not want to make a career out of the military, and they simply complete their contract without further training. These are generally the same folks that do one contract or even a deployment or two before getting out. I have always applauded people who didn't grow up wanting to be a member of the armed forces but enlist in the military anyway. It's simply amazing that young men and women are still willing to voluntarily enlist and fight on behalf of our country even at a personal cost. AIT is where soldiers oftentimes get a little bit of freedom, compared to Basic Training regulations, and they learn how to interact more socially with fellow service members.

When I arrived at Fort Huachuca, Arizona, it was already dark outside and in late January; so it was cold and breezy. I had been told that the mountains were beautiful to look at around Fort Huachuca, but I couldn't make out much more than a dark mass without clear moonlight. So I stopped fighting the sugar high I was on, following the pizza and soda I consumed after Basic, and went to sleep. I woke up bright and early the next day as hungry as I could be. I rounded up the few people I knew from Basic that traveled with me to Arizona, including Isaiah. I remember stepping out of the metal building that would be my home for the next few months and staring at the mountains. I stood there with mountains looming over me in grandeur, while the sun was low in the sky and the air was nice and cool.

I immediately made a mental connection to the hit TV show *M*A*S*H* from back in the day. I used to watch *M*A*S*H* with my grandparents prior to my enlistment, and the mountains in that show looked nearly identical to the ones in front of me there. Because we arrived on the weekend, we had until Monday to explore the installation that would be our home and to get ready to train. On that Monday after reporting to Fort Huachuca, we were brought up to speed on how training would go while we were there. The drill sergeants informed us that because of the surge of troops into Iraq, the demand for our MOS had increased exponentially. With that high demand for our MOS came many soldiers awaiting training, but there weren't enough instructors to handle the influx of soldiers. So, the average wait time between when soldiers were arriving and when they were making it into a class was six months.

There was a mixed reaction by those of us hearing this for the first time, through official channels. I for one was initially extremely upset because I didn't sign up for military service just to sit around and wait. But God's plan was different than mine, and that's exactly what I did. Others, unlike me, were content to spend six months of their contract sitting around in the safety of the United States. They were happy to drink beer every Friday night with no fear of being killed. I was ready to die in combat at this point in my life.

I believe every young man goes through a time where he transitions from boyhood to manhood. For me, that transition meant that I had accepted that my life was incredibly small in comparison to what I was being trained to stand for. I believed so much in the cause of our military's mission, that I was more than willing to die for it.

Even as a (now) thirteen-year vet, when I see someone in uniform, that is what it means to me. It means that even though my time is over, someone else was willing to take my place in the ranks to hold the line firm. America is so blessed to have the intelligence capabilities and physical strength that it does, and that is made possible only because of the men and women whom have sworn the oath to defend our nation.

So there I was, standing in formation, listening to this terrible news of how I would be stuck in Fort Huachuca for the next six months. I am not going to lie and say that I saw any silver lining in that news. I will say that it didn't end up being as bad as I thought it would be. I was able to attend several college courses, I earned a gold German Armed Forces Proficiency Badge (which looked super fancy on my otherwise-bare dress uniform), and most importantly I met a woman.

Her name was Tara, and she was as beautiful as the rising sun with a smile to match. Every time this blond-haired blue-eyed beauty spoke, I just had to listen to her. She was the smartest woman I'd ever met, and I asked her to be my wife before we graduated from AIT. So yes, I not only met my wife while we were in AIT, but we got engaged and married while we were there…all in all about eleven months total (this includes training time and waiting time). While this isn't a book about my marriage, it is most vital to let everyone know that without my wife, nothing I would accomplish after meeting her would have been made possible without her.

Not one day went by during AIT when I wasn't trying to achieve my maximum potential. I had barely graduated high school. I was a mediocre soldier at best during Basic Training. But in AIT I was able to learn in a less strenuous environment. I began learning about human intelligence and how it all worked. I knew I was meant to do it. I was good at it. I stayed up at night to study instruction manuals. I faced challenging situations head-on, instead of beating around the bush and waiting for someone else to solve all of the problems. I learned that I could push my body to new limits, reaching a sub-twelve-minute two-mile-run time, and began to train so that I could get 300 points (maximum points) on my physical fitness tests. I was able to leverage the social skills I developed as a kid for the job I was learning how to do. I was learning how to read body language, I was taking courses in counterterrorism, and I started learning how to understand a radical jihadist and what their core beliefs were. I ended up earning multiple awards for graduating at the top of my class. I opened up my mind and soul to the Army. I knew I could put my talents to use, and I was hoping to save lives overseas.

Not everything was sunshine and gum drops, though, during my time in AIT. Most new recruits are between the ages of eighteen and twenty-two years old, and for most recruits it is their first time away from home. After a few weeks of being at Fort Huachuca, we were able to earn certain freedoms. We were eventually able to wear civilian clothing after duty hours, and were able to put in for day or weekend passes to go off base. Young adults, new found freedoms, and too much time to kill while waiting to start training… was not the greatest combination. Any decent officer (commissioned or non-commissioned) knows that when soldiers have downtime bad things tend to happen. The drill sergeants kept us plenty busy during the duty day, but then we were left to our own devices.

Remember when I said they put us in a big metal building? Well, this building had over a hundred bunk beds and twice that many large footlockers where recruits were forced to store and neatly maintain all their personal and professional items. We called it cell block 4, because CB4 was the building number. We didn't have any dividing barriers for privacy or separation. There were simply a lot of bunk beds and cabinets in one open room. Everything was arranged in such a manner as to give each soldier as much individual space as possible. This was where young men (women had their own building) learned how to live with each other. Living in such cramped quarters, smelling every fart and nasty shoe in the building, takes a toll on people.

Surprisingly, personal hygiene was not high on everyone's priority list. I always assumed it was natural to want to be clean, but I learned there that men are inherently nasty and gross by default. It was far less common to find a young man who cleaned up after himself and maintained good health and hygiene than the opposite.

For the record, I heard these issues were not exclusive to the men. You may be asking why I'm telling you about people's hygiene…I'll tell you.

The Army is designed to perform at the lowest levels possible at all times—or in other words, we were supposed to take care of issues at the lowest level. It always works out best when the boss or platoon sergeant/drill sergeant doesn't have to get involved when there is an issue. We learned the hard way that drill sergeants would take time away from the whole building, or bay, if people showed up to formation not showered, not shaved, or smelling of booze. Did the drill sergeants know we were drinking? I'd hope so, because we didn't hide it. But one of the things we would hide was called a blanket party.

Now, I personally will never admit that I was a part of this, but I saw the whole thing. This type of behavior probably should have bothered me, but it didn't. I didn't have time to get "smoked" (corrective punishment given by the drill sergeants) in formation because some dude was all jacked up and bringing us all down with him. When his peers peacefully tried to resolve the issues, they were met with belligerence and threats. This individual got the shit kicked out of him one night for not being a team player. I learned a valuable lesson that night: there isn't always an easy way to be taught a lesson but there is always a hard way. Many attempts to correct this individual's rebellious and disobedient behavior were unsuccessful, but the problem still needed to be resolved. I made a personal vow that night to never earn a blanket party of my own. This seemingly small incident was much like the saltshaker for me, because it helped to define the soldier I would strive to become.

Retrospective

"You did not choose Me but I chose you, and appointed you that you would go and bear fruit, and that your fruit would remain, so that whatever you ask of the Father in my name He may give to you."
—John 15:16

AIT was a very important time in my life for two main reasons. The first is because it was at AIT that I met and married my wife. We were in the same training program, and she was only a class behind mine. She became my best friend and my confidant. Without her in my life, my life would have turned out much differently. I don't believe I was ready for marriage to such a perfect woman, but she has stuck it out through thick and thin for me. Now that I have found the Lord, I am learning how to support her in the ways she needs to be supported and I am learning to love the way God intended us to love each other. She has been a partner to me at all times, even though I am far from perfect, and she loves me unconditionally. I was blessed by God to have a partner in life such as her.

I found a passion for my job that I didn't expect. I felt gifted to do this type of work, and I now know that my gifts were from God. I had a feeling I would love HUMINT, but there was no way for me to know for sure until I was doing it. In *Jeremiah 29:11, New International Version*, it says,

"For I know the plans I have for you," declares the LORD, "plans to prosper you and not to harm you, plans to give you hope and a future." (Jeremiah 29:11)

Jeremiah sums up in this one verse my entire AIT class.

I learned part of God's first calling for me in AIT, which was to serve my country honorably in combat. But I also discovered that my wife would also be included in that future, and God gave me both in a single (most critical) year of my life. Because of God's grace and anointing, I was fortunate enough to have been selected as honor graduate for my class and was able to make the most of the spare time there.

> "Whatever you do, do your work heartily, as for
> the Lord rather than for men." (Colossians 3:23)

Third Infantry Division

After AIT I really didn't know what to expect when I arrived at Fort Stewart, Georgia. I knew from drill sergeants and other seasoned soldiers that the Third Infantry Division, or 3ID, was a unit that deployed constantly. 3ID did not have a high retention rate (meaning, people hated it there), and it was one of the least sexy military installations around. Now, at that time, I didn't really pay much attention to stuff like that. I just wanted to deploy and do my part. I was itching to succeed—no, to excel. I had a desire and deep yearning to be the best I could be.

Luckily for Tara and me, we were married early enough in advance that we both got orders to Fort Stewart, Georgia. We moved into a small one-bedroom apartment, which was all we could afford on both of our private first class salaries, and I became a Dog Faced Soldier.

I found out while I was in-processing the installation that every morning on loud speakers, strategically placed in the most annoying places, blasted the 3ID theme song. The Dog Faced Soldier song didn't get old until about day 3. The first thing that I noticed when I signed into my unit was that senior-ranking NCOs (non-commissioned officers) weren't common here which was evident because my platoon sergeant was only a sergeant at that time. My new platoon sergeant introduced me to one of the squad leaders, SGT Greg, who in turn was tasked with taking and introducing me to my new squad leader, SGT James. SGT James was a short, small-framed Asian man with a loud commanding voice and zero shits to give about feelings. When I was first introduced to SGT James he walked over, shook my hand, turned around, and walked away. I remember saying something to SGT Greg that I would regret for months to come.

I asked him, "Does SGT James have a Napoleon complex? He is so small and loud." Needless to say, I paid for making that smart-ass comment and was tasked with moving one large pile of sandbags from one end of a parking lot to the other...until SGT James got tired. First impressions do go a long way, and thanks to my sarcasm our soldier/leader relationship was rocky from the beginning.

I found out within a few weeks of getting assigned to 3ID that we would be deploying some time during 2007, and our schedule would be packed with training events prior to our departure. Between January and August of 2007, we spent one month in a pre-deployment field exercise right outside of Fort Stewart; training is conducted before deployments for commanders to deploy their equipment, to identify things that need fixing, and to give soldiers opportunities to spend time away from the flagpole in a simulated deployed atmosphere. We spent another month in Fort Irwin, California, at the National Training Center. This is a training environment where units can "deploy" safely to rehearse and refine war-fighting capabilities. Our unit was dispersed to different units throughout the exercise to fill the intelligence roles assigned us. This exercise is much more for logistics and command implementation than it is meant to be tactical, but there are scenarios that units go through to simulate deployed environments.

During the first mission of the deployed scenario, our team went out to a town filled with locals (or military role-players) to conduct interviews with the local populace. Twenty minutes into this first mission, my entire team, minus myself, was "killed" by a suicide bomber and that left me alone for the remainder of the deployed scenario. Keep in mind; I had zero experience doing the job except for what I learned in AIT. With my squad leader now "dead", I would have to assume his role as well as everyone else's on the team, and I had no idea what all of those roles entailed. I knew through experience that getting accountability of weapons and personnel was vital; so I did that first. Then as the "dead" were being put into the medical vehicles, I continued the mission and began gathering information from the local population about activities in the area. What I didn't know at this time was that the vehicle commander I rode with on the way to this village thought I was also KIA (killed in action), and instead of verifying, he left me behind. So I came out of the building surrounded by role-players – or the local populous – looking at me. I could tell they were wondering if they should take advantage of the situation, by incorporating my unit's mistake into a grand radical gesture, and make me a martyr.

It didn't take long for me to realize I was left behind. To make matters worse, I took my "dead" team member's M-249 Squad Automatic Weapon, or SAW, and I slung my M-4 on my back. The fact that I also had the SAW, with ammunition, meant that I was now carrying approximately 30 extra pounds. I was in blistering California heat, and I was at least 4 miles away from the base. Thankfully, I remembered to bring a map of the area, and I started to make my way back to the base. I had to keep in mind that I was moving through enemy territory the entire time.

After about ten minutes of running with full kit (battle armor and gear) and a machine gun in hand, I saw a sight I'd never appreciated before. A team of three tanks had taken a security posture on the intersection I was coming up on. I had just stopped running as I reached one of the tanks, and as I was catching my breath I inhaled a huge breath of scorching-hot tank exhaust. Everything from my lips to my lungs felt like they were burned by fire. I never knew how hot the exhaust was behind tanks. I was barely able to speak because of my burned throat. I drank the little water I had left, before climbing up the side of this tank and knocking on the entry point with the butt stock of my rifle.

The soldiers in the tank didn't see me coming, because I came up from behind the tank. I also figured they didn't know a soldier was left behind, so they wouldn't expect anyone to come knocking on the tank hatch. Slowly the hatch opened, and the small barrel of an M9 semi-automatic pistol poked out of the hatch. With me looking straight down the barrel of this gun, I identified myself and informed the commander of my situation. God bless that man. Not only did he not embarrass my unit by broadcasting this incident on the radio, but he also let me ride in the tank back to the base. Those men gave me a lot of their water, and they let me play with the tank guns, before we returned to base.

Once we returned, I debriefed all units involved, and the leadership assured me that this type of mistake wouldn't happen again. The Sergeant Major personally accompanied me on all the remaining missions that I went on, for the remainder of this deployed scenario, just to ensure I was never left behind again. He told me to think of him as my personal bodyguard while on mission. The Sergeant Major didn't normally leave the base for these missions, so I just thought it was so awesome of him to go out of his way like that for a Specialist in the Army.

I spent the rest of the exercise acting alone: conducting interviews and interrogations, establishing rapport with other units, writing reports, and so on. I learned how to do my job with my feet in the fire. The first thing that I did was call my first sergeant and I ask what he needed from me each day, what he needed from me at the end of the week, and what he needed by the end of the scenario. I made a detailed checklist as he listed every deliverable he needed from me. I asked him to send me blank templates or forms if available, and I just tackled one task at a time. During these training events, there are cadre (trainers/instructors) that follow and grade/critique each soldier's ability to do their job. The cadre assigned to my team asked me if I wanted to join another team, after the rest of mine was "killed." I respectfully told him I would guarantee progress if he would just let me learn on my own. He did. Theoretically he had an easy job because he only had to monitor me; but he said I kept him busier than any other whole team had in any of his previous scenarios. He was also shocked when he found out I had zero experience, because I managed to successfully navigate every HUMINT obstacle throughout that entire exercise. Before my squad leader "died," I didn't even know what a PERSTAT (personnel status report) was one day, and the next day I was sending in reports required of NCOs, all while producing actionable intelligence for the supporting unit.

According to my cadre, I was the only "team" that collected all of the intelligence in the scenario. I got my first Army Achievement Medal for doing such a spectacular job keeping the mission moving (cadre words, not mine), and to this day I look back on this event as a defining moment of my career. I knew it wasn't the real world yet, but it gave me the confidence to know what I could handle if it ever came to that.

Following that NTC training exercise we all redeployed back to Fort Stewart knowing that we were now officially "ready" for deployment. We had a few months left to get all the pre-mobilization inventory and packing knocked out. We practiced and learned customary/cultural dos and don'ts in Iraq, and we took some pre-deployment leave. One of the most important days of my life also happened after that NTC trip, and before I deployed to Iraq for nearly seventeen months. My beautiful daughter was born right there on Fort Stewart on July 1, 2007. I was twenty years old and in so many ways a baby myself, but I loved that little girl. I was blessed to have two months with her before deploying and leaving her behind with my wife. It was, up to that point, the hardest thing I'd ever have to do.

I didn't know it then, but that deployment coming up would change everything about me as a person. I would come to see some violent and terrible things, instead of holding my beautiful daughter and kissing or making love to my wife. Warfare has been one of the few constants throughout history, but the effects of being in a war are still not easily understood. Losing my life used to have great meaning, and I viewed death as an honor if for God or country; but now that I was a dad, my death was more complicated. Anytime I would consider my death, and I had to think about my daughter growing up without me, her dad, and it shook me to my core.

Retrospective

But Jesus said to him, "Follow Me, and allow the
dead to bury their own dead."
                                        —Matthew 8:22

I learned how to be a soldier at Fort Stewart under very young and
intelligent leadership. SGT James was my first squad leader in the
regular Army. Our relationship started off rather rocky because of the
personality differences between us. SGT James was not a leader that
I would have asked for if I was given a choice. His leadership style
wasn't one that I appreciated as a young man with a big mouth. On
many occasions I put SGT James in a position where he would have
to come down hard on me as a leader. I loved the Army life, but still
had a disdain for people telling me what to do.

I always thought SGT James liked me deep down. I was still too
young to understand that he never once put his own personal needs
above my teammates or mine. I was still too immature and new to
the Army to understand that SGT James was (and still is) an amazing
leader. After years of Army experience, I came to appreciate the lessons and discipline that SGT James instilled into me at Ft. Stewart. I
did eventually come to learn that he was an outstanding NCO, one
whom I severely mistreated and undervalued.

Despite my lack of submission and obedience to his leadership,
he taught me a lot. He taught me how to properly articulate myself,
how to do my job when not in training, how to perform first aid, and
many other basic soldiering tasks. He was the first of many leaders that
would groom me to be the soldier I became later on. I used to really
dislike him for the things he made me do. He always seemed to favor
others by making me do the hard work. Now I see things for what they

were. He was responsible for my life, and he took that responsibility seriously. My own pain and heartache came from a lack of discipline that SGT James was forced to instill into me. SGT James had a monumental task in reining me in and teaching me how to be a soldier.

When we were at NTC and rest of my teammates were "killed", I was repeatedly told that I should return to the main camp. I was told I wouldn't be able to do the mission without my entire team. My cadre offered me the opportunity to go back to base, to eat some good food, and to get some good sleep: all I had to do was give up. I did not accept. I proved the critics wrong by working twenty-hour days and never being okay with what I had already accomplished.

At one point during the exercise, 2 or 3 days into the scenario, the cadre stopped by to let me know that he had given my team an opportunity to come back out to the field and to continue the scenario. He told me that my team had consciously chosen to stay back and to let me continue the mission on my own. At first this bothered me. Up until that point when the cadre informed me that my team decided they wouldn't be coming out to help, I was a nervous wreck and felt completely overwhelmed. I think, sometimes, when we are still holding onto hope that someone else will come along and help to ease our burden, we don't feel the urgency to push and increase our own capabilities. Sometimes sink or swim moments are exactly what we need in order to grow. As soon as I knew for sure that I was on my own until the end, something shifted inside of me. I was filled with a determination and a resolution to do my very best and finish what I started.

By sticking it out, I learned far more than I would have if I had completed the scenario with my whole team. I also developed close ties for a professional network of people within my brigade that would be useful in Iraq. I didn't know it then, but God was preparing me to be able to perform at a higher level even when I didn't have a team to help shoulder the workload. I am forever grateful that God loved me enough to walk next to me there at Fort Irwin when my soldiering abilities were truly tested for the first time.

"The Lord is my Helper, I will not be afraid.
What will man do to me?" (Hebrews 13:6)

SGT James, I owe you an apology for all those months of heartache that I caused you. I hope you know that I used the lessons you taught me throughout my career. You remain one of the most important military leaders I ever had the honor of working for. Thank you for never giving up on me, and for teaching me how to do things the right way. Your task was immense, and you handled it better than I ever could have. Thank you, SGT James.

Kuwait

After the farewell at Fort Stewart, our platoon began the beginning of our Iraq deployment. We started off—staying in Kuwait for about a week—in large, almost-circus-sized military tan tents. Windows were located all over the tent. The walls of the tent were lined with cots, and we all split up according to our squads. During our brief stay in Kuwait we: hung out, worked out, ate four meals a day (midnight chow was clutch), went to ranges, and studied cultural materials relevant to our mission.

Three things about Kuwait stick out in my mind. The first stand out memory for me was of our first time shooting at the range. We needed to verify that the sights on our weapons were good and nothing was shifted in transport. Typical for a 3ID range, there were too many chiefs and not enough Indians. The entire range was unorganized chaos. When it was my turn to shoot, I glanced up from my prone firing position. I saw a man herding camels approximately a hundred yards past our targets. That guy literally looked right at us and then, as if on purpose, scattered his camels throughout the backdrop of our range. We were unable to shoot for the rest of the day. Sometimes I wonder about the mental stability of that guy. I don't know what his intent was that day, but it blew our minds that he was down range of our bullets with his livestock.

My second stand out memory from Kuwait was the "Porta Potty literature." So, in case you didn't know, Porta Potties are often the Army's answer to hygiene needs during training and deployments. Generally, Porta Potties can be contracted at relatively low prices, providing soldiers a human necessity, while boosting the local economy with jobs and income. What nobody tells you is that each shitter has a unique persona. For example, there was a shitter I remember where everyone was supposed to go if they wanted to look at hand drawings of naked women doing things that are not PG-rated. Another shitter was quite literally filled with poems, oftentimes portraying aggression or anger at being deployed and missing home. I'd be lying if I didn't say that when you have to crap MREs, it's nice to have some reading material.

The third and most important thing about my time in Kuwait was getting to know another guy in my unit, Jason. In our tent, he ended up in the cot next to mine. I knew him already but not well. I was very fortunate to come to know him much better in Kuwait, before heading to Iraq. Once we left Kuwait, the activities of daily life for me and the simple joys of port potty literature were a thing of the past.

Retrospective

"Have I not commanded you? Be strong and
courageous! Do not tremble or be dismayed, for
the Lord your God is with you wherever you go."
—Joshua 1:9

The hardest part about being in Kuwait was the feeling of time slowing down. It felt like we were stuck spinning our wheels, knowing we
couldn't go back home but feeling anxious about the unknowns that
were ahead. Having a nomad stop his herd right on our range was the
first time I had seen first hand just how different the populace was in
the Middle East compared to the United States.

Even though we hadn't been gone long, sitting around and waiting for the next hit-time left us all thinking a lot about our families
and the things we had left behind. I spent a lot of this time studying
Arabic and reading materials on the Iraqi culture and working out,
because both felt like they were giving me forward progress instead
of sitting around doing nothing.

Jason helped me work through the personal issues of leaving my
family behind (this was his second deployment) and he helped me
establish a routine early on, which kept my mind and body occupied.
It was Jason that invited me to start going to the gym with him and
to study Iraqi culture. In time, he would become a confidant that I
would rely on daily for advice. He was, and remains to this day, a
great friend to me. I can't thank him enough for his friendship and
guidance throughout this time in my life. *Proverbs 17:17* says, "A
friend loves at all times, and a brother is born for adversity." Jason fit
this verse perfectly as he helped prepare me for war.

I could have just as easily turned down Jason's offers to go to the gym and to study especially since I didn't know him well. Sometimes it is easier for us to keep to ourselves, than it is to socialize and develop friendships. This was such a simple lesson to learn, but it can make all of the difference. We will all experience highs and lows throughout our lives, and many times great friendships can be what helps to get us through those times. God can use other people to reach us and to help us. There are two sides to that equation though. We also need to be available for God to use us to reach someone else. We should take the time to get to know those around us, and care enough to reach out and help when we are able.

Iraq

It took about a week or so after flying into Forward Operating Base (FOB) Kalsu before we finally settled into our quarters, re-zeroed our rifles, and began prepping for operations. Shortly after we arrived on FOB Kalsu and began HUMINT operations, I fought to be removed from SGT James' team. I say fought and not requested, because it wasn't easy. SGT James and I had personality conflicts, which was well known before we ever deployed. He did play favorites, and I was not a favorite. That also was not a shock. The real problem for me came in when I felt he was intentionally holding me back and preventing me from doing my job. He had his own way of conducting HUMINT operations, and I did not agree with him. I was scheduling meetings and he would tell me he wanted someone else to take those meetings. I won't even say that his decisions were wrong, and he was well within his right to make those kinds of calls. But I was trying to be proactive, I wanted to hit the ground running, and he wanted to put a leash on me. Eventually, my request to be moved was granted. I was moved to Jason's team under the leadership of SSG Raul Guerra.

For contextual purposes, it is important to have an understanding of how our teams worked. There are various applications to using intelligence assets in a tactical environment. Our teams were attached to different line units (infantry guys), one HUMINT team per BN or area of operations (AO), and each team would support the line units directly by gathering intelligence that could be utilized on the battlefield. In other words, my job was to talk to all the people that nobody else wanted to, to befriend them, to make them believe I could solve problems that they had, and in return (oftentimes unbeknownst to them) they would provide information to me. Essentially I would find out what mattered to the local people and try to establish mutually beneficial relationships where we would help them as they were helping us. It didn't always work that way, there was a time and a place for everything and there were also hard ways of getting things done. No matter the method, I would take the information gathered and begin putting pieces together, writing it up and letting the people above my pay grade make the decisions on what to do with it. It is that easy, in theory.

What people don't tell you about being an intel guy is that infantrymen hate you. Intelligence soldiers tend to be arrogant. We tend to believe that our interpersonal skills separate us from the people who weren't smart enough to do what we do. I know people in my field that felt above putting themselves in harm's way, because they felt too important. How messed up is that? That was just one thing that separated me from many of my peers; I would never be that guy. The moral of this story is that it's near impossible for a tall, skinny intel guy like me to walk into an infantry platoon that has trained together for months or years and become fluid into their platoon. Intel soldiers don't belong on the front lines for the most part, and it's not because we are too good but because most of us are more of a liability than an asset for that platoon sergeant or platoon leader. We may or may not be good at our jobs, but either way our mere presence alters the line of thinking of the squad assigned to keep us alive. That isn't always a bad thing, but it is always a complication that not many people I knew considered.

I was a very fortunate man. I was proud to be a Dog Faced Soldier, but when I was told my team would be supporting a 101st Airborne BN that was attached to our brigade, I was stoked. I always heard good things about the 101st and now I was going to get to be a part of this chapter of their history. My team and I were further distributed throughout the BN to assist smaller units directly. I was assigned to the Scout Platoon of Headquarters Company (HHC), 2/502, 101st Airborne. This was noticeably the cream of the crop as far as the infantrymen were concerned, and I prepared myself for a challenge when it came time to approach them with my assistance.

I remember walking into their platoon HQ tent to introduce myself. The platoon leader, 1LT Stephens, stood up, shook my hand,

and invited me to sit down and chat with him for a bit. He needed to learn some more about me and see what I had to offer his unit other than inexperience. He treated me with the utmost respect, but I could tell he was just looking at some young kid and trying to find a way to use me. I desired to be the best but had no clue how things were really done, outside of training…so I told the platoon leader and platoon sergeant that. I was up-front with them about my experience level, and I told them I was there to help them. I wanted to be a part of the team, not just a guy who shows up and asks people to go out on a patrol because he has information that may or may not be right. I wanted them to respect me, and more importantly, I wanted to be worthy of that respect.

I remember the first time I asked that platoon to go out on a patrol because of information I had received. I had conducted an interview and I believed the informant to be credible. For reasons worthy of any patriot trying to fix his or her country, the informant provided me a location of a weapons cache. The cache happened to be in my AO, and was allegedly filled to the brim with materials for making explosively formed projectiles, or EFPs. EFPs were making an appearance in our AO at this time, and they were killing American soldiers.

I don't know how the science works behind EFPs, but I can tell you how they work in layman's terms. They are conical-shaped pieces of metal that are stuffed with explosives and topped off with copper or similar metals and then detonated, same as any other bomb. EFPs can be set off manually via hardwire, wirelessly, with sensors, and so on—basically up to the anarchist's imagination—and the explosives melt the copper at such a fast rate that it cuts through up-armored, mine-resistant, ambush-protected vehicles, or MRAPs armor, like a hot knife cuts through warm butter. I would unfortunately become very familiar with how EFP tactics were being used against my brothers in arms, but that story comes later.

I told 1LT Stephens that I believed the informant was telling me the truth and why. This goes against what a lot of people think about intel collectors, that we are supposed to hoard information so that we can have that feeling of authority over others without the information, but 1LT Stephens and I had an understanding. He knew legally I couldn't divulge informant information and that I could tell him no if he asked, but he never would have asked. He did also ask me to understand that he wouldn't put his men's lives at risk unless he felt good about the information. He was honest. He said he knew there is always a chance the information is wrong, and it was his job to think about all the other factors involved with conducting a mounted patrol through two towns known to harbor terrorists.

After some discussion and looking over some area overlays, he decided we would go after the cache. Up until this point, no caches had been found in our AO of this alleged size, and it was worth going out to investigate since EFP attacks were on the rise. It meant so much to me for some reason—that this battle-hardened platoon was willing to put themselves in harm's way, because I received information I believed to be credible and asked them to trust me and my gut. These young men were fathers, sons, brothers, and warriors. They remain to this day my driving force, professionally.

As the platoon circled around the OPORD (operation order) table and board, 1LT Stephens started going through all the necessities for an infantry platoon to conduct a mounted patrol. My job was to brief the intelligence piece. I stood up, wracked with nerves. I looked every single person in the tent square in the eyes before starting my briefing. They probably thought I was nuts, but to me I was showing them the respect they deserved. These men might never come back from this mission that my information and request was sending them on. I was recognizing that. I told them where the cache was and how it was hidden underneath blue barrels, similar to rain barrels, in the outside corner of a mosque. Religious radicalism was rampant then, and it didn't surprise us that the mosques were being used to hide and transport weapons and personnel.

On the way out to the mosque, I was quiet and extremely nervous. We were either going to find something while we were there, or we weren't, and I really didn't want to think about everyone digging for hours just to go home empty handed. I rode in the same vehicle that 1LT Stephens did. I was surprised with how quickly he put his platoon into a good security posture around the mosque, strategically placing personnel and vehicles in case we took contact. When he got out of the Humvee to get the guys to start searching, he told me, "Stay here in the truck, and take all commands from the gunner [who always stays with the truck]."

I replied with a solid "Yes, sir!" and he left.

They searched with mine sweepers and metal detectors for what seemed like hours, before the detectors started to alarm. I was looking out of the almost-four-inch-thick bulletproof glass of the Humvee, watching his men take their fifty pounds' worth of gear off to start digging in various areas.

After about twenty minutes of watching them dig, I couldn't take sitting in the truck any longer. I got out of the truck, walked over to one of privates assigned to dig for explosives, told him to take my place in the truck where the AC was working slightly, and I took his shovel from him to take over. Almost immediately after this happened, I remember one of the squad leaders yelling that they found something buried in the section of turf they were assigned to check. I continued to help dig, never finding any explosives myself, but everyone around me was finding something. We found barrels full of homemade explosives, or HMEs. We found multiple metal cones (two or three of which could have fit a basketball in it) that were meant to be used for EFPs, as well as some materials needed for multiple methods of detonation. We hit the jackpot. My credibility had survived the day, and because I was honest with LT Stephens, we took enough explosives off the street for over fifty good-sized EFPs.

It was some time during the digging before SSG Eads, the squad leader of the private I had traded places with, was walking around trying to find him. I ran over to SSG Eads and told him, "Staff Sergeant, I volunteered to trade places with him to give him a break. I hate sitting around watching other people work."

I thought SSG Eads was going to lose his shit. I knew I didn't have the authority to tell anyone what to do, and after about five seconds of my anticipating getting my ass chewed, he shook my hand and told me he'd never worked with an intel guy that was good at his job and wasn't an arrogant prick. That statement changed my life. I never forgot how good that day felt. I not only had proven on my first mission with them that I was good at my job, but also that I was willing to go out and risk my life too. Most of my intelligence peers and leadership stayed on the base, in their air-conditioned offices, drinking coffee. I knew after this day that I could never be satisfied with my work if I stayed on base and never joined these men. That may or may not have been the right answer; I faced a lot of resistance from my 3ID leadership when it came to me going off base, throughout this deployment. There were times SSG Guerra wouldn't report to our intelligence leadership that I was going out on mission, until I had already left. He took a lot of heat for me, throughout this deployment, in order to allow me to continue producing the way I was.

When we finally got back to the FOB safely, I remember feeling so high on life, as if we had just swooped in like Superman and saved someone's life. Reading daily reports of people losing life or limbs just for driving down the roads of Iraq was stressful, and it felt good to feel like we could depressurize the area by removing the IEDs, even if only for a day or two.

This next story is one of the main reasons I almost didn't write this book.

Following the EFP cache find, I began to refine and increase my operations tempo. I was meeting with two or more informants a day and going out on every single patrol that I was able to with the scouts. I went on overnight recon missions, dozens of raids, conducted interrogations, and most importantly, I was learning a lot from the people that I was fortunate enough to work with. I got into a groove of how to do things and began to trust my gut. When I was talking to informants, detainees, or locals on the street, a weird gut feeling would overcome me when I thought people were lying to me. I would be able to look at them, and depending on how they answered my question or their body language, I would know immediately if they were being honest. I learned how to ask questions and how to follow up with the right questions. I was learning how to construct a crime scene for analysis, how explosives worked, how radicals were pressuring people to commit acts of terror to save the lives of their children or to put food in their kids' mouths.

A few months after our initial EFP cache find, I started getting word that an EFP cell was moving into our AO. Insurgent networks were specifically targeting our area because they wanted to maintain control there. I hadn't known at that time, but when we took that cache off the streets a few months prior, it nearly crippled the cell that had hidden it. We had assumed correctly that EFPs were more than likely out of the area for a while, but what I didn't see coming was how quickly the tide could shift again.

It was early April 2008, and even though we had heard rumors that an EFP cell was moving back into the area, we hadn't seen any real evidence to prove it yet. I had eyes and ears (informants) all over the AO and was confident I had done my job well enough that there was no way a cell could penetrate the AO without me knowing about it. I was wrong, and it cost two American soldiers their lives. To this day I have only told this story to a handful of people, and I pray that I won't be judged too harshly for failing to prevent this attack. I was twenty-one-years-old. I worked eighteen- to twenty-hour days, every day, was taking online college classes, and trying to learn how to be a parent and husband from the Middle East, when my family needed me back home. We knew the EFP cell was coming; we just didn't know when. I should have been more vigilant. I should have known to expect the unexpected.

It was right after breakfast time in April of 2008 when I heard the boom. I was sitting in our team office, when our office was rattled, causing things to fall off my desk. I knew in the pit of my stomach what the sound was. SSG Raul Guerra made a call to confirm that it wasn't a controlled detonation. When he got confirmation, I donned my gear/kit and sprinted towards the tower closest to the black smoke. I thought the wall surrounding the FOB could have been on fire, the smoke was so close. I could smell it, as soon as I left my office. I knew by the amount of smoke and the scrambling of the Quick-Reaction Force (QRF) that one of our convoys was hit. I ran to the front gate, which was a place I was very familiar with. A Ugandan security force was responsible for perimeter security on the FOB. The Ugandans guarding the gate were waving Americans through the gate as if security protocol didn't matter anymore. The attack happened within a few hundred yards of our front gate and within eyesight of the guard tower. I didn't know how bad it was at this point or which unit got hit, but there is a nauseating feeling about getting sucker punched right outside the same place we slept and ate.

I was able to join the QRF as they left to support the convoy, which wasn't the first or last time I would find myself in a tough spot for not having clearance to leave the FOB from my direct superiors. I meant well, but I still had a hard time following the rules. Waiting for people to give me permission to do something, just seemed counterproductive. So, I left on my own accord, and I wasn't the only one. When the area was secured and cleared of any further devices, we began clearing out the MRAP that was hit. Two soldiers were killed in that attack, and a third soldier lost his legs. An EFP, one of the largest that we knew of to come through our AO, was emplaced using tactics and techniques that immediately put me on edge.

I knew just from the location, and how the attack happened on the ground, that this was a complicated attack. The line of sight from the guard towers was easily a kilometer or two in all directions. There was no way the people responsible for the bomb looked different than any of the locals that frequented that road; if those responsible looked out of the ordinary, the gate guards would have either opened fire or at least reported suspicious behavior. Black smoke was pouring out of the MRAP as soldiers were forming chains to remove all the sensitive items, weapons, and ammunition out of the vehicle – then it hit me. I saw someone pass an item from inside the truck and place it in my hands… I almost threw up and cried at the same time. It was a chunk of flesh from one of these brave men who just gave their lives. I became numb after that. Once we were done emptying the MRAP and I was done writing up my notes, I walked back to the base.

I took a shower to get the blood off of me and changed my uniform, before I went to the guard tower to ask them what they saw. I can't remember the kid's name, but I do remember how shaken he was. I could tell he felt guilty for not having seen the bomb, but then I guess I felt guilty too. It was one thing to find an EFP cache and get it off the streets; it was something else to hold a chunk of another man's flesh and see what an EFP could do to one of the Army's most advanced convoy vehicles to date. The armor didn't stand a chance.

I was on fire for justice now. I had seen death firsthand, because of a bomb that I was supposed to have been able to prevent. Where was all of my training? How did I let this happen? All these thoughts rushed through my mind as I was interviewing the kid from the guard tower. He told me he had been up there for hours, and he hadn't seen anyone that would have been able to plant a bomb so close to the FOB. I asked him some follow-up questions and then I looked for the guard roster for the previous twenty-four hours. I tracked down all of the guards who were present over a twenty-four-hour period and interviewed them as well. I asked if they saw anything suspicious or out of the ordinary. None of them saw anything that was worth taking note of—that is, until two days later when the kid from the tower came and found me.

He told me he remembered something that might be signifi-cant. He told me about this van that he saw drive through that same spot just a few minutes prior to the explosion. The van was traveling west on the road situated furthest north of the FOB boundary; when it slowed down momentarily in the area of the explosion, then sped up again. Now, if I'm being honest, my first reaction when I was hearing this was rage. How could this kid not have remembered this before? Why was he just coming forward about it now? Why didn't he warn someone? But then a spiritual kind of calm came over me. I took a deep breath, and I began to truly listen and understand him. He wasn't able to see that while the van gradually slowed down the north-facing side sliding door was opened, and a cunning man known as Abu Zara took this cleverly disguised EFP and placed it out of a moving vehicle. This was a spot that Abu Zara had pre-se-lected long before that day. Then they drove the van less than a half-kilometer away, never losing line of sight on their device, and detonated that device wirelessly. It took me and quite a few other very intelligent people—including 1LT Stephens, SSG Guerra, and even a retired Georgia Bureau of Investigation agent—to put all the pieces together. When we finally did, we were concerned. This attack wasn't like most of the attacks we had seen or thwarted so far; this attack required precision and planning. The location, the device, the detonator, even the van used were all meticulously planned out and rehearsed prior to the explosion. These weren't low-level criminals; they were trained explosives experts, and they had just hit me square in the face with reality. They were in our AO, and they meant business. My arrogance and inexperience had, in my opinion, cost two men their lives. I think about them every day of my life.

I put everything that I possibly could into taking down the entire cell that was responsible for that attack. Once the guard told me about the van, that was where we started, and we continued to pull at the thread until there was nothing left to unravel. I continued to work twenty-hour days, but following that EFP attack my tempo increased exponentially. Many nights I fell asleep at my desk while writing reports. I started having problems sleeping. My team leader was constantly yelling me at for not sleeping and eating enough. I got to the point where I was completely depleted from months of working very long days and not being able to sleep during the few hours I wasn't working each day. I knew I needed to be able to get some sleep, so I start drinking just enough whiskey or Nyquil to be able to fall asleep for a few hours, before hitting the grind again. Nyquil was a $4 bottle of liquid sleep that I could get at the Shoppette (military convenience store) on base, and I ended up addicted to it because I wasn't able to fall asleep without it. By June or July (only three months after the explosion), I was drinking half a bottle of Nyquil a night, just trying to get the picture of the MRAP out of my mind. I began to distance myself even further from my wife and daughter, from my leadership, and if I'm being frank, I began to watch the old me fade away.

I didn't have much time to feel too bad for myself in Iraq because within weeks of Abu Zara killing those American soldiers, the scout platoon and I found ourselves in a hectic hornet's-nest environment that we had provoked by targeting the insurgents in our area. One such day we had gotten word that an Iraqi police checkpoint was hit by a VBIED (Vehicle-Borne Improvised Explosive Device), right outside Tunis's (the town was due west and nearest to our FOB) southern border, and the Iraqi police were all killed. When we arrived at the checkpoint to assess the damage done, I could see blood and body parts everywhere. I remember distinctly seeing a face of one of the local policemen on the concrete, whom I'd had multiple friendly conversations with. Yes, I said I saw his face on the ground. Seeing it made me think about *The Texas Chainsaw Massacre* Hollywood hit where the maniac literally peeled the skin off people so that the face could be worn as a mask. That's what this looked like, and I wish I could say I don't see that face every day, but I do. There was a little hut where the guards would gather for heat and for electricity in the road median; where the police could check identification of incoming traffic to Tunis—that hut was gone. The debris was splintered all over the road, leaving little to the imagination of what happened.

I remember feeling so nauseous, knowing that these men died less than a few kilometers away from where we slept, and I didn't know about it beforehand, again. That whole day was nothing but a blur of pulling security, interviewing the locals surrounding in the vicinity, and helping console the Iraqi police whose comrades were murdered only hours before. The smell of smoke, gunpowder, and explosives was still in the air. We knew that this was a direct result of policies implemented and raids carried out in our area of operations. We were squeezing out the bad guys in the area by hunting them down one at a time, and they were lashing out as a cornered animal would before it becomes prey to the predator.

After that long day, we returned to the FOB and discussed the following day's mission; which would have us driving right through the area where the police station was hit, to a local dairy factory that made delicious yogurt. The scout platoon's company commander was going to attend a leader's meeting with local sheikhs. During that mission to take the commander to his meeting, I rode in the captain's vehicle because we were anticipating taking contact. The scout platoon wanted to ensure they didn't have any non-infantrymen in the assault element where a good number of injuries are normally sustained during attacks. I remember leaving the FOB and finding the lack of people outside and in town alarming, as did everyone else in the convoy. No kids, no people walking amongst the early-morning market, no police outside at the police checkpoint where the attack happened the day prior.

No sooner had we passed that same checkpoint before the gunshots started raining down on our convoy. I remember seeing a guy stand up from behind a berm on the eastern side of the road where we were taking contact with an RPG on his shoulder. It's amazing how slow you see things when you feel like you are about to die. I felt transfixed upon this grenade that had thick plumes of white smoke behind it swirling in our direction; that was when we noticed they were targeting our truck. I remember seeing this whiz of white smoke fly past the windshield of our Humvee, missing us by less than two feet, and smashing into a mud wall less than ten meters to the right of our vehicle. As I was sitting directly behind the commander, who was sitting in the front passenger seat, I had a particularly clear line of sight to this grenade that was still smoking and sticking out of a house.

I remember hearing the captain say something along the lines of, "That was close, SGT Calhoun, you should go take a look at that RPG."

I almost laughed and asked the captain what he thought I would be able to do, seeing as I didn't know the first thing about disarming grenades and didn't want to learn on a live grenade. On top of that, he seemed to have forgotten that we still had troops taking fire. He quickly came back to his senses and went fluidly into becoming a command-and-control element that could help the now-dismounted scout platoon work their way through the fields in which our assailants were now fleeing. I don't remember the precise details of how many bad guys those scouts killed that day, but I do remember how badass it felt walking into a meeting with local sheiks, relatively on time, after having just endured an ambush and acting as if it were all in a normal day's work.

Because we were so close to the FOB, the Explosives Ordinance Disposal guys were able to make quick work of the grenade stuck in the dairy farmer's wall, Civil Affairs was able to cover expenses, and we were able to move out in time for the meeting. Although I had no part in this fight other than gathering intel on the surviving assailants later on, I always wondered what would have happened if that grenade had gone off? Or had struck our vehicle?

We were almost over productive with the amount of information we were gathering after the ambush. We weren't going to allow anyone to shoot at us and get away with it. We became a vigilant and cohesive team of American soldiers, out for justice. The locals came to know the scouts as the "Painted Gun Platoon." When the bad guys found out we were in the area it was almost comical watching them, from aircraft videos later on, scattering in every different direction. The "Painted Gun Platoon" made them aware that their desire for jihad wasn't as great as their desire for survival, which was questionable if confronting these Americans.

I spent a lot of time down at the front gate with the Ugandan guards. I briefed them to call me, if anyone showed up saying they had information or intelligence, and they didn't have a point of contact already. So the guards would call me when there was someone at the gate with information, and they would even call me if they didn't know where to direct someone who was at the gate. The relationships I established with the gate guards paid dividends many times.

One day a guy showed up to the front gate of FOB Kalsu saying he had information about the location of a Jaysh Al-Mahdi (Mahdi's Army, Shia radical group) weapons cache. I brought the guy into my team's designated meeting room, and he began telling me all the details about weapons he had seen people hiding in his neighbor's yard. He was a terrible liar, and I could easily tell he was trying to get his neighbor in trouble for some reason. That didn't necessarily mean that there weren't weapons or that the neighbor wasn't a bad guy, but it was obvious to me that his intent wasn't pure. What he didn't know was that we were already planning on heading down that way that very same day. So I told him he could come with us and show us where the weapons were; then we could even possibly reimburse him for his troubles.

To my surprise, he agreed and even asked for a ski mask to hide his face. The drive out to his house was about an hour long, and as we turned onto the last semi-hard-surface road before reaching his house, I heard a deafening popping sound from behind our vehicle.

As we stopped to assess our surroundings, we found we were not taking fire but that the vehicle behind us had struck a small IED. After about ten minutes, the dust settled. We realized right away that the vehicle was still mission-capable. I don't even remember the tire being blown, although it may have been. The driver of my vehicle and I realized that we had just driven on top of the exact same spot where the bomb was located; but, for some reason, it didn't go off. It was a hair-raising realization to have, especially right after the RPG incident, but I still never associated it with God's role in my life. We were yet again able to continue our mission after being targeted. The informant we brought with us wasn't fazed at all about the fact that we had hit an IED less than a kilometer from his house. We all believed he knew the IED was there. We continued on to his house, so that he could show us where the weapons cache was, before dealing with any of his transgressions.

He hopped out of the Humvee and began to run toward a tree line. The guy started running from one tree to the next. He stopped at about eight different trees to pick up eight different explosive devices. He also spent a little time standing around, scratching his head, as if confounded that there wasn't more stuff to be found. He kept circling around and going back to one particular tree that he said he felt sure was where his neighbor had stashed something. Once he was done bringing us the explosives—which by this point we were positive he had himself emplaced to try and get his neighbor arrested—I turned him around, put him on his knees, zip-tied his hands together behind his back, and searched him again, just in case he had a hidden explosive device on him at some point during his charade. We brought him to the Iraqi police station while en route back to the FOB to turn him over for questioning. I didn't find out until months later that he was a supply runner for JAM and was trying to ditch his weapon stash—out of which the RPG fired at us came from—in the backyard of his neighbor, with whom he had been at odds for years.

I still look back on that day and thank God for protecting my brothers and me from the bomb that could have easily killed everyone in the vehicle. That was the closest I'd ever been to an IED going off. It wasn't even a very big IED, but it scared the crap out of me.

74

Events like those will change how a man views the world. When you spend over a year of your life fearing that you are the next IED victim because every time you turn around someone in Iraq is getting blown up, it just changes how you think—at least it did for me.

Toward the end of the 2008 summer, we had rounded up a good chunk of the IED cells operating in our area. In an effort to try and get the remaining cell members, the 2-502 led a battalion-sized raid on a small village and surrounding rural areas known to house insurgents. I was one of many different assets on the ground during this particular raid. Because of my knowledge of the area and my informant's house being in the target area, it was decided that I would ride onto the objective with a supporting element. The supporting element was tasked with clearing the area near my informant's house, so it was logical to ride with them. The scouts filled their seats with infantrymen because they were heading for the most hostile area. It didn't matter to me whom I rode with; but after this mission, I never took for granted how efficient the scouts were.

After certain elements had been inserted via Blackhawks, our element drove in from the southwest. As we entered the village, one of the MRAP vehicles got tangled up in low-hanging power lines crossing the road, which caused mechanical issues in the MRAP. The turret in that MRAP started turning on its own and wouldn't stop, as a result of the energy surge from the power lines. The gunner, with all of his gear, was stuck in that turret as it spun around. Just as he started to feel the flesh of his torso reach the point of tearing, one of the other passengers in the vehicle realized what was happening and hit the emergency release. The gunner had red streaks across his torso, where his flesh had been on the verge of ripping. I'm not sure what would have happened to that guy if he hadn't been freed from his seat, but ever since then, I have carried a seat belt cutter with me in all military vehicles. The thought of being contorted and twisted to death just sounds terrible.

While I didn't know any of this while it was happening, we did notice that the power went out in the section of town we were driving through. Since we were already anticipating taking enemy contact, the seriousness of our situation changed a bit. It's hard enough to look for

IEDs at nighttime, but to do so with zero electricity lighting up the town, it was near impossible. I was riding in another vehicle with some guys I didn't know in the headquarters company, and their mission was to drop me and my interpreter CJ off at a certain house. Our goal was to talk with an informant to get time-sensitive information about insurgent bed-down locations. We knew we were in the correct area, but we didn't want to kick in everyone's doors looking for insurgents unless we had to; knowing exact locations worked best. The rules were changing. We needed credible intelligence to allow any commander the peace of mind to make a decision that could potentially cost Iraqis their lives by sending Americans into their homes looking for known insurgents. For security reasons, the informants are never aware of when missions like this one will take place.

I still struggle with the looks of sheer terror on the faces of children and women, when they saw scary American soldiers standing in their bedrooms at 2:00 am, grabbing their father/husband by the scruff of his neck and dragging him into another room where CJ and I would question him and try to get time-sensitive information. While CJ and I were talking to my informant, the group of guys that dropped us off were supposed to be clearing houses near the one we were in and then escorting CJ and me to another location where we would continue our interviews. The convoy we rode in stopped about two kilometers away from our target house. CJ, about a squad's worth of guys, and I had to walk to the house. When they were done clearing what needed to be cleared, we were supposed to walk back to the trucks together. After about twenty minutes of talking with my informant, CJ and I went outside to speak with the squad leader. To our surprise, we weren't able to find him. There were three other military-age males in the house we were in, and they were all walking around freely, as if there hadn't been an American in their presence for at least a few minutes. They told CJ that the other Americans had said something on the radio, and then all took off at a slight run back the way we had all come.

The other soldiers we were with had completely forgotten about CJ and me. Now, CJ and I were two kilometers away from the closest American soldier, with an entire village to traverse through to get back to the vehicles, if they were still there. Once we all came to the realization that CJ and I had been left behind, the looks CJ and I were both getting didn't need interpretation. The Iraqis were surprised, but they didn't show any signs of hospitality or a desire to assist us. The looks we were getting were those of people entertaining thoughts of turning American soldiers over to the local radicals. When CJ and I both realized this, we left the house and started briskly walking back the way we had come. I had my M4 and my M9 on me, but since CJ was a civilian, he wasn't authorized to carry a weapon issued by the military. Fortunately for me, CJ and I had spent considerable time on the range shooting, and I knew firsthand he was one hell of shot with a sidearm. So I unholstered my pistol and handed it to CJ. We didn't need to say anything to each other, because we both knew how bad this situation could get if we didn't get back to the main element.

That was one of the longest walks of my life, and even though my mind was telling me to run like a coward and get back to safety, my gut kept telling me: just keep walking, don't look around a lot, and don't talk to anyone. I was on edge, and CJ and I both realized about the same time we were being watched by seemingly random military-aged males. They were periodically coming out on their rooftops to get a look at us, and then they would say something into the cell phones they had in their hands. It felt like only a minute after seeing the first guy that a dog came out of one of the houses, less than six yards to our left, and lunged at CJ. The dog was trying to take a bite out of him. I kicked the dog square in the rib cage as hard as I could, and it yelped and scampered away to catch its breath after having it knocked forcefully out of its lungs.

I thought CJ was going to shoot that dog, and I don't know what would have happened if he had. I am still impressed that CJ not only managed to evade the lunging animal, but he showed extreme restraint when others might not have. CJ knew just as well as I did that the quiet and our constant moving were the only two things going in our favor. We didn't want to shoot anything, because if it triggered a reaction, CJ and I were obviously ill-equipped to handle it.

As we were getting closer to where the vehicles had dropped us off, two things happened simultaneously. First, I noticed that a small, green-and-white pickup truck with four military-age males had started creeping behind us about one hundred yards back or so. We also heard a radio call with my call sign; something that wasn't heard very often. The squad leader had gotten back to the vehicles, and thought for some reason that the entire convoy was moving out and that CJ and I had left without their knowledge. In other words, they thought we had left already and took off as fast as possible to try and find us. Once they got to the trucks, they assumed we had gotten a ride with someone else to the next objective and went there themselves. Thankfully, the squad leader went and found the platoon sergeant and confirmed that my position was unknown. He immediately turned back around with his three-truck element, while calling for me on the radio. They came around the corner to where CJ and I were walking, with our friends in the little pickup truck watching the whole time.

Once we were back in the Humvees, CJ gave me back my sidearm, and we told the squad leader about the truck following us. The pick-up truck hadn't even turned around yet, before they had those men at gunpoint and made them get out of the vehicle. They didn't have any weapons, but they had two handheld radios, and after we interviewed them all, we found out one of them was a target that we had been searching for. He was a low-level guy, but we wanted to make it a clean sweep, hence our flushing them out via BN operation.

All in all, that was a great day, because we came home safe, caught a bad guy, and have a story to tell that could just as easily have gone the other way for CJ and me. It wasn't until that night that I remembered my NTC trip and getting left behind by a unit that didn't know me well. It was at that moment that I realized I had been unintentionally trained to react to getting left behind, because I had done it before. I didn't let my natural reaction of freaking out occur. I knew what to do, because I had a test run in training, and after that incident I studied the proper courses of action just in case it ever happened again.

I could write an entirely different book about how the scout platoon and I tracked down and either killed or detained every single one of the cell members involved in the EFP attack that took two American lives right outside of our gate; but, in my opinion it would be an incomplete book because we never got the leader. My entire deployment to Iraq lasted 17 months, and came to an end before I could catch Abu Zara. I personally gathered intelligence on the driver, on Abu Zara, on the supplier, on the members of their early warning networks, and on where the explosives were coming from. All while continuing all of the other operations I was juggling. But no matter how hard I tried or how many sleepless nights I had, I would never find that piece-of-shit coward who wasn't man enough to fight an American head-on. His cell members all broke during interrogations, leading to the imminent downfall of the entire cell.

There are so many more stories that I could tell about my time in Iraq, but that isn't the purpose of this book. I had the privilege of working with the Scout Platoon, 2/502 Airborne Infantry Regiment, for approximately fifteen months. I believe an angel was with us. We didn't take any casualties in the fifteen-month time period we got to work together, despite many near-fatal encounters. I went out on multiple missions every week, but I don't remember even one day that the Scout Platoon didn't go out on a mission. God was looking out for us then, just like he is right now.

Retrospective

"And He will wipe away every tear from their eyes; and there will no longer be any death; there will no longer be any mourning, or crying, or pain; the first things have passed away."

—Revelation 21:4

Iraq was literally the best of times and the worst of times for me. I was very fortunate to have been placed on a team with Jason. He kept me very centered and made sure I wasn't overextending myself. After the EFP explosion outside of our FOB, everything changed for me inside. From that point on, I wanted only to make sure our area wasn't ever struck like that again. Jason and my team leader, SSG Guerra, were constantly on me about not sleeping or eating enough, telling me to take breaks and slow down occasionally. Jason even confronted me about my Nyquil addiction, which made me respect him even more as a friend.

We need to surround ourselves with friends that will call us out for making poor decisions, even when we don't want to hear it. We also need to listen and appreciate when someone is trying to help us to see something that we aren't currently seeing. If we don't allow ourselves to be corrected and helped by those around us who care for us, then we are going to suffer more in this life than we need to. We need to be careful not to ignore and not to push away any source of truth and honest criticism in our lives. God will put people in our lives that can and should help us; Jason was a great help to me during this long deployment.

We took apart that cell and it felt good; but, since that deployment, I realized I left a part of myself there in Iraq. I failed to catch the one person responsible for killing such good and loving soldiers. The death of those two soldiers still weighs heavily on me. That remains a struggle for me, even though I know with absolute certainty that it isn't God reminding me and bringing up my past failures. I see the vehicle they were killed in every single night in my head, but God's grace is sufficient for me. I did everything that I could to not let their deaths be in vain. My guilt is what drove me to give everything that I had to offer during those long months. I was humbled so completely by this event, that I believe God was able to use me for the remainder of this deployment. I wasn't perfect, I was a punk in a lot of ways, but what I credited to "my gut" before, I now believe was the Holy Spirit guiding me. God's power was made perfect in my weakness. I was all in after that. I was young but extremely motivated to do everything I could to prevent more American deaths. God took my motivation and drive and helped me make it effective and fruitful.

> "The Lord is my shepherd, I shall not want. He makes me lie down in green pastures; He leads me beside quiet waters. He restores my soul; He guides me in the paths of righteousness For His name's sake. Even though I walk through the valley of the shadow of death, I fear no evil, for You are with me; Your rod and Your staff, they comfort me. You prepare a table before me in the presence of my enemies; You have anointed my head with oil; My cup overflows. Surely goodness and lovingkindness will follow me all the days of my life, And I will dwell in the house of the Lord forever." (Psalm 23)
>
> "You will not be afraid of the terror by night, or of the arrow that flies by day." (Psalm 91:5)

When we started picking up momentum, I was going out on missions every single day with the scouts, and we rarely came back without information or intelligence. We were on a hot streak, and the insurgents were feeling the pressure. I remember life slowing down, when that RPG was coming toward our vehicle, almost as if it were surreal. I felt detached from my body, watching it run through the motions. While I was watching the scouts maneuver on the enemy, the grenade was hissing as it stuck out of the farmer's wall.

Surreal moments became frequent for me, and they would often happen to me while in the middle of interviews or conversations with informants. I would feel an urge to ask questions that I hadn't previously planned on asking and wouldn't have thought of on my own. I was relying on my "gut," as I would call it, during that time, because my ability to discern truth from fiction was becoming more accurate. I know now that it was the Holy Spirit guiding me.

I could tell if a person was lying to me many times before the words were translated. I started to think it was my skills that were improving, and then I'd have a dream about that blood stained MRAP that I had helped to recover. My humility would return, and my drive to do more increased. That was how Iraq was for me, an emotional roller coaster of a ride.

I have taken the time to confront my past and embrace these memories of mine. I have come to understand that all of my "luck" was not a coincidence. I don't think it is coincidence that I was in a vehicle that drove over at least one known IED that didn't go off, but then struck the vehicle behind me without giving even one of the passengers so much as a headache or damaging the vehicle. The RPG not going off. CJ and I having a pickup truck full of unfriendly military-aged males follow us for roughly two kilometers, after being left behind by the convoy, but catching up to our unit unharmed. We successfully detained or killed every single member of Abu Zara's EFP cell, without one single casualty or combat-related injury to the scout platoon members. These were all thanks to, and because of, God. The Lord never once left me alone in Iraq, and we had great success because of His presence around us.

SSG Raul Guerra was such a blessing me to throughout this entire deployment. He truly enabled and supported me to be able to do my job. I would get into trouble on a somewhat regular basis, by breaking the rules to get my job done. If I didn't think intelligence was making it past my chain of command, I had established a relationship with someone high ranking and outside of my chain of command, and he often encouraged me to come to him with what I was working on. That individual was able to influence the missions the scouts and I went on; he was able to authorize or move things along for us. I also went on missions with the scouts multiple times each week, and my intelligence chain of command didn't want me leaving the FOB. SSG Guerra would back me up continuously even when it meant getting an ass chewing himself. He saw the results of my work, and he was willing to go out on a limb for me because of that. He would always come back from chow with a Mango in hand, and whenever I stirred the pot with our chain of command he would yell at me while eating his mango. I won't ever look at a mango without thinking of SSG Guerra. He died in Afghanistan on July 4, 2012, and he is greatly missed.

It amazes me when I think of everything that I did up until this point in my life. I was definitely a rule breaker. I had made many mistakes. I was arrogant at times. I was more than willing to break through or go around obstacles that were standing in my way, when I thought I was right, even when it meant ignoring the authority placed over me. There are so many things that I would do differently, if I were put in a similar situation today. I choose to believe that I could have found a way to be effective at my job, if I had approached the obstacles I faced with a different/better attitude. The amazing part for me is that God was willing to use me, even while I was not doing and saying all of the right things. God can use anyone. Just be prepared to be humbled, and be prepared to work hard.

WLC/Air Assault School

After Iraq a lot of things changed for me personally and for our unit, which is normal after a long deployment. Personnel changes happen frequently, and some of us were getting ready to change duty stations while others would remain with the unit. For those of us staying with the unit, it was time to get some military training in and then get ready for the next deployment. I had gotten promoted toward the end of the deployment, so I was a sergeant and now a team leader. We had new leadership from the battalion level all the way down to the company level.

When a soldier gets promoted to the NCO ranks, they are required to attend training that will teach and enable them as new leaders to perform and function properly within their units. So off I went to Fort Stewart's Warrior Leader Course (WLC) to learn how to be an NCO. I actually enjoyed my time there, because I found the tactical training very easy plus we were getting food and plenty of sleep. I studied the Ranger Handbook and FM 7-8 (infantry rifle platoon and squad) in Iraq to try and learn how to better integrate into the scout platoon. The Ranger Handbook is essentially a basic tactical manual for Rangers, and that time studying it paid dividends. The only thing I didn't like at this academy was our having to recite the NCO creed over and over again, while waiting in line for chow. We weren't permitted to eat until we properly recited the creed. I'm not going to lie. I managed to forget the creed a whole lot faster than I learned it, but I definitely understand why they made us memorize it. Being an NCO is an enormous responsibility and privilege.

I was in great shape, and it showed during the Physical Fitness Test (PFT) on day one of WLC. To attend any military school, the first thing required of all soldiers at that school is to pass a PFT. The

Army standard is to only train soldiers within regulation, which failing PFT scores are not. The PFT has three events: push-ups, sit-ups, and the 2-mile run, in that order. As we were all in our push-up lines, waiting to be tested, there was a big group of Rangers near me. They were all talking about how they were going to show everyone up and were discussing which of them would get the highest PFT score. I never said a word to them, but I decided in that moment that I wanted to beat every single one of them in that PFT. My motivation level for doing well skyrocketed. I did end up beating every single one of them, and I earned the Iron Sergeant award for getting the highest PFT score during that WLC class.

At the end of the course, I also placed within the top 10 percent of my class, earning the highly coveted Commandant's List award, which decorates NCOs with superior leadership qualities. WLC was a good confidence-boosting moment for me at that point in my life, because when I thought about Rangers or guys in higher-tiered units, I always envisioned these Olympic athletes. But here they were, a bunch of guys, bragging about how badass they were, but were beaten by a skinny intelligence guy. I'm pretty sure they were all legitimate warriors, but it felt good for me to know that I had earned a place at the table of respect. Just because I was a POG (person other than a grunt) didn't mean I wasn't capable of competing with guys who are generally expected to maintain a higher level of physical fitness.

After WLC I was able to really meet my new BN commander and CSM because they were invited to my graduation ceremony (first time our BN ever won an Iron SGT award). After the graduation ceremony, my BN commander came up to me and handed me a BN coin and told me since I did so well, he was going to give me a four-day weekend. I jumped at that four-day weekend like any other young father and husband would have.

When that mini-vacation ended, I came back to work. Our unit was transitioning from an armor brigade to a light infantry brigade. Because of that transition, I found out that our BN had been given two slots, for the first time ever, for an Air Assault course at Fort Benning, Georgia. Our BN was having a PFT competition for those slots. The two soldiers with the highest scores in the BN would get to go.

I want to take a quick second to give some context as to why this story is funny to me. Our CSM was an engineer and was in love with the engineer company in our BN. He actually stood in front of our formation before the PFT and told everyone that he didn't expect anyone to beat out the engineers. He was an engineer, and that meant engineers were by default the best soldiers in the BN. Not only did his engineers not get the two highest scores in the BN, both slots went to HUMINT soldiers. I got one slot, and one of the high-speed female soldiers in my platoon, Marcia, got the other slot. As petty as it may be, I really enjoyed seeing the look on CSM's face when two intel soldiers bested his engineer company. I was tired of being looked at like some guy who couldn't understand what "real combat" was like, simply because I was an intelligence professional. I was determined to set and achieve high goals. I would not allow others to put limits on my potential.

Air Assault school was a very short and physically demanding course that ended with some badass rappelling from a tall tower and helicopters, which is just some adrenaline-filled fun. Sure, guys have done cooler stuff, but how many people get to say they have rappelled out of a helicopter? I can't imagine it's too many, and I was glad to be one of them. After Marcia and I returned from our Air Assault graduation ceremony, we were given duties to help train and assist other people with passing Air Assault school standards. We devised a training plan that would help the CSM feel better about sending his engineers to Air Assault School.

The class following ours gave our battalion eight slots for Air Assault, all of which went to male engineers in our battalion. Of those eight soldiers, only two graduated the course; the rest of them either failed or quit the PFT or obstacle course. That really made poking fun at the engineers easy and fun to do. They talked a lot of shit; it was good and healthy for them to get a dose of humility every once in a while.

While all this was going on, I also found out that I wouldn't be getting orders out of 3ID, as I had hoped. By this time I had been stationed with 3ID for about three years, and typically after three years orders would come down to move a soldier to his or her next duty station. Many of my friends and fellow soldiers in 3ID were being given orders to leave, but it apparently wasn't in the cards for me.

I was proud to have served with the 3ID, but I didn't want it to be my life anymore. I had also become a little accustomed to working with the scout platoon during my deployment to Iraq. The scout platoon was different from my unit in that everyone pulled their own weight in the scout platoon. In regular Army units, you will find many people who are lazy, or on medical profile. I was finding it hard to cope with all the soldiers on medical profiles, which excused them from having to do various physical labors and heavy lifting. Medical profiles are extremely important, and some soldiers really need them from time to time; some soldiers just abuse what medical profiles are intended for, in order to get out of hard or unpleasant work. So a few carried the load for the many, and I was tired of carrying the weight of others. These circumstances birthed my desire to earn my way into an elite force. I wanted to be part of a team of soldiers who would all pull their weight to achieve the mission.

I really started struggling with a feeling of strangulation. I had reached my limit of stress with work and the exhaustion of always giving one hundred percent. I ended up telling my wife that I had too much on my plate and that I had nothing left to offer at the end of the workday. I eventually asked her for a divorce and asked her to take our daughter and leave. If something had to give, I knew it couldn't be the Army, so I thought it had to be my family.

Retrospective

"Do you see a man skilled in his work? He will stand before kings; He will not stand before obscure men."

—Proverbs 22:29

My time spent at WLC and Air Assault School was important because that's when I began to take on leadership positions and responsibilities. I learned a lot at both the WLC and Air Assault courses, but the main thing that they both did for me was boost my self-confidence. While I admit that I became more arrogant after exceeding the standards of both schools, that confidence is what helped to inspire my need to test my worth at Special Forces Assessment and Selection (SFAS or Selection for short). It wasn't until after Air Assault that I realized I had reached my maximum potential with 3ID, and I was ready for the next challenge. I felt like a saturated sponge sitting around waiting for the next tide (deployment) to come in.

When my wife left, I realized how lonely I really was in the world. My wife and daughter were my closest family, and I had just sent them away because I didn't know how to be a soldier, husband, and father. I didn't think my wife could understand the stress I was under or that I needed to drink the stress away. At this point in my life, I felt completely void of any emotion other than anger. I put everything I had into my work, but I didn't put everything I had into my family. I thought that I could claim to not be a quitter, just because I hadn't quit anything professionally. Yet, I was choosing to quit being a husband, and I was choosing to quit on my family.

Darkness can creep in, whenever and wherever we don't overcome it with light. I never stopped to think about what I was doing to my family. I didn't understand how to overcome what was making me angry or clouding my judgment. I didn't have spiritual discernment or the Word of God to help me to see the unseen enemy. When I look back on this with spiritual reflection, it is obvious that I was under spiritual attack. Evil was working to isolate and discourage me. I had driven my family away; my friends were getting orders to move; and I didn't have hope of another fruitful deployment with this same unit.

Before Selection

It wasn't until about a month or two after Air Assault School and after my family moved to a different state that I really began having a hard time with life. I was drinking on average a six-pack of beer a night; sometimes I polished off a whole case by myself in a weekend. I was having a hard time finding the motivation to work—not that I was becoming lazy, but more like, I had lost the drive that I had in Iraq. I still had potential, but something was missing.

I was growing tired of Fort Stewart and the "Dog-Faced Soldier" song. I hated having to sit around on Friday evenings doing motor-pool maintenance or plucking weeds. I was sick and tired of getting yelled at for having my hands in my pockets or for wearing my hat like a country singer instead of a soldier. CSM was all about maintaining Army regulations and he made a constant point to find me whenever possible to highlight something I was doing wrong, rightfully so.

I was feeling restless and wanted to leave the Third Infantry Division. I loved the experience, but I knew it was time for me to go. That's when things started to get spicy for me. I had never considered trying out for Special Forces before this point in my life. In Iraq I was fortunate enough to train alongside a Special Forces task force to locate and secure captured American soldiers. Even then, I never saw myself wanting to be a Green Beret.

I always viewed myself as more of an aspiring James Bond than a John Rambo. I don't know many soldiers who were worth their weight and weren't incited to jealousy, when seeing Special Forces (SF) recruitment posters or Green Berets walking around. I think many of us would see those posters or SF soldiers walking around, and wonder if we had what it took to achieve what they had. I think that is healthy and needed; we should all have something to reach for and to be inspired by. What red, white, and blue bleeding patriot doesn't want to don that prestigious presidential award? Those guys always looked like they had their shit together, wore their sunglasses everywhere, and always had at least one hand in their pocket.

You had better believe these things caught my attention, so I decided to inquire about it—gather information if you will—just to see what it was all about. I sat down for one of the recruitment pitches where the guy tells you all about: the different schools you would go through, the types of missions you would be doing, the exotic places you could go, and the badass shit you could do. All it takes is passing Special Forces Assessment and Selection, successfully graduating the Special Forces Qualification Course (SFQC, or Q-Course for short), then earning your spot on an Operational Detachment Alpha, or ODA.

Not everyone who I worked with knew what Green Berets did, but we all knew about some of the more famous stories following 9/11. Stories of Green Berets nearly destroying the Taliban. We had all seen the SF guys in Iraq. They were dressed in civilian clothes all the time, until it was time for a mission. They could be seen at all sorts of odd times throughout the day, coming and going through their own private gate, and occasionally leaving through one of the main FOB exits. When we saw them going out a gate they were kitted up, in uniform, and ready to accomplish their mission. I always felt safer knowing we had an ODA on the base, because I knew the assets that brought and what that meant. If we were ever messed with we had some of America's best, running and gunning, to neutralize any combatants.

I remember coming back from that recruitment briefing pumped up. I knew that my chances of making it through were slim, but I had already accomplished more than I thought I would by this point. I wanted to find a road less traveled. A few different people in my BN already went to Selection, but no one from my BN had ever been selected. Not one Green Beret had ever started their career from my battalion, so it felt as though the odds were stacked against me.

I began to train hard, every day, to prepare for Selection. I heard the stories: people's skin coming right off their feet because of the road marches, people becoming so dehydrated that they passed out and died before help could come, and people getting attacked by poisonous snakes while out in the woods alone—oh yes, I had heard the stories.

I knew that I was going to struggle more than most would, physically. Keep in mind, at this time I might have weighed 150 pounds. I was in good shape, but I knew that I was never going to gain fifty pounds and bench-press cars with my physical build. For the longest time I compared myself to others, because I was never stronger or even as strong as my friends. At least one of them was always faster, smarter, or more technically savvy than I was. I was scoring well and beating others on the PFT, but that didn't mean I was stronger or faster. I couldn't even explain why I was beating many in the PFT.

My advantage had never been my physical strength or speed, or even intelligence. Don't get me wrong, God blessed me. I considered myself to be in shape and intelligent, but my advantage was elsewhere. My body frame and type wasn't made to carry 65- to 125-pound rucksacks for long distances. I would learn to mentally overcome that weakness. I had a lot of weaknesses that I would have to mentally overcome.

I rucked three to five times a week at different weights, durations, and distances for months (all on top of the daily PT (Physical Training) being done at my company and my volunteering to run remedial PT for PT failures at the end of every workday)—all to prepare for Selection. I was doing PT with the recruitment office for a while before my battalion commander found out and complained. Not sure why this guy had it out for me, but as a sergeant in the military, I had always assumed people just looked out for their soldiers and peers. If a soldier of mine came to tell me he wanted to go to SFAS, I would do everything in my power to make that happen and would be honored to have known the man willing to push his limits for Uncle Sam.

When my battalion commander found out I was going to Selection, the first thing he did was deny me access to a promotion board, which I was already slotted to attend less than a week later.

Then he called me into his office, invited CSM into his office, and shut the door so nobody could overhear the conversation. Then they both broke all professional boundaries and began personally and professionally insulting and belittling me. My commander stated that there was no way someone like me could make it through the pipeline. I stood there, and listened to all of his threats and attacks against me, without responding. Before I was allowed to leave the battalion commander's office, he said to me, "When you fail to get selected, SGT Calhoun, you will come back to this BN, and I will personally ensure that you never get promoted or leave this unit. This is your family, and only a quitter would leave their family six months before a deployment."

Retrospective

Do not be deceived: "Bad Company corrupts good morals."
—1 Corinthians 16:33

I had every reason to not pursue the avenue of Special Forces. I was unlikely to succeed. I was berated; made to feel as though my aspirations of being a part of more rigorous training, more dangerous missions, and a faster-paced military unit was somehow quitting on my unit. I had heard fatal stories of soldiers who had gone before me and tried to earn the Green Beret. I saw friends go to Selection and fail; those friends were bigger and stronger than me. I was promised a miserable military life and career upon my seemingly inevitable return to 3ID, if I failed or wasn't selected.

Though times may seem impossible, and we may be discouraged or mocked, God is with us. God made a way for me. God used all the discouragement I had and turned it into motivation to succeed. This was one of the bigger steps of faith I have taken in my life, but God is faithful, and my step of faith was not misplaced.

"Do all things without grumbling or disputing; so that you will prove yourselves to be blameless and innocent, children of God above reproach in the midst of a crooked and perverse generation, among whom you appear as lights in the world." (Philippians 2:14–15)

Sometimes letting go of the familiar things in life can be challenging or even scary. I could have stayed with the Third Infantry

Division for another deployment and been successful, but the yearning in my heart for more was overwhelmingly powerful. I believe now that the Holy Spirit drew me to that SFAS recruitment briefing. The Holy Spirit was at work deep inside, pulling me away from the Third Infantry Division and pushing me into the glimmer of hope that I was meant to do more with the blessings God was going to bestow upon me.

> "He saved us, not on the basis of deeds which we have done in righteousness, but according to His mercy, by the washing of regeneration and renewing by the Holy Spirit, whom He poured out upon us richly through Jesus Christ our savior." (Titus 3:5–6)

Throughout my entire life, I can see how God worked everything, even the bad, together for my good. I can't say that enough. If my wife and daughter were still with me and I didn't have the free time that I did, I would not have been able to train and prepare each day the way that I did. Those countless hours that I trained were absolutely critical for me.

God also worked the backlash that I faced with my commander and CSM for my good. I want to use this venue to thank my battalion commander for acting in such a childish manner. He and CSM spoke to me and made me feel like an outcast for wanting to join an elite Army unit. That really bothered me. The words spoken to me that day in the commander's office fueled me each day that I was in Selection. I left his office feeling like crap but very determined to never look him in the eyes as a quitter or failure. The hatred I felt toward my commander was a greater motivator to succeed than any SF recruitment poster could be.

Special Forces Assessment and Selection

I flew from Savannah, Georgia, to Fayetteville, North Carolina, enroute to Fort Bragg. Fort Bragg is home to the Eighty-Second Airborne and the Special Forces Command. Fort Bragg is also where soldiers go for SFAS and the SFQC. It was September 2009, the weather was warm during the day with a possibility of chill during the night, perfect weather for attempting Selection. I took the military shuttle, with nothing but my packing-list items in a duffel bag, from the airport to Fort Bragg. I didn't know what to expect, but I wasn't going to take any chances and show up with too much stuff to have to carry.

The shuttle driver pulled up to this run-down barracks building on Fort Bragg and told me, "This is it."

I looked at him and said, "You can't be serious."

He completely ignored me. I hopped out and walked into the barracks building. I was met by the fire guard/reception desk. I told the soldier behind the desk my name, and he shuffled through some papers until he found my name on some list. He told me to rack out in an open bunk somewhere. We were leaving the next morning, and he said the cadre are oftentimes not very nice to people who aren't packed up and ready to roll. This wasn't my first rodeo, so I expected to play some Army games, but what I was about to go through would be much more than that. I walked to one of the nearby Shoppettes that night, grabbed some snacks, and then went back to the barracks to get some sleep.

I was one of the first people standing outside with my gear the next morning waiting for our ride. We all hopped on the old

Blue Bird buses that showed up, and they took us out to a place called Camp Mackall. The mere name of Camp Mackall tends to send waves of emotion through me. If you have been there, whether your experiences there ended in happiness or pain, nothing is free at Camp Mackall. There are no "fuck fuck" games (term often used when students aren't following instruction). There are great men training other men to become greater men. Every man there has to earn his own keep. The Special Forces courses are run so efficiently I think it would surprise some Fortune 500 companies.

The cadre at Selection are famous for their mundane attitudes, and for always being willing to achieve mental superiority at any given time. The cadre at Selection are the first people that will ever assess a soldier in terms of trainability, leadership ability, and team cooperativeness —all of which are critical for a Green Beret to be successful in his career. Even the students evaluate their peers, after certain phases of training.

We would rate and compare the performance and attitude of our peers. If there were 20 students total, we would have to place all of our peers in positions/ranks of 1-19 (we didn't evaluate ourselves). So, we would have to rate someone first, someone last, and everyone else in every position in-between. Most of the time we were also given pink and blue cards to give out if we needed/wanted to: blue cards were meant for someone that may have gone above and beyond, and the pink cards were meant to indicate someone we did not want to work with (for any number of reasons). The blue and pink slips were anonymous, but we did write on those cards why we were giving them, and the recipients were told what those cards said. We were told what was on the cards, so that we had every opportunity to improve.

We have all known someone who never put in the work himself or herself, but have reaped rewards because of others grouped with them. Well, the cadre can't be everywhere, and with this peer system, they don't have to be. Part of the concept is that the strong will separate from the weak naturally. The weak will either quit or will be physically or emotionally unable to complete a phase of training. If all else fails, the people who are putting in the work have a venue to tell cadre in these peer evaluations how the team feels about each individual person. People can peer low for multitudes of reasons, but I tended to notice that the rankings were fair and accurate.

I won't give too much about Selection away, but it's broken down into phases. The first phase is pretty much a standard phase in any Army school, in that the PFT is the first event, and I was simply amazed at how many people failed the PFT. This was no regular test, but nonetheless, failing on day one is simply unacceptable to me. I remember watching the guy in front of me during the push-up part of the PFT doing what I would have considered immaculate push-ups. The cadre grading his push-ups kept repeating the same number: 17...*thump*...17...*thump*...17...*thump*. I could hear his chest bounce off the ground, but he never got credit for more than seventeen push-ups. I was wondering if it wasn't some kind of test. At the end of that two minute push-up event the guy stood up, and the cadre looked him dead in the face and said, "Candidate, you failed to meet the required number of push-ups for this event, get back in line, and prepare for the next event."

The guy looked around, glanced in my direction briefly, then looked at the cadre and said, "Why even waste my time if I already failed?"

Then he walked away to the main office where candidates were told to go if they were going to quit or voluntarily withdraw (V-DUB, as those familiar with the term called it).

I was up next. I knew I had to start strong and make every push-up count. I started pumping out perfect push-ups. Even with my lanky frame and long arms, my chest was bouncing off the ground. I could hear the cadre counting: 17...*thump*...18...*thump*...19... *thump*...20...*thump*...20...*thump*...20. Wait a minute, he stopped counting at twenty. As my body continued to do as perfect a push-up as I knew how, I was debating internally. Was this it? Was I getting cut already? What was I doing wrong? Then I decided that if I was going to fail, I would fail giving 100 percent. I pushed that ground as hard as I could for the entire two-minute period. I left it all on the ground, let the sweat all drip down to the earth.

I stood up and the cadre said to me, "Candidate, you have failed to reach the required number of push-ups to pass the push-up event, go to the end of the line, and prepare for the next event."

That was it. I looked toward the office where the other guy had gone. I thought about how embarrassing it was going to be when I went back to a unit where the highest-ranking officer treated me like trash, but I didn't head to the office. My feet involuntarily shuffled to the end of the line. My chest was heaving and my arms throbbing, from the first event. I told myself I would try and ask later if he could tell me what I did wrong, but not until after the PFT. The guy behind me got upward of sixty-five push-ups. He never had a number repeated; nobody else in my line would. That greatly enhanced my fear of failure.

When it was finally my turn for the sit-up event, I lay down and waited for the command "Begin." One of the other candidates was adjusting his hands on my ankles to get comfortable before holding my feet for two minutes. I heard the command and began doing sit-ups like my life depended on it. I remember the cadre counting: 39...*thump*—my back hits the ground, 40...*thump*...40 *thump*...40 *thump* . "Oh no, not again," I thought, "what could it be this time?"

I just kept doing what I was doing, thinking that maybe this was just their way of politely saying they didn't think I had what it took. After two minutes, I heard the same spiel as before and then I walked over to the run line for the last event: the two-mile run.

We were not allowed to have watches at all during my three-week Selection course. So we didn't have a way to keep track of our speed during the 2-mile run. They just wanted to see how fast we were willing to go, with everything always on the line. I was disheartened by this point, but I still managed a respectable finishing time. I finished long before a majority of my class. I wasn't very strong, but I could run like Forrest Gump, no joke.

After the PFT, they formed us all up into a giant rectangular formation. I want to say there were over three hundred candidates, each of us with our assigned number: mine was 37. They called out more than one-third of the formation but never called number 37. They told the rest of us to conduct personal hygiene and check the whiteboard. The whiteboard is where we received all direction. It could change anytime. At 0225 a formation time of 0230 could be written on the white board. It was all about taking accountability. We learned as a group to monitor the board constantly, taking shifts. I never once heard about the PFT again and never saw the PFT failures again.

People would disappear at night. Somehow, nobody on shift ever saw these guys leave. Most would wait until everyone fell asleep, and then they would creep out, wanting to quit in silent shame. This happened throughout the entire SF training pipeline. I guess it is hard for some men to look others in the face and admit weakness. I embraced it. I accepted the truth and never let it define who I was.

Most of the people that make it all the way through Selection will tell you about team week—where the candidates must work together in simulated extreme environments. During team week we were pushed to all bodily limitations. Our ability to handle extreme duress while maintaining an operations-oriented mind-set, even during times of excruciating pain, was being assessed. Team week was hell for me; it really was. I was easily the weakest person when it came to carrying water cans: something the cadre picked up on quickly. But even when I hit muscle failure, I would drop the can and use my other hand. At times I was switching them every two steps, just so nobody else would have to carry my weight. Some guys crushed these events; others got crushed…like me, but that's not the story I plan to tell. If you want to know about team week, go there.

To make it to team week, all candidates have to pass the infamous star course. The star course is a land navigation course where each candidate is given a map, a compass, and a protractor to work with. Everyone carries a minimum of forty-five pounds in their rucksack, but that doesn't include the MREs and water weight, nor the rubber "dummy" rifles that we had to carry as well. We all had safety gear, and it's all quite regimented, but it doesn't feel like it to the students. I had very minimal land navigation experience prior to this course, so I was very nervous. At Fort Stewart the land navigation course was swampy, nothing but pure swamp. We would walk on the roads or be forced to wade through chest-high swamp water. Those were really the only two options. We never failed to see a gator or feed a couple thousand mosquitos, at Fort Stewart. But I had never had to move through such varied terrain, particularly at night. Fort Stewart was swampy, but it was all very flat. There were no hills, valleys, or major natural terrain features…just swamp.

The star course covered more than a twelve-kilometer distance, and we had a limited amount of time to get a set number of points— meaning even if you knew what you were doing, time was of the essence. We did receive some excellent training from the cadre on how to conduct proper land navigation techniques. But to be honest, when you are only eating one or two MREs a day and sleeping an average of four hours a night, it's hard to be mentally alert and physically active. Over time our bodies began to tire and ask for the food it normally gets. That, on top of stress and lack of sleep, takes a toll on anyone's learning retention. I did learn some things, and on the first of two separate test days, we were given our first opportunity to go find our points. The points were four-foot-tall white posts, located anywhere and everywhere a person could imagine out in the North Carolina wilderness, and impossible to see at night if not for the glow sticks the cadre would put on them (at least most of them). Even with the glow sticks, the points were very hard to recognize from any significant distance—meaning, you had to know what you were doing to find them.

That first night we all lined up. The cadre did a safety inspection, making sure all candidates had water, food, and safety gear, while simultaneously giving the candidates our first grid coordinate. When the cadre told me my first point and started to walk away, I asked him where the other points were, and he told me, "Your next grid coordinate is on the white post, located at your first grid coordinate." I was shocked because it was a new technique for me, but I got down to business and spent the next eight hours only finding my first two points.

I knew that I needed help, but all the guys who found all their points were allowed to go back to camp and sleep. So then I was really feeling lost and up Shit Creek, because I had failed the first land navigation test and had no foreseeable way of passing on the second attempt. I was sitting around, approximately four hours before the next land navigation course began. I was exhausted, feeling physically drained from walking and running through the woods with a heavy rucksack on my back. I remember asking God to help me to find all of my points and pass this course.

(Let me just take a time out here to say: I was not a practicing Christian. I was as non-Christian as any Christian can get. But that old saying "There are no atheists in foxholes" doesn't just apply to foxholes. I think throughout human history, we have all had a moment in our lives where we reach out into the nothingness, asking for a sign. Begging for some kind of intervention from God, just to know that we aren't alone— not only there in the middle of the North Carolina woods, but here in the universe—that we all have a collective purpose.)

I was going over my notes, trying to figure out how I was ever going to pass the star course. I knew from my first night of testing that I wasn't capable of relying on my previous land navigation experience. As I was starting to feel my destiny slip away, a guy sat down next to me. He introduced himself, and I wish I could say I remember his name, but sadly, I don't. Anyway, he sat down next to me on the ground, and he asked me how my first run at the star course went. I admitted to him that I felt a bit over my head, because this just isn't something I had done before. I was essentially learning land navigation while going through Selection, and it was not working in my favor. He pulled out his map and protractor and spent the next three hours talking me through how to properly read a map and how to tell where water would collect and where I could expect to find the draws (very densely wooded areas, which are the bane of a candidate's star course existence). As thick as the vegetation was, it was hard to maintain a proper azimuth with the compass and maintain a pace count. Plus, it's just plain creepy at times, walking around the woods at night. We were charging through the areas where large animals tend to go to bed down, out of the natural paths and surrounded by brush. He showed me how to take the map markers and color parts of the map to help better highlight certain terrain features, making map checking while on azimuth much easier to do.

He told me in our conversation that he was some type of property surveyor and that before he enlisted into the 18 X-Ray Program, he used to do this kind of stuff for a living. The 18 X-Ray Program is a program designed to take recruits off the street, and instead of sending them to regular Army units before they are allowed to attend SFAS, they attend a very rigorous physical course after their initial military training that prepares them for a successful Selection class. If they get selected, they are moved directly into the SF pipeline. In essence, they can become a Green Beret with less than three years of military time and zero regular Army experience. They are the privates of the Q-Course, if you will. Cadre often treated them a bit more harshly, in an attempt to ensure they were capable of handling the stress of being a Green Beret. With about thirty minutes to kill before the next star course event began, I shook this guy's hand as he walked away, and I don't remember seeing him again the rest of my time in Selection. I always hoped he got selected, but oftentimes I wonder if he wasn't some kind of angel, sent to make sure I had just enough knowledge to keep moving forward. I think about his small act of kindness often and about how much my life changed because of the time he spent with me. He spent hours teaching me, when he could have been sleeping like the rest of the guys were.

As we lined up for the second and last attempt to find our points in the darkness, I noticed, as I had the night before, how dark the sky was and how little moon was visible. The sky was cloudy, and the air was cool. After sitting around all day long in the sun, it felt good to have that late-night chill running through the area. We were given our first points, as the cadre inspected all candidates for required safety equipment. Before starting, I took a knee, set down my rucksack, pulled the headlamp out of my pocket, and turned it on its brightest setting available, which wasn't much because only red light was allowed. The idea is to minimize the amount of light that could jeopardize a mission, by training using only enough light to remain mission-ready. Red light doesn't travel as far and is therefore preferred over white light in tactical settings, if light discipline must be broken. I plotted my point on the map. Using the declination diagram at the bottom, I was able to determine which azimuth I would use on my OD green lensatic compass to get me to my first point. I stood up, collected my stuff, and took one last look around, before stepping into the darkness.

My first point was a long trek, at least six kilometers away. As soon as I stepped out of the staging area, my confidence boosted. Something about being away from everyone made me feel more at ease. I had done my homework this time. I knew from the lesson I had gotten earlier that I could use major terrain features, such as a paved road and a stream, to guide my steps. So I could use my compass only to keep general direction, and I could move at a faster pace until I hit my target intersection. Once at that intersection, I could move on to the next leg of the movement; or if the point was close enough, I could shoot a straight azimuth from that intersection (we called this last position the *attack point*) and walk my way into the area my point should be. I hadn't quite made it to my first attack point, only having walked/run for about an hour and a half, but I was getting pretty close. As I was getting closer to the attack point, I realized I had mistakenly overlooked a field that was directly in my path, which is never good news.

We always avoided walking through open fields if we could. In the real world, we all knew that open fields meant no protection from any organized attack without a long movement under fire. So, I decided to skirt around this small field, thinking it shouldn't add any more than ten to twenty minutes to my walk. I knew my attack point was on the other side of the field. I felt like I could almost see it. I moved west, hugging the field's southern tree line, until I reached the western tree line of the field. I cut north, always keeping this field on my right-hand side. As I was heading north, I heard and then saw a pickup truck traveling at a high rate of speed from west to east, highlighting the road that I was using as my back stop. Perfect timing, I thought. The intersection I was targeting was within eyesight and now illuminated by headlights.

Just as I saw the taillights disappear, I starting moving again. Almost immediately, I felt my foot fall through some tall grass into a hole in the ground. I had stepped into the hole heel-first; so my foot folded upward, forcing the top of my foot and shin to form a narrow V shape. As this was happening, my body, rucksack and all, was already in motion, anticipating the next step, which caused me to fall at an awkward ninety-degree angle landing on my side. Somehow, my rucksack frame hit me square on the nose in the fall, causing it to bleed. At the same time I heard a crunching and small *pop* sound come from my right ankle, which was trapped in the ground. I cried out in pain and made a failed attempt at grasping for my ankle immediately after hitting the ground. I recognized that it was my ankle that made the sound, but I couldn't reach it. My foot was stuck in this hole: about twelve inches deep and just wide enough for a guy like me to strain an ankle in. I collected myself and then propped myself up on my left knee. I used my dummy rifle as a crutch for leverage as I pulled my right foot out of the hole. I knew from ruck marching at Fort Stewart that if my ankle injury was severe enough I couldn't take my boots off. If the swelling was bad enough, I wouldn't be able to get my boots back on. I decided to take a ten-minute break. I elevated my foot and started to feel very sorry for myself. I felt like such a failure. I was failing to pass land navigation, and now, to top it off, I had an ankle that couldn't bear any weight on it.

I was sipping some water from my canteen, contemplating how I was going to manage the next few hours. I knew I was close to my first point and had at least six hours before the test was over. I figured, worst case, I would just limp to the next point and wait there. So that's what I did. I was feeling defeated and didn't even look at my map or compass after the strain. I quite literally just happened upon my point...walked right into the post. It was easily visible, but I was looking at the ground and sizing up the ground for each individual step I had to take. Once I had reached that point, I got the grid coordinate for my next point and wrote it in my little field notebook. I sat down about a hundred meters from the post and made the decision to just try to make the next point before the time ran out. It was only four kilometers away, and I didn't see any low-lying areas that would make traveling difficult on the map. Making the decision to keep trying was easier for me than quitting.

I stood up with my back against a tree, then bent down to grab my rucksack. I slid the rucksack over one arm. As I tried shifting the weight of my rucksack to get the other arm through the other strap, I realized my left foot was caught in one of the tree roots. The momentum of my rucksack as it transitioned from one side of my body to the other, while my foot was stuck, caused me to fall with my foot facing one direction and my body falling another. My right ankle was immediately forgotten, as the searing-hot pain from my left ankle shot up my leg and straight into my brain. I knew it was injured before I even tried to put weight on it. As I sat on the ground, my eyes welled up with tears. I knew I wasn't ever going to be the strongest or fastest soldier, but I had never felt so frustrated with myself. Even though this kind of injury is extremely common, having it happen twice, once on each ankle, within an hour time period, wasn't an easy pill to swallow.

I sat there contemplating failure, trying to find a peaceful place to retreat to in my mind. I failed because I thought back to my time in Iraq and how I felt when Abu Zara bested me by evading capture. That failure stuck with me, almost attaching itself to my soul. I remember telling myself in Iraq I'd never fail my brothers in arms again. I remember leaving the office multiple times to go sit by myself on one of the HESCO sand-filled barriers, just to cry and process my emotions for having failed my fellow soldiers. Now I was here in the United States out in the middle of nowhere with two extremely swollen and aching ankles, only one of four points found, with no hope left. I thought about my wife and daughter. I thought about how I would have to tell them that I was too physically weak and incapable of being a man that could wear the Green Beret. I was subpar, at best.

Then suddenly I got this surge of energy to stand up. I said out loud to myself, "I am going to walk until my feet fall off. I won't quit."

As I was standing by the tree, I put my ruck on, snapped up my canteen pouches, and then flipped my dummy rifle around to put the butt stock on the ground and hold it by the barrel. I used that dummy rifle as a crutch, placing my palm on the front sight post, to help support my body weight. Now, I'm a pretty tall guy, at six feet. I was fortunate to have an old M-16 dummy rifle, this one and only time, because it was longer in length than the m4 dummy rifles. I was looking for any natural walking sticks to use instead, but with how the land is maintained there, it was difficult to find hardwood just lying around that could be usable as a walking staff. I sure didn't have time to fashion one with my pocketknife. I managed to get three of the four points that night, and other than falling down a few more times, reinjuring my ankles, I actually managed a decent pace and somehow didn't get lost at all. Because of the lesson I had gotten earlier from the random 18 X-Ray, I knew how to traverse the terrain using the map, saving my feet and ankles from extra pounding. Speed was no longer a concern of mine, because I was unable to move fast. Instead, I spent more time planning my route and utilizing the techniques that I was taught, than I spent worrying about running through the woods at night. I was glad to be over with the event, win or lose.

Fortunately for me, I never heard another thing about not getting all my points. I just kept taking instructions from the whiteboard. I would deal with not getting selected when it happened. Keeping my head in the game, managing my pain, and maintaining realistic expectations with my injuries were my primary focus now. As we were bedding down for the night after the star course, I took my boots off. I was amazed at how easily they slid off my feet. I had been wearing my damp socks for an entire day at this point, and I rolled my damp socks off my feet and onto the floor. My feet looked like they had been in a swimming pool for hours, and both of my ankles were extremely bruised and swollen. I pulled out my baby wipes and baby powder (both essential for good foot hygiene in the field) and proceeded to clean and powder my feet for what would be (unbeknownst to me) the last time they would see outside of my boots for the next five days.

The next morning, I gingerly cleaned off my feet, threaded my blisters (used a sewing kit to thread string through the blisters, leaving the string inside the blister to allow drainage), and put a new pair of socks on. I loosened up all the laces on my boots so that I wouldn't put any unneeded pressure on my ankle, and I slid my foot into my boot…or at least that's what I tried to do. I realized the rookie mistake I had made when I really took the time to notice how badly swollen my ankles both were. I didn't know how I was going to get my boots back on, but I had five minutes to be in formation to start off team week. How was I going to make this work? I thought. I didn't have time to think about not being able to handle the team week events. I was just trying to focus on getting to formation. One step at a time is always the best way to achieve any goal. I took the laces out of my boots completely and spread out the thick material as far as I could and winced and shoved both of my feet into their respective boots. I laced back up, grabbed my ruck, and went to formation.

The next few days of team week were really hard for me. I ended up fracturing multiple small bones in both of my feet during team week on top of the sprained ankles I had already sustained. I didn't dare take my boots off again until team week was over. I knew I'd never get them back on, when I was sustaining new injuries daily. I accepted the reality that they were permanently attached until this was over. Even in pain, I always volunteered to carry the collective load first, even if only for a step or two. I made it a point to bust my butt, because I knew I would be peered out if I wasn't able to contribute. I thank God, even now, for helping me to keep putting one foot in front of the other.

Once team week was over, we were given some time to rest and grab some good food at the DFAC. The night that team week ended, the whiteboard told us to form up the next morning outside of a specific building. I don't remember the exact number of people standing in that formation with me. Our formation was at least a hundred meters from the building. Every fifteen minutes or so, the cadre would call for our numbers. The wait felt so long, but eventually I heard it: "thirty-seven!"

I backed out of the formation and hobbled/jogged to the building where I was informed of how I did at Selection. They told me about my peer ratings, my performance, pointed out my weaknesses, and pointed out the very few things they noticed of positive nature. During this evaluation report, the cadre showed no emotion. I felt sure I hadn't made the cut.

He looked at me and said, "Candidate, you have been selected to attend the Special Forces Qualification Course. Exit the building, and report back to your unit for orders."

The feeling of elation I felt that day lasted for months. With God's help, I had managed to push through emotionally and physically, even when my body was failing and my hope was gone. I knew I wasn't strong. Looking back on it now, I know without a doubt the Holy Spirit was with me during that entire course. God would use me for things in the future, but not until I went back to Fort Stewart to rain on a certain BN commander's parade, with a letter of selection in hand.

I will be honest and say that I peered in the bottom half during Selection. I also didn't get great leadership marks. My lower ranking hurt my pride, but it was accurate. Selection highlighted every area that I needed to improve in. I can at least say that I didn't peer last and I never received a pink slip, in Selection. I was one of the weaker people on my team, but I always volunteered for duty, and I always gave everything I had. My peers noticed that, and I therefore earned a lower but sufficient peer rating. The guys who benefited the team the most physically or via leadership deserved the best ratings. If I wanted to have a high peer rating, I'd have to earn it.

Retrospective

"In the same way the Spirit also helps our weakness;
for we do not know how to pray as we should, but
the Spirit Himself intercedes for us with groanings
too deep for words." (Romans 8:26)

I can look back on Selection and see God in my life. God sent a selfless person to spend invaluable sleep time to help teach me what I needed to know about land navigation to pass Selection. If it had not been for him, I wouldn't have passed that land navigation course. I simply wasn't skilled enough at terrain association to meet the time requirements. It's not a coincidence that this guy randomly approached me, that he had been a land surveyor (very knowledgeable about maps), and that he taught me techniques that allowed me to progress after I sprained my ankle(s). I also want to highlight that at that time, all the students who had passed their star course, on the initial attempt, were back at base sleeping and eating. Only those of us who needed to make a second attempt were still in the staging area of the land navigation course.

I didn't know what injuries I would sustain on that second attempt, but God did know. God knew exactly how to prepare me for that night. God didn't prevent me from sustaining those injuries; we aren't promised a life without struggle or hardship. God did get me through that night, though; we are promised that God will be with us even in the worst of times.

I woke up one night while in the process of writing this book with an overwhelming feeling that the man who helped me was an angel. I can't say for sure, but I find it strange that as knowledgeable as he was, he was still hanging around the people who had failed. I have done some research on angels, and I now believe that he was a ministering angel.

When I told my wife this, she agreed that she thinks he was very likely an angel. She also told me that even if he wasn't an angel, his being a professional surveyor and having failed the first time were very important details. Angel or not, God used him in my life to teach me what I needed to know to be successful. I'm beginning to understand more and more that God uses our weaknesses or failures, for others just as much as for ourselves. If your opinion is that he was a man and not an angel, I hope you would agree that he didn't deserve to fail or deserve to have to go through that course again. He wasn't likely to fail the first time, with his knowledge and expertise. He was there that day with an opportunity to help someone—me— and he did.

No matter what we face or go through in life, we have to know in our hearts that God is in control and that His plan is greater than ours, for our good and His glory. More importantly, when we go through tough times in our lives, we need to look for the opportunities that God will give us to help one another. Helping others in our own trials can often be a source of great joy for us and a lifeline for them. Whether that man understood what he did for me or not, he threw out a lifeline for me that day.

As I was walking through the woods, using my dummy rifle as a crutch, I was actively hoping a cadre would drive past me so I could get in his truck and quit. I prayed for something to happen that would help my pain. Even though I was looking for a way to quit, I was also putting one foot in front of the other. I continued walking toward my points simply because I had nowhere else to go. If it had not been for God's grace, I wouldn't have made it through Selection. It's hard to describe what going through team week at SFAS was like with two severely sprained ankles. Every time I wanted to and was trying to quit, there was no one around to hear. Once I was near a cadre and had the opportunity to quit, I was somehow okay enough to try a little longer. I was getting brief relief from my pain: just enough relief that I felt I could give the next event a try, and then the next event, and so on.

As I look back on this experience from a spiritual standpoint, I know I was not experienced enough to have passed that course on my own. I was physically weak and broken; I was not a great leader; and I kept largely to myself. But God helped me in the times when I had nothing left to give, to keep putting one foot in front of the other. Even with the physical training I had done to prepare for the course, I never anticipated fracturing multiple bones in both feet or spraining both ankles. My doctors told me I likely over-trained before Selection, and that could have contributed to the stress-fractures. Unfortunately for me, my muscles wouldn't have been strong enough to carry that weight if I hadn't trained as hard as I did.

Jesus let me give everything I possibly could, and then He would give me just enough strength to do it again. Cadre were constantly driving all around, nonstop; it's not a coincidence that I didn't see a cadre after my injuries. These are all very small things, but added together, plus the gift of hindsight, I know God used that situation to qualify me for His future purpose. The Lord was with me in my weakest moments, and my success in getting selected... To God be the glory.

> "The Lord is the one who goes ahead of you; He will be with you. He will not fail you or forsake you. Do not fear or be dismayed." (Deuteronomy 31:8)
>
> God only ever asks of us the things He knows we are capable of doing *with His help*.

After Selection

Upon my return to Fort Stewart, I hobbled into my 1SG's office on crutches. The metatarsal fractures and ankles so swollen that finding the separation point between my ankle and calf was nearly impossible. The colors surrounding my feet, from the ankles to the toes, were deep purple in color with swashes of yellow and brown mixed in. As I waited for the 1SG to give me permission to speak, I couldn't help but feel apprehensive about how to inform the battalion commander. I knew he would more than likely give me a second dose of the bullshit he was spewing the last time I'd seen him. Fortunately, I now held the golden ticket out of that unit, regardless of what he thought. The 1SG invited me to sit down. I filled him in on my being selected, and I informed him that I would have orders cut within a few months assigning me to Fort Bragg to attend the Special Forces Qualification Course. My 1SG congratulated me and told me he would inform the BN commander and CSM. I thanked him and hobbled out to the PT formation, having managed to evade the "Dog-Faced Soldier" song that particular morning, in high spirits.

That day was a day of storytelling and physical pain. I had such a hard time walking, trying to decide which foot to put all my weight on every single step because they both were throbbing with sharp pains. Telling my platoon how Selection was and what it was like that day kept my emotions high throughout that night.

The next day I showed up to formation still in pain and on crutches. Just as the company had finished stretching in preparation for a cardiovascular event, the battalion commander showed up and asked for me by name. I fell out of the formation and moved to his position with my chin held high. In my mind, there was nothing but contempt for this petty man. But I owed him the respect due his rank, so I told myself I would treat him the way his rank requires; soon I'd be out of there anyways. He began by congratulating me for getting selected, and then he asked how my feet were doing. I was pleasantly surprised at his demeanor and by his questions, until my company had finally departed on their run. Once we were alone, he told me to drop the crutches; we were going on a run.

I remember laughing, because I thought he was joking; it sounded funny to me for about two seconds. But then I realized he was serious. I told him I was on a profile and wasn't able to conduct physical training. He then told me, "Drop the fucking crutches, we are going for a run!" So I did. We ran almost six miles that day at a seven-minute pace. Normally this would have been cake, and I'd have embarrassed this prick, but the best I could do was keep up that day. I listened to him berate me for six miles, without responding once. Upon our return to the company, I noticed our company had been dismissed already from PT for breakfast and personal hygiene, because their personal items and outer PT garments weren't stacked neatly in formation anymore. My crutches were exactly where I left them, and as we stopped running, the battalion commander walked straight to his office. He never spoke to me again in person.

After some healing, and because I wasn't Airborne-qualified, I had to attend and pass Airborne school before any orders would be cut for me to be reassigned to Fort Bragg. My battalion was responsible for cutting my Airborne orders because I was an NCO that was assigned to their battalion. It sounds easy to understand, but for some reason, my battalion S-1 wasn't going to cut my orders to attend Airborne. I had less than a week to report and was being told by my S-1 that the battalion commander refused to approve the orders. So they couldn't type them up. I was forced to go the Special Forces recruiting station where I had signed up for Selection and told the master sergeant working there what was going on. He made one phone call, and after fifteen minutes of waiting, he told me he had just gotten an e-mail that my battalion commander had been talked with and my orders were being cut. He also told me that it wasn't uncommon for SF candidates to receive this type of resistance when leaving a unit to pursue the SF career.

I walked back to my battalion S-1 to get the orders and could hear my battalion commander yelling from his office like a child, "If he wants to leave, tell those motherfuckers to write his goddamned orders."

I was sad in a way that I would be leaving this unit, which had become my home, in a negative way. I felt a sense of pride being there, until this commander showed up.

I know people oftentimes don't like the people in charge of them. Even now, having been a military leader myself, I understand how the loss of a stellar soldier can affect a unit. But I just hated that me trying to become a better soldier had caused the worst in a person to come out.

I want to make sure that it's very clear that I am not writing down what happened to bash my old battalion commander. I am just trying to paint an accurate picture. If anyone attempts to join SF and faces this type of opposition, I hope I am making it clear that you are not alone or to blame. I also want to emphasize that we should not be deterred in the presence of obstacles.

I personally want to thank you, sir. You know who you are. The way you treated me before I left for Selection is in large part what got me through Selection. I more than likely would have quit after spraining my first ankle, if I had a welcoming home unit to go back to. But you closed that door before I even walked out of it. So again, thank you, sir, for being the motivation that pushed me through the gate that few men have walked through. I sincerely wish you the best. You taught me more than you probably wish you had by treating me like garbage. I saw firsthand how God can take a terrible situation and use it to better His servants.

I ended up getting my orders and reported to Fort Benning, Georgia, for Airborne School, right on schedule.

Retrospective

"Behold, all those who are angered at you will be shamed and dishonored; Those who contend with you will be as nothing and will perish."
—Isaiah 41:11

In life, we will face people who will try to tear us down. We will face obstacles. I'm reminded of Moses. He sent a leader from each of the twelve tribes of Israel to recon or scope out the land of Canaan: The Promised Land. That is a good representation of the promise of something in the face of the uncertainty and hardship that discourage us. In this story, of the twelve leaders, ten would rather turn back and not risk failing when facing an opponent that was perceived to be bigger and stronger. Those ten did not believe they could overcome the inhabitants of Canaan and as a result did not pursue the rewards promised to them by God: a land of milk, honey, and much fruit. It is hard to start a journey when we believe we will not be able to finish. It is hard to pick a fight if we believe we will lose. It is hard to risk everything for the mere chance of something more. For the two leaders who were not discouraged, God was with them, and their reward was great.

God will always bring us through our struggles and our journeys, even when we don't feel His presence. He wants us to remain strong in Him and to rely on Him as our only source. The giants I have faced look different than the giants others do and will face, but God will always be greater. Something else I have learned is that here on earth, if we live our life for Christ, there will always be more giants to overcome.

"For our struggle is not against flesh and blood, but against the rulers, against the powers, against the world forces of this darkness, against the spiritual forces of wickedness in the heavenly places." (Ephesians 6:12)

During Selection I thought a lot about my wife and how terrible I had been to her. I remember thinking to myself, during many nights, that I wanted to call and talk to her, just to hear her voice. After I got selected, I went down to Florida where she and my daughter were living, and I asked her to forgive me and to take me back. In a miraculous fashion, she did. Even though I have been a less-than-perfect husband, since I have found Jesus, my love for her has exponentially increased.

Airborne School

Airborne school is probably the most nerve-wracking military school I ever attended. There is just something completely unnatural about jumping out of a perfectly good aircraft. I had known only a few people who had graduated Airborne school while I was at Fort Stewart, and they all acted like their shit didn't stink. I was curious as to what the talk was all about. Keep in mind, I knew I wasn't a fan of heights at this point, but if they could do it, why couldn't I? I had done Air Assault school, and that had made my butt pucker. I couldn't even fathom jumping out of an airplane from a much higher altitude with no rope to hold on to. Truthfully, I had no idea how afraid of heights I truly was until the first jump.

I won't go into much detail about the course itself for a few reasons. The most prominent being that even if I laid it all out for you, it still would never do it justice until you were on the aircraft and about to jump out that door. The chances of a chute not opening are extremely rare, but however unlikely, it is a possibility. Therefore, there are methods taught at the course that help a jumper keep a tight body position and teach them to remain calm if they need to reach for their backup parachute's pull handle. The likelihood of both chutes not opening is extremely rare. Generally, deaths caused by parachute failure result from a violent exit from the aircraft that render the jumper unconscious or dazed, or the jumper could panic and forget to pull the reserve chute.

From the inside of the aircraft, there are very few windows. So it feels like being packed into a sardine can. There was actually a benefit to how packed in and uncomfortable we were: I wanted out of that plane. By this point, we had rehearsed the actions on the aircraft so many times that I knew what to do. I knew to repeat the commands I was given to those behind me, without having to give it any thought.

The Army is amazing in this way. The Army will take a person that is petrified of heights and rehearse so many times that even in times of great fear that person's body will go through the motions.

It was cold outside when I went through Airborne school. But on the aircraft, between my nerves and the body heat from being cramped alongside my peers, I had a thin film of sweat on me. I would be lying if I said I heard any of the commands from our Jump Masters that first flight. I do know that I began shivering once they opened up the two rear personnel doors, one on each side of the aircraft. The wind whipped through the aircraft, invading my uniform and sending chills down my spine. I couldn't believe I was about to jump out of a plane. What if I freeze up at the door? I had never failed to commit before, but this was different. I legitimately contemplated my life. Even as a stranger to God, I remember begging Him to protect me and keep me safe during this jump.

When we got the "Hook up" command, it snapped me back to reality. I'm not sure I honestly believed in the hopeful prayer requests when I whispered them, but when a man nears a life-or-death moment, my experience has told me those prayers tend to get answered right away. I was going to find out. I hooked up my static line to one of the long metal cables running alongside the aircraft on both sides. I stood there grasping my static line as instructed. I ran through the last equipment check and static line inspection, and then waited for the Jump Master to come by and check my gear as well. As the Jump Master walked toward me, hunched over, on the seats we were all just sitting in, he was checking our static lines. The thirty-second command was passed along using the phrase and the hand signal. We each made eye contact with the jumper behind us, making sure they were ready to go as well.

We were all nervous, I had contemplated death, and now I was just numb. I saw the red lights above the doors turn from red to green. In a moment, the Jump Master at the door stuck his head out one last time, checking for the drop zone, and yelled "Go!"

There are a lot of things a person can be trained to do; but just in case my legs locked up, I told the guy behind me at the last moment, "If I freeze, kick me out that door!"

He laughed at me and gave me the thumbs-up. I turned back around and in step with the man in front of me shuffled to the door. I approached the step and, afraid to look down, was staring at the parachute of the guy in front of me. But when he jumped, I had no choice but to see the tiny trees and roads flying by at such a fast pace; the wind was racing faster than I'd ever heard before. I remember saying Jesus's name and then jumping out of the aircraft.

My eyes were closed, and my feet and knees were tightly together as I jumped into the turbulent wind. I had my hands on either side of my alternate parachute, which is standard in case the main chute fails to deploy. My chin was tucked into my chest, and while keeping this rigid body form, I counted one…two…three…four… My parachute ripped out of the pack and deployed beautifully. I was twisted beyond measure, but my parachute opened, which meant survival, and I was immediately grateful to God for that, but now I realized the bad news.

I was one of the skinny guys, but I would come to realize that I tended to fall at a faster rate than other folks. I distinctly remember passing multiple people that jumped before me, on the way down to the ground. In training cadre tell you what happens when someone steers their chute directly above someone else's chute; it basically results in the lower parachute stealing the air of the higher parachute. I'm not a scientist and I am terrible at math. So don't ask me how it works, but believe me when I say that it does. The last one hundred feet of my fall were petrifying. I saw the ground approaching at an alarming rate. I knew beyond any doubt I was going to have a hard landing.

In Airborne School, there were so many jumpers and it was difficult to steer my chute away from those below me. I was already falling too fast for my liking, and right before I hit the ground I went right over someone else just before they landed. It was like hitting a pocket without any resistance and then free falling the rest of the way. I remembered what they told us in training: to keep our feet and knees together and slightly bent. The idea is that by keeping the extremities together and keeping the joints loose: injuries should be less likely. Ideally, we are supposed to fall in such a way that the impact is spread out over our whole bodies, instead of any single body part taking the brunt.

I hit the ground feet-first, traveling backward with the wind. I remember my butt slamming into the ground, then my head, knocking my Kevlar helmet loose, and then flipping feet over head and landing on my stomach. As soon as I hit the ground, the breath in my lungs was expelled harshly, but I hardly had time to notice because I was being dragged backwards by my parachute. I could hear the Airborne cadre, who I had seen before landing, standing on the bed of a pickup truck with a megaphone in his hands.

"Pull your canopy release, pull your canopy release!"

I instinctively yelled back at him, saying things no Christian should, out of shock. I hit the ground hard and lashed out instead of doing what my training had taught me. This only happened one time. Each jump I completed gave me a better understanding of what to expect and how to handle myself, gradually increasing my confidence level each time. While my fear of heights may not have gone away completely, by the end of this course I was confident in saying that I had faced my fear of heights head on.

Retrospective

"Hear, O Lord, and be gracious to me; O Lord,
be my helper."

—Psalm 30:10

Airborne school is a rite of passage for paratroopers. In World War II, troops from the 101st Airborne jumped out of aircraft into Normandy, as a means of putting American troops behind enemy lines at a rapid rate. If you haven't seen the HBO series *Band of Brothers*, I highly suggest you watch it. It shows in-depth the type and effect of warfare paratroopers bring to a fight.

I was terrified of heights before Airborne school, and I can think of no better analogy of committing to Jesus Christ than that of jumping out of an aircraft for the first time. Being a paratrooper and effectively living life for Christ have a few things in common. They both require a leap of faith. They both require that we train and educate ourselves on proper practices, and what to do if something is amiss. They both require us to be prepared for the worst-case scenario. Neither promise that everything will go smoothly, and in the end they both require that we do everything we are supposed to and then let go of control.

The loss of control is a scary thing. I only ever focused on getting out of the aircraft and on my chute opening. I hadn't really considered how hard the landings could be. How often do we make choices without overlooking or failing to consider all of the implications? My chute opening wasn't a promise of a soft landing. The true test of my endurance would come at the end of the jump. I survived that landing and would jump many more times in my military career; unfortunately for me, I can count on one hand how many soft landings I would have. All of the training I received in Airborne School could only teach me how to best mitigate the risks, not to eliminate them completely.

When we choose to face the darkness, the heights, or the temptations, it is more important that we always trust God than allow our fear to hinder God's plan for us. Remember, it could be decades before the task you were put here for starts to bear fruit; but if you put your faith in God and are obedient to His will, you will bear good fruit.

> "I am the vine, you are the branches; he who abides
> in Me and I in him, he bears much fruit, for apart
> from Me you can do nothing." (John 15:5)

Take the leap of faith; don't be afraid of what could happen. If it is God's plan and we follow Him, He will make our path straight. I am more afraid of not fulfilling my purpose than any of the obstacles I may face in pursuit of my purpose.

WLC/BLC

After Airborne school, I went back to Fort Stewart to officially sign out of the installation and move on to the next chapter of my life. Once the family and I moved into on-base housing at Fort Bragg, I reported to the first phase of training in the Special Forces Qualification Course (or the pipeline). It wasn't until I arrived at the in-processing station that I was informed I would have to attend the Special Forces mixed version of the Warrior Leader Course (WLC) and Basic Leader Course (BLC), which was located at Camp Mackall. They told me that even though I had exceptional marks from my previous WLC class it just didn't matter, because I didn't have BLC yet. Both WLC and BLC were required, to get waived past this first step. This course ended up being an eye-opening experience for me, and even though I lost blood and sweat there, I learned a tremendous amount. This course tested my physical limits and pain threshold within the first week.

The first thing that I remember distinctly was called the Burpee Mile. For context, I will first explain what a burpee is.

It begins in a standing position. As a person swings their arms back, they bend their knees slightly, legs shoulder-width apart. And as the arms swing forward, the person jumps hard off the ground, raising their arms in the sky, trying to reach as high as possible before landing on their feet and dropping immediately into a push-up position. Completing one push-up and then jumping back up to a standing position is the end of one repetition. Many NCOs have managed to correctively train their soldiers using this technique.

Our cadre had a different idea, though, and with no warning or opportunities to gather gloves, they told us to do burpees to a location we knew to be exactly one mile away from the spot we were in. We were to stay on the concrete road the entire time. The process for the exercise remains the same. The only difference being that a person will jump up and forward instead of straight up in the air. It's basically long-jumping a mile with push-ups in between jumps.

I considered myself to be in great shape at the time, but without gloves, I didn't make it even one hundred meters before having the first shard of glass in one hand and a pebble embedded in the other. There was sharp, hot pain every time my hands hit the pavement, which also happened to be scorching hot at the time. We were not allowed to walk in-between jumps. If we were seen walking, the cadre would force us to start from the beginning. It was just a means of exerting authority and discomfort on us, to make us want to quit. Some people like myself had the misconception upon arriving to the Q-Course that the cadre would no longer treat us like they did in Selection: begging us to quit. I thought we had "passed" the hazing phase and would now be turned into warriors. What I didn't know was that a majority of people that get selected don't make it through the entire pipeline; it gets harder and harder every step of the way.

Once I made it to about the seven-hundred-meter mark, guys were starting to reach the finish line. I noticed that most of them were shirtless. They had ripped their shirts into two pieces, to cover up their hands and giving them some type of protection. I had failed to consider that there were no females at our location; we were at Camp Mackall. I needed to start thinking like a Green Beret now. I wasn't going to be training like I had at Fort Stewart. I was going to have to start thinking outside the box and use my "better to ask forgiveness than permission" personality, to accomplish my mission. I eventually finished. I was shirtless by the end, as I followed the example of the other guys for the last three hundred meters. The t-shirt didn't do me a whole lot of good, by that point, since the damage to my hands was already done. I was heaving, my lungs hurt, and my muscles were pumping as they circulated the blood going through my body.

Only in an elite unit will you put over a hundred people through something like that and see many of them smiling at the end. I was one of the people smiling once it was all over. I was both proud of my accomplishment and ashamed that I had been three hundred meters behind the fastest person. I couldn't know this then, but I would never come first in a run again. My days of being among the more physically fit soldiers in formation were over. We washed up and treated the open wounds on our hands, before going to the NCO professional development classrooms for the day's block of instruction.

One of the cadre (who will remain nameless because he is still actively kicking the crap out of bad guys) was a real asshole when he was in instructor mode. He was the kind of guy that would bring back old army methods. He would let people speak freely if they didn't like what he said, but If we did speak out against him, we had to meet him in the dojo on the compound. I was never a huge fan of combatives (hand-to-hand combat training), primarily because I was never great at them. I had no idea this cadre was a partner at a UFC gym near Fort Bragg and that he fought for fun. I have always enjoyed watching people, who know they are about to fight, before they begin to fight. You can tell who a person really is when the threat of violence is introduced. Generally people will shy away and avoid it. To be a Green Beret means standing up and fighting back, even if it means losing or dying. This meant something to the cadre, and they didn't want weak people in their regiment. I respected that and wasn't surprised when my classroom got the phone call to leave the classroom and line up outside the dojo. I knew the cadre was going to personally fight every single student in our WLC/BLC class, because I heard him talking about it a few days prior. It was easy to recognize who was afraid and who wasn't. Not everyone here came from a background of school ground fistfights. Many hadn't been in combat at all, and now they were going to have to fight a trained Green Beret and professional fighter.

As the people in my class stood outside the dojo, the cadre opened the door from the inside and yelled at us to get in line and to take our shoes off before entering his dojo. We would enter the dojo one at a time, walk to the center of the mat, get on our knees across from the cadre who was already kneeling when we walked in, shake his hand, and then fight for two minutes or until submission. Not surprisingly, there wasn't a huge rush to the door; only a handful of people, including myself, pushed toward the front. I ended up being third, which I was okay with. It would give me two opportunities to study his technique and less time for my adrenaline to wear off.

The first guy in lasted about a minute before he was put into an arm bar. Both the guy in front of me and I watched it happen with smiles on our faces, because of how flawlessly it was executed. The cadre reversed his body position so fast that I don't think the poor guy had a chance. He was soaked with sweat after only a minute, so I was convinced he gave his all and that I was going to take an ass whooping. The second guy was up. He went in and appeared to flail around for about thirty seconds before tapping the cadre's leg as a sign of submission. He stood up, smiling toward the door. I assume it was a smile of relief that he submitted before he was physically hurt. The cadre saw straight through it, came up behind him, spun him around, picked him up in some WWF-style fashion, and slammed the guy on the mats. Then he proceeded to mount his back, forcing the guy's stomach to the ground. He calmly slipped his hand in between the student's chin and neck, before the student knew what was happening. I saw the student tapping the arm of the cadre, trying to tap out. The cadre waited until right before he passed out before letting go and telling him to open the door for the next guy: me.

I walked up to the cadre, maintaining eye contact the entire time. I might not be a big guy, but I was not a punk and wasn't going to let this guy make me think otherwise. I foolishly convinced myself as I walked across the mat that the cadre was probably already tired, after two rounds, and that I should go for the throat right off the bat. What seemed like a logical plan began perfectly. I shook his hand and tried to quickly slip past him. I slammed my forearm into his mouth in an attempt to wrap my arm around his throat. I think I hit a nerve, because my whole forearm was numb. I thought maybe I overestimated his height and that was how I missed his throat. He was much shorter than I was and stocky. The idea that he saw my attack coming and tucked his chin before I could get my grip didn't cross my mind. He stood up with me on his back, took a step forward, and tucked his shoulder to roll me off his back. While I was on my way down he put a hand on my chest to push me down faster. He slammed me into the mat and forced all the air out of my lungs, before kneeling on my chest. He was about to finish the match, so in a last-ditch effort, I grabbed his wrist and pulled it into my chest as hard as I could. As he was trying to get his hand free, I wrapped my legs around his arm, trying to put him into an arm bar.

He literally laughed out loud, before he put me in a wristlock and put his knee down on my chest again, releasing my grip on his forearm. I am not ashamed to say that I tapped within seconds of the wristlock. I had never been in one up to that point and can fully appreciate seeing a 120-pound corrections officer force a much larger convict to the ground using only a finger or wristlock. It really is amazing how effective they are. As soon as I tapped, he released and helped me to my feet. I didn't get a "Good job" or clap on the back, nor did I deserve one, but he didn't body-slam me from behind either.

I just lost a sparring match. In the real world, if a man from a different military had defeated me in hand-to-hand combat, I would be captured or dead. The cadre was showing us how our situation could look, if we were to face someone in hand-to-hand combat with our current abilities. He fought over thirty of us that day, one right after the other. I don't remember seeing him drink water or take any breaks, and he won every single match. There were a couple different students that I thought came close to getting the better of him, but he maximized on his opportunities before they did, every single time. After he had wiped the mats with us, we went back to our classrooms and continued class like normal. Of course, we talked about who got their ass kicked the worst and who lasted longer before tapping out.

The next day, however, that same cadre told us about the next phase of training. To pass this WLC/BLC class, we would need to participate in a boxing/combatives tournament. The cadre divided us into two big circles. The cadre called two of us at a time, by name, to the middle of each circle. Nobody knew who was boxing whom. We just knew if we didn't fight like we meant it, we had to fight the same cadre that whooped us before. It really surprised me to see so many people try to get out of sparring; as if they were going to be able to avoid conflict their whole lives and wanted to prove it here in the Q-Course. That wasn't going to fly. We all knew that after they made an example of the first person. The cadre I spoke of before came down into one of the rings, holding one of the students by the scruff of his neck, telling the whole class that he was trying to get out of fighting. He then forced the guy to put gloves on, putting some on himself, then he told the guy to hit him in the face. The cadre stood with his gloves behind his back and let this guy hit him in the face, before dropping him like a sack of potatoes with three blows to the face.

I felt bad for the guy at first because I hate seeing violence inflicted upon people who can't handle it, but then I realized, that was the point of the training. This wasn't just anyone off the street; this was a man that was trying to earn the Green Beret.

"Weeding out the weak" is a phrase that students hear often in the Q-Course. It's not about being hateful or targeting people out of spite, which is hard to understand when you are the target of the harshness. The cadre were teaching us a lesson. Some of the guys in the same circle as me had never been punched in the face before; they had never been choked out until their vision narrows and truly felt the helplessness of being overpowered. Having another man cause you to pass out, from lack of oxygen or blood to the brain, is a humbling experience. There is just something about having another man put his arms around your throat and slowly apply pressure until you pass out that makes you contemplate life from a different perspective. On one hand, it is a frightening to accept that there are some people that I could not physically prevent from taking my life; but on the other hand, I sleep great at night knowing these are the types of men that give terrorists nightmares.

When my name was called, I stepped into the ring, touched gloves with my opponent, and then went to town for over a minute in a barrage of fists to his face and midsection. Because of my lanky demeanor, I am often overlooked as a physical threat; that has worked to my benefit on multiple occasions and is a trait that I have learned to appreciate. I remember taking a few shots to the face, but once I got into the zone, I wasn't coming out until I had won. The round lasted two minutes and was exhausting. Toward the end my opponent was heaving for breath and unable to throw a punch out of exhaustion; so I was confident I would win the match, and I did.

Since I had won, I would move on to the next round, where I fought someone about the same height as me but much bigger in build. This guy didn't fold as easily as the first guy, and even though I was laying some good shots on him, he was giving as good as he was getting. I would like to think that we were about even as far as judging went, up until the last ten seconds of the round. I threw a right jab at his nose; he dodged it and sent an uppercut my way, laying me on my ass. Now I didn't get "knocked out," but as he helped me to my feet, I knew that the fight was over. It only takes one good shot to change the course of a fight, something good to remember when facing greater odds.

When the day was over, we had all fought at least two or three rounds and had cheered on our buddies as they fought for honor and pride. Green Berets don't do what they do for the glory. They just want to win and to be the best. If you ever go to a military school and are looking to see if any Green Berets are in class, look to the front of line…that's where you will find them.

Retrospective

"Blessed be the Lord, my rock, Who trains my hands for war, And my fingers for battle."
—Psalm 144:1

When I think back to the month I spent at WLC/BLC, the above-mentioned scripture comes to my mind. WLC and BLC are leadership courses, and this was the first of many courses required to pass the SFQC. The entire purpose behind any leadership school is to teach a person how to take charge of a situation and what to do while in charge.

It didn't matter to anyone at this course that I had already spent a month of my life at a WLC class already. The whole point of this WLC/BLC class is to set the standards of NCOs on an ODA. We were given access to military manuals of all kinds, and we gave each other classes on different leadership responsibilities. Above all that, we were getting face time, in small groups, with Green Berets. In my small group, we got to speak with a Green Beret who had just gotten back from a deployment and had fresh information and tactics to share with us, which we eagerly soaked up.

As Christians who are trying to walk our lives with Christ, don't we also listen to the testimonies of others that have been walking with Jesus long before us, to be encouraged and inspired? The same way that I used to listen to stories from guys returning from a deployment is how I now listen to the testimonies of God's children who have fought the good fight and have been victorious.

Things like the burpee mile resonated with me because even though every single person completed it, there were a few that looked defeated just at the sight of their bleeding hands. Instead

131

of focusing on the mission and the end goal, they focused more on themselves and the pain they were in. I was among this group for a brief moment before I embraced the pain and started to look at the exercise for what it was: a physical fitness activity designed to hurt and to remind us that even though we aren't in Selection anymore there are physical and mental hurdles that could take us out of the course anytime.

Most of the PT we did at WLC/BLC was out in the woods and running through creek beds. None of it was "fun," but everything had its purpose. They made us crawl through hundreds of yards of concrete irrigation canals, at night, without flashlights, filled with snakes and spiders, and for cadre delight they threw in tear gas. At face value, this sounds terrible, but how else do you tests a man's ability to endure terrible situations? Special Forces soldiers aren't asked to complete missions that are easy, and we train like we fight. Trusting that God will use our environments and situations for His purpose is similar to knowing that there was always a purpose behind the actions of our cadre.

God allows us to be tested, to make sure we are committed to the decisions we have declared to Him. Similar to how there are many men that think they have what it takes to become a Green Beret, there are many people that believe they can handle being used by God. Have you read the stories of those who have been used by God? Preparation and testing comes before the Green Beret can be earned, and preparation and testing often precede an anointing to be used by God. Both come with a lot of responsibility.

Physical fitness in elite military units can be quite overwhelming, but to the brave men trying to don the Green Beret, these are the opportunities to test their own limits. I feel like WLC/BLC (in the SFQC) was when the journey of renewing my mind, to develop a mind of an operator, really started. As a student, when running through a creek bed at 5:00 a.m., in cold weather, I didn't see the value in the struggle. But now that I have spent time on an ODA, I understand why they ran us into the ground. Green Berets can't worry about their feet being wet or not eating or not sleeping, if there is a mission to accomplish;

it's really that simple. The mind cannot give way, before the body gives out, if we are giving all we have.

> "And do not be conformed to this world, but
> be transformed by the renewing of your mind,
> so that you may prove what the will of God is,
> that which is good and acceptable and perfect."
> (Romans 12:2)

Language Training

After WLC/BLC things started to get interesting as I began the foreign language portion of my training. After finding out I had been selected, I remember having a sergeant major sit down with me and ask me which language I wanted to learn. I said Spanish, because who doesn't want to learn Spanish? He didn't think that was funny. I ended up getting assigned the Pashtu language. Pashtu is spoken in various provinces of Pakistan and Afghanistan. I was less than thrilled, but at least it meant I would have a chance to go to Afghanistan as a Green Beret.

I'm not going to spend a lot of time talking about the lesson plans of learning Pashtu, but I will say that I struggled trying to learn it. I spent eight hours a day, five days a week, sitting in a classroom, learning how to speak the language of future Afghan counterparts. It was hard to sit in a classroom for that long, forcing my brain to learn a language that didn't make a lot of sense to me, but I did it.

Every time I thought that class was getting boring or that it wasn't for me, I would think about my enemy. SFC George E. Vera was the cadre I was assigned to, during language school. He would remind us of every reason it was important to know the native language during a deployment. During language we would report to SFC Vera for PT in the mornings, and he would put out any administrative due-outs that we had that day. He was also used in a disciplinarian role for any students that ran into legal or course troubles. I used to show up to his PT sessions, music blasting, windows down, and the warm North Carolina breeze on my face.

He was the first cadre I was truly able to interact with professionally and who was personable with us. That is not to mistake kindness for weakness, because he was as fierce a man as I have ever known. He had something in common with all the cadre I had encountered up to that point: something about the eyes caught my attention. It reminded me of the thousand-yard stare that I had heard referenced when reading about World War II, Korea, or Vietnam veterans. There is just something different about a person who has seen combat: real combat. Their eyes could look right at you, and then sometimes right through you. He gave me the nickname "Joker" at some point for being a smart-ass, which is right on par for my personality. He had seen combat, and he knew that we were part of something much greater than ourselves. He knew people that were in the ranks with him when he attended the Q-Course who were no longer with us. I could just see it in his eyes. He knew that even though many of the men in his formation were decorated soldiers and NCOs, he knew that none of us had ever had the experiences he had as an operator. It was his job to make sure we kept on the straight and narrow. He was an excellent instructor: going out of his way to help us train and prepare for the next phases of training. I learned a lot from SFC Vera. He is one of the most courageous men I have ever had the honor of meeting.

I remember distinctly one morning formation with SFC Vera. He informed us that there had been a fight in the gym on base. A Q-Course student got into it with an 82nd Airborne soldier. Many 82nd guys ended up joining in, and the Q-Course student got his ass beat. SFC Vera also told us that they discovered that other Q-Course students had been in the gym, when the fight started, but they didn't back him up. He proceeded to tell us that if we ever saw a brother get into a fight that we better not leave him there on his own. SFC Vera further told us not to worry about getting into trouble for fighting, if we are backing up a brother; he did say if he ever found out that we left a brother on his own that he would crush our nuts.

My respect for SFC Vera increased after he told us that. He was teaching us what it meant to be a part of the brotherhood. He was giving us a clear understanding of what it looks like to be a man who can be trusted by an SF team. This type of teaching has a place. A Green Beret can be behind enemy lines and only have a few other operators with him. If he gets into trouble, he needs to know that his brothers would stop at nothing to get him out of that trouble.

I'd like to take a moment and fast-forward to fill you in on why MSG Vera is a name my kids will grow up recognizing.

On 7 August 2015, less than three months before I got out of the Army, MSG George E. Vera and 1SG Andrew McKenna were on Camp Integrity near Kabul when their base entrance was struck with a massive Vehicular-Borne Improvised Explosive Device. MSG Vera and 1SG McKenna exposed themselves to the VBIED blast as they pulled wounded soldiers to safety. MSG Vera was shot during his efforts to secure the perimeter and 1SG McKenna was Killed in Action. MSG Vera and 1SG McKenna earned the Silver Star for their heroic actions.

MSG Vera is the definition of American badass. I thank God that I was fortunate enough to have gotten to know him and learn from him, during this language course. It is because of men like McKenna and Vera that our country is great. I will never forget the sacrifices made by them and the many others who gave this country everything they had to offer.

The culminating test at the end of any Army language course measures the student's ability to understand verbal communications and to speak to people in the target language. Language school was about as exciting as sitting in any old classroom for eight hours a day can be, but SFC Vera used to reinforce the training by reminding us that we would be able to train indigenous forces with this training. The one mission that Green Berets own exclusively revolves around training people from the target country and teaching them basic soldiering tactics in their native language. I think a lot of people tend to overlook the importance of communication in a target language, but without being able to talk to our allies or enemies, how can anything be accomplished?

Take the Navy Seals for example. They generally do not receive language training (to my knowledge) because they are a direct-action unit—meaning, their missions don't revolve around training the local populace. They are more of tactical-precision-type unit and are very good at what they do. They were never designed to do what Army Special Forces was designed to do.

Green Berets live in the long game. We are trained to survive with minimal resources and are able to accomplish any mission by, with, and through the local population. We go into hostile territories, with only an ODA, to chip away at hostile foreign entities from within; all of which can only be done using a common language.

It takes a long time to learn a foreign language if you are like me. So I wasn't surprised when people started to get DUIs and began to quit the program because they just weren't that vested in the program. I think it shows a completely different side of Army soldiers.

A common misconception is that soldiers are uneducated and join the military because their lack of education leaves them with no other choice. Special Forces soldiers are some of the military's brightest military tacticians the world has to offer. I will take an ODA over a SEAL platoon any day of the week (I'm a little biased). Just to attend Selection, a person has to have a high GT score, which is a test result that shows the individual is capable of learning new things quickly. A lot of the men I personally served with had bachelor's degrees, master's degrees, or some type of civilian certification (welding, electrician, plumber, Security+, A+, etc.). I want to say we even had a self-made millionaire in my WLC/BLC class. So education is something most of us were very familiar with. During deployments and long training exercises, it was common to see someone pull a textbook or notebook out of their bag to knock out some homework or to study for a college class. I was made aware during this language course just how intelligent my peers were.

I did not have a degree at this time, and I was not breezing through this class. I was also working out twice a day: once in the mornings as a platoon, and once in the afternoon in the weight room to try and get my weight up. So I stayed extremely busy throughout the course.

Like I said before, the end of language school ends with a test of verbal dialogue to base a soldier's fluency in their target language. I got an above-average score on my final test—meaning, I was able to move on to the next phase of training if I could pass the gates.

Retrospective

"And how is it that we each hear them in our own
language to which we were born?"
—Acts 2:8

Learning a foreign language during this training seemed like forcing
a square peg through a round hole, for me. I studied for hours and
hours and still felt barely able to have even a basic conversation. The
program was only six months long at the time and was the hardest
intellectual challenge I had ever faced up to that point. I found it
much harder to sit in a classroom for months than it was to be out in
the woods training. I also needed people around me reminding me
of how important my learning this language was, and I couldn't lose
sight of the fact that this course was necessary in the overall goal that
I had: graduating the Q-Course.

I found that reading the Bible was a lot like learning a foreign
language. I will explain more of how my picking up and reading the
Bible came to pass in the later chapters of this book, but I experienced a lot of the same difficulties when I started to study the Bible
that I faced in the language course. It was difficult to wrap my mind
around and digest a lot of what I was reading, at times. Once I started
to read the Word of God, though, I couldn't stop. The harder it was
to understand, the more I would study and try to understand. I have
found that there are answers to the questions that I have; I just had
to devote my time and seek those answers.

I am very intentional about reading the Bible every single
day. When I stopped studying and using what I had learned in
the Pashtu class, it started to slip away. Sometimes I will watch a
show or a movie and I will understand what is being said, if they

are speaking in Pashtu. But if I truly want to be able to speak and understand Pashtu again, I would need to refresh and start studying again. Pashtu isn't a priority for me at the moment, so I don't currently partake in any of that. Learning and understanding God's word is a priority for me, and I know that if I want to deepen my understanding and not regress, then I have to devote my time to reading it each day.

> "This book of the law shall not depart from your mouth, but you shall meditate on it day and night, so that you may be careful to do according to all that is written in it; for then you will make your way prosperous, and then you will have success." (Joshua 1:8)

I explained that many of my peers were very educated and intelligent, but it was still critical for us to spend six months learning the language of the people we would be deploying to work with and train. No matter how educated or informed we were about tactics or anything else we would be training the indigenous forces on, it wouldn't have benefited our target audience at all if we couldn't pass that knowledge on to them. Special Forces understand the importance and the value of being able to converse with someone they need to train. This principle is true when spreading any message. When we try to spread the Gospel, we need to be able to reach and communicate with the recipient. In Acts 2:8 (referenced at the beginning of this retrospective), what caught everyone's attention was the disciples speaking in the audience's many native languages.

Something strange happened to me during this language course that I almost forgot to write about until my wife reminded me. Less than a month into this course, I got an e-mail from a government agency saying I had been recommended by name for a certain spot in a more elite intelligence-gathering unit: if I wanted the job. This was the kind of job I dreamed about, and I don't think it's a coincidence that the e-mail came when it did. Remember, many of us were restless and not happy about sitting in a classroom learning a foreign language for six months. If there was a time that this offer would have swayed me, this was the time.

I responded to the e-mail. I told the guy about my situation and that I wouldn't be able to live with myself if I quit the Q-Course. I needed to know if I had what it took to graduate. It wasn't until my wife mentioned this story to me that I was able to fully appreciate the Holy Spirit working in me. Everything in my body and mind knew that job was perfect for me, but something heavy just sat on my mind when I thought about taking the position and quitting the course. The Holy Spirit was hard at work, trying to show me the right path. We can't allow ourselves to get distracted by every shiny object or dream opportunity. There will always be a different path we can take, but it is important to allow God to lead us where He wants us to go.

"There is a way which seems right to a man, but its end is the way of death." (Proverbs 14:12)

The Gates

Next up were the gates. We had to pass these gates to qualify us for the next phase of training. These gates consisted of a passing the PFT with a minimum of 70 points in each event and a total score of 260 or higher. This is different than the regular Army, which requires 180 or higher total score with a minimum passing score of 60 points in each event. Quite a difference in the expected baseline. Men who didn't enjoy physical fitness often ended up quitting or failing events—primarily because to maintain the level of fitness required, many hours of free time must be spent in the gym instead of on the couch at the house. That type of life isn't for everyone, and that is a big reason that I have such great respect for my brothers who wear the Green Beret. I scraped by physically on a lot of the physical requirements, passing all of them but never coming in first (not by a long shot). I was competing against men who could easily play professional sports but didn't. I have seen some of the country's most lethal warriors push their bodies to extreme limits just because they can.

A twelve-mile ruck march was also required, in a three-hour time period, with sixty-five pounds (plus water) in the ruck. The routes were always hilly and dusty where these ruck marches were conducted, in the back woods of Fort Bragg's range roads. Two or three weeks prior to this gate, after our language training was over for the day, we were given the opportunity to ruck the twelve miles to learn the course. Our cadre bused us out that evening and gave us a safety briefing as we all checked the weights in our packs one last time. SFC Vera gave us the route and all the safety point locations, and then he told us to get on the starting line. When he said go, we all began running down the road. We were trying to capitalize on the adrenaline for as long as possible, before settling into the long monotony of silent darkness.

This trial run was intended to help us understand how prepared we were for the upcoming gate. I never understood why ruck marching was so challenging for me, but even with my long legs and fast run times, I couldn't keep my pace in sync with my peers. I had to jog to keep up with their long rucking strides. Of the hundreds of ruck marches I've done, either alone or for military training, I've only ever failed one road march: the trial run of the course for this particular gate. There were approximately 200 students partaking in this trial event. Roughly 30 students finished with an acceptable time, myself not included. I never worried about passing physical fitness tests before, because I worked my butt off to make sure I didn't have anything to worry about. I knew when I failed that night that I had something to be worried about.

I can recall how terribly hot and humid it was that day. Rucking those twelve miles in the evening, instead of the customary early morning, made a big difference. I remember getting cramps in my legs so bad that night that my hamstrings seized up on multiple occasions. It's quite a painful experience. When you are jogging, ignoring the pain and burning in your legs, trying to focus on the finish line, and your leg seizes: you fall down. Each time, I fell on my hands, knees, and elbows, while getting a good smack in the back of the head from my rucksack. There were over twenty heat casualties that night. One guy was even taken to the hospital because his muscle cramps were so severe.

I don't really know what happened that night. I have no excuses for my failure. But for those of you who know the type of person I am, you understand how this failure ate away at me from the inside. After that night, I slept, ate, and drank ruck marching. I stayed hydrated. I focused on healthy eating. I even tailored my workout routine to compliment my leg muscles. I had to pass this gate. I couldn't make it this far just to fail a simple ruck march.

The morning of the actual twelve-mile gate, we showed up around 0400 and were stretching while the cadre got the safety points set up before starting. It was a nice cool day. I ended up finishing in two hours and twenty minutes: my fastest twelve-mile ruck march time.

There was only one gate remaining to get into the next phase of training, which was passing the land navigation course. Land navigation is one of the few things that is hard to train for, especially when you aren't very good at it. SFC Vera set our class up for success, though, and gave us a few opportunities to get out in the woods alone with our maps and compasses. Just like in Selection, I wasn't shy about my lack of abilities or confidence, when it came to land navigation. I learned a lot from my peers, and SFC Vera, as a result of my asking for help. By this time, Selection felt like it was years ago. No matter how much I studied a map, when I was dropped off in the woods, my perspective changed. Lots of things can happen when you are all alone, in the North Carolina woods, looking for little white posts. I knew this firsthand and was thinking back on my Selection days as we were traveling out to the land navigation staging area for our final gate.

The drive out to Camp Mackall always seemed to take forever. All I could think about was how poorly I had done the last time I did a land navigation test. My ankles never fully recovered from the injuries sustained during Selection. I swear they throbbed in anticipation of the abuse they were about to endure again. I found that once I sustained severe sprains in both ankles the first time, it was much easier to repeat later. I have sprained an ankle on almost every land navigation course I have ever done since Selection.

As we hopped off the trucks, we lined our rucks up in formation, pulled out an MRE, and ate it; showing the cadre that we had eaten at least a majority of it. I found it curious that they were concerned about our food intake. Looking back on it, it makes sense that they wanted to know for certain we all had food in our bodies, to mitigate the chance of internal injury from lack of nutrition. The cadre did a safety inspection: making sure we had an MRE in our ruck, water in all the required canteens, and that we had the safety equipment required of all students taking a land navigation course. They gave us our points, and I began to plot them on my map. I identified my azimuths, my backstops, and my attack points. I learned in the past that by being slow and meticulous in the planning phase, I could save hours of physical exertion. I was going to stick with what I knew worked.

I remember finding my first point in less than an hour. It was about six kilometers away, but I was able to get there pretty quickly because of my route planning. My confidence was soaring, when I got to the point that was very dimly illuminated by a blue glow stick. It was sitting in the bottom of a small draw (densely vegetated area surrounding sources of water), surrounded by brush. The surrounding brush was extremely dense, and I was trying to figure out how to get in to the point. I started to think that more than likely the cadre knew of a path to this point, and it was probably around on the other side of the draw, nearest to the closest road. I knew from past experiences that trying to chop my way through a draw is nothing but a waste of energy and will hurt me more in the long run. It was better to slowly walk around the point until I found the path the cadre used. It took me about twenty minutes to get to the other side, but the path was clearly visible. It looked as if a bear or large deer had trampled through the brush into the very small clearing that the post was in. I was so excited; everything was working out perfectly.

My next point was just over seven kilometers away, and the first leg required that I go back the way I had just come. So I began to move around the thick brush back through the path I had made to get to the first point. There was a fallen tree that was blocking my path. I had already successfully maneuvered over the tree on the way to the first point; now it was time to maneuver over it one more time. This tree was very large. I am six-feet tall, and when I was straddling the tree I was also essentially sitting on the tree. I swung my left leg over the tree first, and with my left foot standing firm I swung my right leg over. When I pushed myself off the tree, I lost footing with my left foot, not realizing I was standing on a rock slick with moisture. My left foot slipped and didn't get a foothold until firmly seated between two rocks. Unfortunately when my foot got stuck, the rest of my body didn't stop with it. I twisted my ankle, once again. This changed things. I wasn't going to get a second chance at this. If I didn't pass, I would get recycled—meaning, I'd be sent to the beginning of the class following the one I was in. I couldn't have that; it would extend my graduation by two months. I got back up and moved as quickly as I could to where my next point should have been. That's right, I didn't see my point anywhere. I had just spent the past five hours walking and only had one point to show for it. I only had three hours remaining to find the other three points. I knew my time was short. So instead of freaking out, I sat down and took off my ruck.

One of the small tricks of the trade is to be comfortable when you can, because you may not have the luxury of comfort when you expect it in the future. I studied my map and assessed my location again, using a variety of techniques that I was taught during Selection. I knew precisely where I was, but to be sure, I decided to walk to an intersection on the other side of my point just to shoot an azimuth from it and ensure that I was right. I spent the next three hours combing the area, breaking through brush, trying to systematically find that point. Approximately thirty minutes before the end of the test, I noticed a handful of guys that were walking around the same area I was; I assumed they were looking for the same point.

Once the exercise was over and I knew I had failed and would not be able to move on to the next phase of training. I asked some of the guys that had been in my area if they were looking for the same point that I was. I gave them the grid coordinates of the point, to make sure there wasn't any confusion. Every single person that had been in that area was looking for the same point I was. Seven of the eight people in the area were now looking at getting recycled or removed from the course. See, in the Q-Course, you could be recycled up to one time per phase of training, or the cadre could refuse to grant any recycles. The cadre were constantly assessing the students, and they would determine whether or not a student should be given the opportunity to have one more chance at passing. We all walked to the road, put our rucks in the back of a pickup truck, and got our rides back to the staging area. I was headed back to Fort Bragg. I failed to accomplish my mission.

Retrospective

"The steps of a man are established by the Lord, and He delights in his way. When he falls, he will not be hurled headlong, because the Lord is the One who holds his hand."

—Psalm 37:23–24

I struggled with the stress that the gates brought into my life. In less than a month's time, I failed to meet a standard ruck march time during a rehearsal ruck march, and I also failed to successfully complete the star navigation course... again. Those two failures may or may not seem like a big deal, but they both greatly affected my self-confidence. Failing to achieve or meet a standard is simply unacceptable for any Green Beret, and the cadre there let us all know it.

In regular Army units, after events like these, we would all sit around the finish line and talk about life, as we watched our peers come across the finish line. In the Q-Course our cadre didn't want to see us cheering for our peers as they neared the finish line, because these events were meant to be completely on the individual. There wouldn't be anyone cheering for you to keep walking when you got sent to Afghanistan in the middle of nowhere with just your ODA. It was just expected that the people who deserved to be there would pass their gates. So you can imagine why my confidence was shattered when I failed the first ruck march. Even though I passed the actual ruck march a few weeks after this happened, it was another stark reminder that nothing can be taken for granted here in the Q-Course.

Failing land navigation was an even more serious blow to my confidence. I am ashamed to admit that if SFC Vera had approached me at that time and told me I didn't have what it took, I would have walked away from the Q-Course and wouldn't be writing this book. The devil took a firm hold of my mental reigns after getting bused back to Fort Bragg. I was ready to quit because I didn't feel like I was good enough to be in the course. I was tired of spraining my ankles every time I stepped into the woods. I was tired of failing in land navigation. I lost sight of my motivation for being there and for a short period of time was in a deep state of depression. I hadn't invited Jesus into my life yet, and didn't recognize that the devil was trying yet again to force my hand. The devil knew my confidence in my abilities was a weak point in my armor. So instead of seeing this failure as an opportunity for reflection and for more training, all I could see was the shame of having failed something that very few of my friends and peers struggled with. It wasn't until years after this small window of my life that I realized God uses the bad situations for our good. It took many years, but I can now look back and see that it was during these hardest of times that God was able to get me to a point where He needed me to be. My failures kept me humble.

> "And He has said to me, "My grace is sufficient for you, for power is perfected in weakness." Most gladly, therefore, I will rather boast about my weaknesses, so that the power of Christ may dwell in me. Therefore I am well content with weaknesses, with insults, with distresses, with persecutions, with difficulties, for Christ's sake; for when I am weak, then I am strong." (2 Corinthians 12:9-10)
>
> "Whoever exalts himself shall be humbled; and whoever humbles himself shall be exalted." (Matthew 23:12)
>
> "Therefore humble yourselves under the mighty hand of God, that He may exalt you at the proper time." (1Peter 5:6)

This chapter is dedicated to the bravest and most courageous man I've ever had the privilege of knowing personally.

Master Sergeant George E. Vera, sir, you are an American hero, and I want to take this opportunity to thank you for all the help and guidance you gave me professionally. Even when I failed, you treated me with respect and encouraged me to keep my head up and to train harder. Those were the words I needed to hear, and I thank you for the critical role you played in my life. It has been my greatest honor to say you were one of the men responsible for pushing me past my personal limits and into a great American military unit. I pray for you often, and my family all know who you are and pray for you as well.

Second Chance at Land Navigation

I knew I was going to get another chance to come back out here and try again for the next class, because that's what the cadre told me once I got back to Fort Bragg. I was relieved that I wasn't out of the course completely, and nervous because I had to go back out there again in less than two months to try again. I studied my butt off. I was spending hours a day in the woods after coming back to Bragg, just so I could learn the finer intricacies of land navigation.

I asked friends for help, and I received it. I was now attached to a different class, so I didn't know any of the people here. Getting to know them was my next priority. I spent months upon months with the group of guys in my previous class. I knew them, and they knew me. We had adapted well to each other's strengths and weaknesses and had outstanding camaraderie. Now I would only have a couple of months to get to know my new teammates before we went on to the next phase of training: SUT, or Small-Unit Tactics. I started to spend a lot of time with my new teammates, and we all became good friends. I became very close friends with a few of the guys, including SGT Clint Loughmiller. He had come from a similar Army background and, like me, felt way out of his comfort zone being in the course. We went to multiple ranges while waiting for the next SUT class, and he taught me a lot about how to shoot properly.

When the day finally came to head back out to Camp Mackall, I felt prepared for the land navigation. It was much colder this time, though, and my rucksack was much heavier because of the cold weather gear I was carrying. If I got lost, I didn't want to freeze to death. We lined up and got inspected, as was the procedure I knew so well. After the cadre gave us our first points, I took off into the darkness to climb over this mountain of a mental hurdle I was dealing with. I could feel doubt just resting in the back of my mind, telling me I couldn't do it before and that I was going to fail this time too. I got to my first point, only three kilometers away, without a hitch. I found it easily, and it looked like the next point was going to be easy to find too, but there was a problem.

We all heard rumors about a certain point that was extremely challenging to get to, because to reach it, a two-hundred-meter stretch of six-foot deep water, called Scuba Road, stood between the two stretches of land.

I could try and come at the point from the path most guys took, but I also considered coming at it from a different angle. I would be trading in a long route in knee-deep water for a short route in deep water. My choices weren't appealing either way, but after a few minutes of internal debate, I decided to take the shorter path that crossed the deeper water.

There are a multitude of things that must be considered whenever soldiers are near bodies of water, such as waterproofing the contents in the rucksack, maintaining a water-free rifle, factoring in the temperature of the water and the air on land, and most importantly, being able to swim the two-hundred-meter distance. I had learned about waterproofing in Selection; so that wasn't an issue. Since I waterproofed my rucksack, it was usable as a flotation device to help carry my weight across the water.

It wasn't until I had just put my boot bottoms in the water that I considered the health risks for doing this. The water was cold as ice, and I'm pretty sure the only reason the water wasn't iced over was because it was running water: belonging to a creek system that fed into a larger river system. If I swam across the creek in my uniform and boots, I was going to have a couple problems. First, it was not easy to swim in a military uniform with boots on, a rifle in hand, a rucksack, and doing so in a silent/tactical manner. Second, once I got to the other side that was when I was concerned for my safety. After I got out of the water, the much-colder air would have a chance to seep into my soaking-wet skin. Oftentimes people will get frostbite if extremities are wet. My extremities would have been wet and exposed to cold air for minutes by then.

I had a spare uniform in my rucksack; so I could swim over and change as fast as possible, and then move on to my next point (only about five hundred meters away). However, that would've left me without any dry uniforms, because I would also have to swim back across to the mainland where the rest of my points would end up being. Even if I decided to put my wet uniform back on for the swim back, to keep one uniform dry, then I was looking at carrying around a wet uniform for the duration of the land navigation course. A wet uniform would be heavier than my current extra dry uniform; I wasn't intentionally doing anything that would add weight to my rucksack.

I decided to do something unorthodox: I opened up my rucksack, took off my uniform and boots that I was currently wearing, and sealed everything up in my ruck. I decided if I was going to swim, I could do it naked. Then I could put on one of my dry uniforms briefly while finding the next point, and then repeat the process again in reverse.

As I stepped into the water, a cold shiver went up my spine, and I began to kick my legs like a frog. I was holding the ruck in front of me and using it as a mobile buoy. I got about halfway across the creek, before I really started to get cold. My chest felt heavy with every cold breath I took, and my legs began to sting and go numb. I eventually lost the ability to swim; my arms just wouldn't work properly. To my surprise, as my feet began to search for the bottom, I felt a huge piece of concrete underneath my feet: there were concrete stepping-stones that covered the bottom two or three feet of the creek. I stood there, water up to my nipples, wondering if I could have just walked the entire way. Of course, they wouldn't let students risk drowning out here. I eventually made it to the other side. I used a T-shirt to towel off, pulled out my thermal military-issued sleeping bag, and hopped my naked butt right inside of it. I lay there for about twenty minutes, until my body heat came back to me and I was able to feel all my fingers and toes.

I put my dry clothes back on and went to get my second point. It didn't take me long to find it. Within an hour, I had crossed Scuba

Road for the second time, again doing it naked. The second time I walked all the way across on the huge concrete blocks. When I got to the other side, as I was taking my last step out of the water, the leg that was bearing the weight on the concrete block slipped. The rocks or cement blocks were covered in green algae and could easily be used as a slip-and-slide. I hadn't taken into consideration that my floating rucksack was supporting some of my weight while I was crossing the creek. So I didn't slip until the last step, when I put all of my weight on the slippery rocks.

As my left leg slipped backward toward the water, I instinctively tried to find proper footing with my right foot. My right foot found a place to make an attempt at breaking my fall; that was when I realized my foot was stuck and I was falling away from it. I heard the *pop* before I felt the pain; but the pain soon followed. I grabbed my right foot and pulled it out of the nook it had gotten stuck in. Then I grabbed my ruck, which had floated away about four feet, and hobbled onto land. I pulled out my T-shirt to dry myself off, pulled out my sleeping bag to warm myself, and then got dressed. I wrapped my foot in an ACE bandage that I was allowed to have now. In Selection they did not want students conducting first aid on themselves, for safety reasons. Some people would push themselves to such limits that they ended up in precarious situations and would injure themselves permanently; all because they weren't willing to quit.

Almost the exact second I had finished lacing up my second boot, a cadre walked around a thick growth of underbrush. I hadn't seen him on the way in, so I assumed he must have driven up and parked when I had been on the other side of the water getting my point.

He stood there for about a minute before slowly saying, "SGT Calhoun, why in fuck did you just wade across Scuba Road butt-ass naked?"

I looked him dead in the eye and told him, "Sergeant, I didn't want to get my clothes wet; because I wouldn't have a spare uniform if I needed to change later, and wet clothes makes the ruck heavier, which isn't cool either."

He told me to keep my clothes on and then told me about a story of a guy who nearly died on the far side of Scuba Road a few years prior. He hadn't waterproofed his ruck properly, and crossed the water fully clothed. He was soaking wet, along with all of his spare uniforms, boots, socks, and sleeping bag. Apparently he tried to start a fire; but he was hypothermic and wasn't able to think straight. They found him about an hour away from death: inside his wet sleeping bag, propped up against a tree in a sitting position with a whistle in his mouth. The only reason the cadre found him was because he had put the whistle in his mouth before falling asleep. His lips tightened around the whistle as his core body temperature dropped, and during each exhale there was a slight whistle sound. Hearing this story made me grateful that I made the decisions that I did to keep my clothes, boots, and rucksack dry.

It was at this time I really noticed how much time I had spent getting my second point; I burned through an additional two hours of time. I took stock of my situation and began a pro/con list in my head. I knew I only had two points remaining. I had plenty of water and dry clothes; so things could be worse, but not by much. I had sprained an ankle, again, and I had approximately three hours left to find my last two points.

My next point...well, my next point was the exact same point as the one I wasn't able to find last time. I knew I recognized the area when I glanced at the map on the far side of Scuba Road; but it only really hit me when I was planning my route where exactly I was headed. This was terrifying, and my mind clouded with doubt immediately. The thought of quitting did cross my mind. I just didn't want trek to where this point was supposed to be ... again and not find it ... again. The good side to this point was that it was only about three kilometers away, and once I was within a kilometer of the point everything looked familiar. My last attempt with this particular point got me very well acquainted with the area. I knew where to travel to avoid the dense surrounding terrain; which allowed me to traverse through mostly open terrain and to find that point within thirty minutes. I walked right up to it. It was less than thirty meters from the tree I had used last time to rest on while plotting my combing methods in search of this point. Now I personally believe that point had been taken down or forgotten about, before my first attempt in the last class. I would never know for certain, though. Thankfully, I didn't have to struggle with finding this point for a second time.

I plotted my final point using the grid coordinate attached to the white post and discovered that this point was about eight kilometers away: pretty much right back to the staging area. I found all my points, with almost an hour to spare.

Retrospective

"This I recall to my mind, Therefore I have hope. The Lord's lovingkindness indeed never ceases, For His compassions never fail. They are new every morning; Great is Your faithfulness."
—Lamentations 3:21–23

I look back on this second chance I was given as such a blessing in disguise. My initial failure humbled me so much that it almost became detrimental to my confidence level. Being humbled never feels good and it comes at a price, but I can say with absolute certainly that pride would have cost me the Q-Course. Looking my new teammates in the eyes and telling them I was there because I failed was not an easy thing for me to do. The devil knew this about me; just like he knew every time I sprained my ankle, I would think about quitting. This time, I even had a cadre there so that I could quit, but something inside me just never let the thoughts vocalize. After reading *Ephesians 6:16*, where Paul tells us to take up the Shield of Faith to extinguish the fiery arrows of the evil one, I realized that my moments of doubt were the arrows being used against me. I just didn't have the knowledge to shield myself then.

"Pride goes before destructions, and a haughty spirit before stumbling." (Proverbs 16:18)

Finding that same point, which I failed to find during my first land navigation gate, in the same spot I remember looking last time, frustrated me. It was a hard pill to swallow: just thinking that I failed and was set back two months, because the point truly hadn't been marked. The ease with which I walked up to the point during the second attempt and other students that also missed this same point last time were not helping me to push away the thoughts of unfairness. These weren't thoughts that I wanted to be bogged down with, but I think so much of our culture teaches us to be upset about any perceived unfair treatment. I didn't even know for sure that I hadn't just overlooked the same point last time, and yet I was upset at the thought that it might not have been marked. The point of the Q-Course isn't about being fairly treated: it is about overcoming obstacles. Successful completion of the entire course is dependent upon finding a way to overcome fear, doubt, pacifism, and other things. This course challenges every individual's desire to be on an ODA on so many levels. Be it a mental challenge, physical challenge, or institutional/structural challenge: there is something there to challenge anyone.

After I found that point, I found a sense of reassurance within myself. I knew I wasn't great at land navigation, but I needed to know I could find that point. No matter where you go or what school you go to, people will always try justifying why they failed or quit instead of pushing through until the end. It is all but guaranteed that I will fall, stumble, fail, or be set back, throughout my life. I just hope I never fail to get back up and try again.

> "Do not lie in wait, O wicked man, against the dwelling of the righteous; do not destroy his resting place; for a righteous man falls seven times, and rises again, but the wicked stumble in time of calamity." (Proverbs 24:15)

I am certain now, after much reflection, that the devil used every moment of weakness to try and force me to quit. Even though there were times that I wanted to quit, eventually, and without fail, the calm realization that I just had to keep putting one foot in front of the other would come back to me. Every time the pain in my ankles felt too much to bear, a sense of relief came over me. There may be a scientist out there who can tell me why and how I felt that relief; but at the end of the day, even the greatest of doctors have a hard time believing the complex nature of our bodies happened at random. If there is even a chance it's not random, that means it's by design. If we were designed by something, why can't it be the God of Abraham, Isaac, and Jacob? I know the truth now, and it has set me free. The devil was yet again thwarted in stopping my progress, and SUT was up next. I thought I was walking alone at the time, but I can see looking back that the footprints up to this point weren't mine at all.

> "Consider it all joy, my brethren, when you encounter various trials, knowing that the testing of your faith produces endurance. And let endurance have its perfect result, so that you may be perfect and complete, lacking in nothing." (James 1:2-4)
>
> "Simon, Simon, behold, Satan has demanded permission to sift you like wheat; but I have prayed for you, that your faith may not fail; and you, when once you have turned again, strengthen your brothers." (Luke 22:31-32)

Small-Unit Tactics—
Squad-Level Training

The next phase of training was SUT, located at Camp Mackall. SUT was about three and a half (almost four) months long, from start to finish: if every test was passed on the first attempt. Squad-level training was the first portion of SUT, and was followed by the platoon-level portion of SUT. Throughout the entire SUT course, every student was rotated through different team positions. Each time we were in a leadership position, we would receive a grade and feedback from our cadre. Our cadre would tell us if he was recommending a GO or a NO-GO and why. People who haven't attended Ranger School will often compare SUT to Ranger School, which is a sore spot for the Ranger qualified folks, but they do have their similarities.

Before starting the tactical phase of training, we spent about two weeks doing nothing but shooting. We shot pistols, rifles, shotguns, M-249, and M-240B machine guns, until our fingers blistered. Our cadre achieved what I thought was impossible and made me *not* want to go to a range. I learned how to shoot from multiple angles and while moving. I learned how to transition from an assault rifle to my sidearm in one smooth motion: never losing control or positive identification of my targets. We were taught techniques for tactically reloading and maintaining a steady firing posture.

The whole idea behind courses like SUT is to teach students basic tactical skills, and then apply those skills to a simulated training environment. My team became a very tight-knit team. We ate together; we slept in the same bay; we cleaned together; we conducted missions together; and most importantly, we helped each other. Everything we did, we did for the good of the group. We did

PT every morning with our cadre, and then we learned the finer intricacies of warfare from some of the most lethal warriors our country has ever produced. There are multiple phases of SUT that a student must pass to graduate from that phase of training. They wanted to test us in small ODA-sized elements, swapping us around into leadership positions at random, to evaluate if we had what it took to "don the beret."

Even though we had come to work well together, the Q-Course is designed to bring out the worst in people. There were a few members of our group that started to show poor leadership qualities when under duress. When poor decisions were made, the cadre would find a way to demonstrate the consequences of those decisions. Our failures to work together as a team, under poor student leadership, after being sleep- and food-deprived, made life more difficult than absolutely necessary. The cadre started killing team members off using artillery simulation rounds, which are extremely loud and simulate incoming artillery. When a team member dies, the team has to carry that person and the equipment that they had, which is no easy feat since our rucks were already over a hundred pounds each.

We would go out into the woods for almost a week straight, conducting mission after mission, without a break. Then we would come back to Mackall on Sunday to grab some hot chow at the famous Camp Mackall DFAC, shower the days' worth of crud off of us, do some laundry, go to church, and then get back to the grind.

Our cadre for this phase of training were ferocious when correcting a student. Our team had two main cadre for this phase, and they crushed us for every mistake that we made. There were tasks that we could do on day 1 but not on day 4, because we hadn't slept or eaten for three of those days (one MRE per day). It was easy to hate the cadre because of their attitudes and bitterness toward the students. It didn't matter what happened; there would be no excuses. If one person failed, we all failed. When we all failed, it generally meant we were going to be carrying our "dead" teammates and their hundred-pound rucksacks. That was how we learned not to mess up. Every time we made a mistake, we paid for it in blood, sweat, and tears.

I don't think a day went by that I didn't contemplate quitting. I had better sleep in Iraq than I did out in the six-foot-deep foxholes we had to dig every night before conducting patrol base activities. It was designed to suck. As a leader, if I didn't accomplish my mission when put in charge, I went home, period. It didn't matter if one of my teammates was the one doing the wrong thing; as the leader, you had to take responsibility for the results. That is what the real world is all about. The cadre were training us and testing our abilities; because if we succeeded, one day our decisions and actions could impact more than just ourselves.

Our cadre would try to pit us against each other, trying to help force the team to come together and make a decision on who deserved to be there and who didn't. As students, we didn't have any kind of authority. As teammates, we were each experiencing what it would be like to be on an ODA with the men in our teams. When everything about our situation and environment sucked, and then we would see someone on our team cutting corners or not carrying his weight, it made us angry. We didn't have to accept that behavior, and we would tell the person they needed to leave. Poor attitudes or lack of intestinal fortitude, from one person, could bring down the team. Some guys just didn't seem to understand that we were all miserable, going through this rigorous course, but as long as we kept it together, we would all come out as Green Berets.

I remember one night in particular during SUT that personal conflicts came to a head. We had failed to execute a proper ambush, because the officer in charge had mismanaged his resources and failed to ensure he had communications up and running—both huge no-no's. After the exercise, the cadre had us lined up alongside the dirt road we were on, shoulder to shoulder, pulling all our sensitive items out to get accountability of them. He was berating us, telling us how we all would've died if this was a real mission. He was stressing as hard as he could to us, without explicitly stating it, that we failed to accomplish our mission because of a certain captain who wasn't willing to swallow the pride pill. I won't say his name because nobody should be judged for going to a school and finding out they aren't cut out for the job. This guy wasn't getting it, though. Every time he opened his mouth, we either heard some story that glorified him or one of the people he was lucky to know. We just wanted the guy to stop talking, if I'm being honest. He was a typical complainer: never being a part of a solution but always vocal to highlight the failures of someone else.

It's important to understand before I tell you what happened that in this phase of training, the rank you had before the course is situationally "irrelevant"—meaning: there was no pulling rank on someone out here. This training was meant for every single one of us to have a go at manhood and see if we had what it took, period. The cadre only wanted the best to pass; we just wanted to eat and sleep; this captain just wanted to make sure everyone knew all the excuses for why he wasn't able to hold up his part of the job. It was this captain, in fact, who interrupted our cadre as he was chewing us out that night on the side of the road. He pointed out where the cadre had "misspoken" at some point, because the captain didn't want to be called what he was: the weakest link.

Our cadre had enough of this guy's mouth and told us to grab our rucksacks and put them up over our heads. My rucksack was anywhere between 65 to 120 pounds, depending on whether or not I was carrying ammo for the machine gun or had eaten MREs or expended ammo. It wouldn't have mattered if my ruck had been ten pounds: I wouldn't have been able to hold it above my head for any extended period of time by this point. I was physically drained and so fatigued that I felt like I was living my life in slow motion, as strange as that sounds. I struggled to get the ruck over my head for mere seconds at a time, but I never quit trying to get it up. I eventually went down on one knee to give my body a better chance at lifting the ruck; I hoisted the ruck over my back, as if I was going to wear it, then sunk both hands underneath the shoulder straps and lifted straight up. I forced my arms to lock at the elbows, and then stood up on both feet: successfully keeping my form for as long as was tolerable. Just as the burning in my muscles became too intense to bear any longer, this captain started to grumble about the situation not being "fair." As I watched him struggle to keep his rucksack held over his head, my temper began to rise.

During the Q-Course I very rarely complained out loud because I already considered myself to be slightly out of my weight class. I definitely didn't want people thinking I was a whiner. This captain, though—he was the textbook whiner. He barely let that first grumble leave his lips, before my rucksack was on the ground and I was closing the distance between the two of us faster than his brain could process what was going on. As I closed in, he realized I was heading toward him and dropped his ruck on the ground: making a gesture that was supposed to portray authority. I had moved past the point of rank mattering. We were a small tight-knit group of men, and we were having issues with this captain every night. Some of the guys could carry 120-pound rucksacks in each arm, but I couldn't. I for one was tired of listening to this captain talk us into crappy situations.

I got up in his face, our noses only two inches from each other, and I told him, "You need to shut the fuck up, sir. I refuse to carry you another step of the way."

He yelled back in my face, saying I had better show him the respect he deserved and that I couldn't talk to a captain in the United States Army that way. I told him his rank didn't mean shit in the woods; we were here to weed out the weak, and that he was the weakest link. Everyone around us was dead silent, to include the cadre, waiting to see what would happen. If I'm being honest, I expected to get into a fistfight with that captain, then and there. I was mentally prepared to beat the living tar out of this officer who was degrading the team's health and morale with his negativity.

You see, Green Berets are often in very crappy environments and shitty living conditions, but you will never hear a Green Beret complain about his circumstances because he always knows it could be worse. Green Berets don't have the luxury of being overwhelmed and second-guessed; the team leader (officer in charge of the team) is the extension of the US government in a foreign country and should act accordingly.

The incident didn't end up turning physical. That night was the one and only night that our cadre didn't force us to run, with our dead buddies on our backs, to our patrol base location after actions on the objective. Our cadre didn't throw artillery simulators behind us to increase the stress levels and simulate incoming artillery, while conducting movements. I believe our cadre had been waiting for someone to correct that captain for his terrible attitude and poor performance.

At some point that evening, the captain silently collected his equipment, walked out of our patrol base, and voluntarily withdrew from the Special Forces course. I felt bad for a while afterward, because I knew how I would feel if someone said those things to me. I already didn't consider myself worthy to stand alongside the men next to me. Hearing someone reinforce my weaknesses would have been detrimental to my career, because, more than likely, I would have agreed with whoever was telling me I wasn't good enough. It wasn't until a year or so later (when deployed to Afghanistan) that I began to understand why the choice I made was the right one. Just because he was a captain didn't mean he was good at what he did, and the stakes were higher on an ODA.

It's an important life lesson: learning that just because someone is in a position of authority doesn't make him or her right. This isn't to say I was right either; just that I was able to make peace with my actions when I realized just how important the team leader's role is on a team. If no one ever said anything and that captain managed to weasel through the course, he could have gotten my friends and brothers in arms killed because of his inability to operate under duress. If he would lose his cool in training, where we knew our lives weren't in danger, how would he act when bullets started to fly? Fortunately for us, we never had to find out.

There were a lot of things to worry about, while at SUT and out on patrol. We had to worry about the cadre; they were always waiting for us to fall asleep while in our patrol bases or for us to make some mistake while conducting our missions. They wanted to weed out the weak, and we as students just wanted to get to the next day. Every day that went by was one day closer to going home.

Sleep deprivation was something that we were all struggling with, since we were going three or more days without sleep at times. There was one incident in particular that I find amusing now and that illustrates just how tired we were. We were in the woods, doing patrols, when we were told some VIPs (high ranking military officials) were coming out to see us. So we were moving to the location where the CSM and Commander were meeting us. They were coming out to check on our training and to see what we were doing. If my memory serves me correctly, one of the Captains on our team was briefing the CSM and telling him what we had been doing. The rest of us were nearby carrying out patrol base tasks. One minute, our teammate was standing in front of the CSM, having a conversation. The next minute, he hit the ground. Mid-conversation, in front of the CSM, while standing: he fell asleep. The CSM watched him go down, and then took a knee to address him and see if he was okay. When our teammate came to and asked what happened, the CSM told him he passed out. Of course he responded with, "no I didn't." The CSM then asked when the last time we slept was, and the cadre confirmed that it had probably been more than 72 hours.

Another thing we had to worry about was the terrain on which we would be navigating. The woods in North Carolina are as varied as any forest I've seen. There are variations in elevation, flora, fauna, and weather—all of which enhance any training environment. There were places that were easily traversable during the day and were nearly impossible to walk though at night. The weather was a concern because rain would cause all the water sources to rise and would soften the forest floor.

One night, it was pouring rain while we were patrolling through the woods. I was leading my squad as the point man when all of a sudden I felt myself fall through a hole barely big enough to fit my body, let alone my rucksack. For about half a second, my rucksack prevented me from going underwater completely; but then the resistance gave way and I was completely submerged in darkness. Poof, gone. I want to put this into context so that you can truly appreciate how scared I was. It was pitch-black outside. We were wearing soaking-wet uniforms, boots, equipment vests, and hundred-pound rucksacks on our backs. We were carrying our weapons, and using only our night vision goggles to see where we were going. With all of my heavy gear on, I was wedged in hole full of water and more than six feet deep.

The guy behind me had been scanning his sector and was looking in a different direction when he heard the commotion of me falling. By the time he looked back at where I had just been, I was gone. He actually walked past my hand, which was now sticking out of the ground and waving; I was trying to get someone's attention. It was the man after him who noticed and grabbed my hand to begin pulling me out of the mud and water. As he was pulling me up, I was pushing off the sides of the hole with my feet trying to step/walk myself upwards and out of that tiny hole. Once my head was out of the water, I gasped for air, and our cadre heard the commotion. The cadre turned on his white light to see what was happening; by that time, there were already two more guys helping to pull me out of that hole.

We were on a mission and limited on time, so I did a quick sensitive-item count, wiped down my rifle, and got back into my position at the front of the patrol. I walked the remaining four kilometers in my heavy mud-laden uniform, in near-freezing temperatures. By the time we completed that mission, my toes were numb and my lips were blue. Warming up that night in dry clothes was a godsend, and I have never taken the "out of the dryer" feeling for granted since this incident.

I'm not sure how long I was underwater in that hole. I know it was long enough to start worrying about not being able to breathe, and long enough that I began frantically waving my hand hoping my teammates would see it. This entire incident was handled so smoothly and was in sharp contrast to what I had experienced in regular Army training. My teammates pulled me out of that hole and went right back to their positions, without saying a word. My team leader checked me out quietly, asked if I was ok, and then we continued mission. The fact that I almost drowned did not change the fact that we had a mission to accomplish. I became excited by the thought that these were my brothers now. I was standing next to people that could face down death and never take a backward step. This further solidified my desire to remain in the ranks with these brave men; just to stand in their ranks was such an honor of mine.

One night that sticks out in my memory during this phase of training came after our squad had gone approximately three days without sleep. Our mission was to set up a linear ambush, late at night. To fully grasp the story it is important to understand that conducting an ambush is a very extensive task. The assaulting element was relatively close and parallel to the road we were targeting. They are emplaced quickly and quietly. The assault line is where the machine gun and claymore mines are set up to be utilized in the ambush. There were two, two-man security elements, one element on the left and one on right side of the ambush, both about two hundred meters away. I was on the right side security team. Both of the security positions had a radio to communicate with the assault element. The security team's entire mission was to tell the assault line when the target was nearing the kill zone. We were basically an early-warning network.

This particular night after my partner and I had been emplaced in our security position, we waited for what seemed like hours for the target vehicle to arrive. Prior to its arrival my partner fell into a very deep sleep. I realized he was asleep and tried to wake him up with no success. I wanted so badly to sleep, and could feel my body involuntarily doing the head bob. Then, I saw something that absolutely terrified me. While looking through my night-vision goggles (NVG), I saw a very large figure. This figure was at least 15-20 feet tall and was completely black. It had what appeared to be some sort of cloak or robe on because I wasn't able to see either of the legs or feet. This figure had very large wings that seemed to have been tucked behind it's back. The head and face were indistinguishable and appeared to look similar to a person wearing a hood and standing with their head slightly bowed (no facial features were visible). It looked like a large angel was standing between the assault element and us. The most terrifying detail was the sword it was holding. The angel looked as if it were leaning, or resting its hands, on a very long sword. The point of the sword was in the ground and the hilt was about chest height on this angel.

I was so terrified by what I was seeing that I shook my partner vigorously, until he woke up, so that I could ask him if he also saw it. He looked in the direction I was pointing and told me he didn't see anything. I told him matter-of-factly that I believed I was actively hallucinating and in doing so saw what I told him looked like the angel of death. He laughed at me and ended up going right back to sleep, against my wishes. This angel did not move at all. It did not speak or identify itself. I wasn't able to take my NVGs off long enough to let my eyes adjust to the darkness, while on mission and waiting for our target to show up. So I was not able to get a good look at it without my NVGs; but with my NVGs on, I was able to reacquire a visual of it every single time I looked in that direction. I took my NVGs off multiple times to let my eyes briefly rest, thinking it was a hallucination. Every other time during our training when I struggled with what I was seeing, it would be different each time I looked in the direction of the object: sometimes moving or altering shape while I was still staring at it. This time, regardless of how I tried to logic what I was seeing away, I wasn't able to make it disappear.

I was physically and emotionally shaken because this was something that looked very real to me. I wanted to sleep so badly, my eyes were burning and hard to keep open. My body was physically exhausted, and my partner's heavy breathing wasn't helping me want to stay awake. Even with all of those factors, I was not able to fall asleep. I wasn't able to stop looking over my shoulder every ten seconds to see if anything changed. The figure never moved.

While this was going on, all of a sudden, I heard the quiet sound of a Humvee rolling down the dirt road that we were all supposed to be watching. Our target vehicle managed to get almost directly in front of my position before I heard and saw it. I immediately got on the radio to tell the assault element, but I didn't even receive one acknowledgement that they had heard my transmission. As I continued to radio the assault element, the vehicle was moving into the kill zone. Once the vehicle was in the kill zone, the assault element should initiate the ambush and shoot to kill everything inside of it. The vehicle was nearly 200 meters away from me, now, in the kill zone, and not one single person opened fire. I have now assumed that everyone had fallen asleep. I was only able to see the taillights of the vehicle at this point. I could see that the lights were well within the outer kill zone limit. Since I hadn't heard back on the radio from the assault element, and because they hadn't engaged the target, I took a shot at the vehicle from my security position. This is not something that I should have done. I knew it when I pulled the trigger, but for some reason I just felt compelled to shoot. As soon as I opened fire, the entire assault element engaged and destroyed the target. After firing my rifle, I looked back at the spot where the dark figure had been, and it was gone.

My next thought was that maybe I shouldn't have taken the shot. I was worried I had ruined the ambush. My partner had woken up when he heard me firing and immediately tried figuring out what was going on. I filled him in on what had happened, and he apologized for falling asleep again. I wasn't upset. I would have been asleep right there next to him if not for this figure showing up and keeping my attention.

When the mission was over, the security elements were the first to arrive at the road for sensitive items accountability. The cadre approached us right away. He asked us, in a very aggressive tone, which one of us had taken the shot. At this point I was concerned that I kicked off the ambush too soon. I didn't know for sure if everyone was asleep; it was possible there was something wrong with my radio and the assault element could have been waiting to engage for a reason. So I was second-guessing myself, when our cadre confronted us. I told him I was the one that fired. He asked why, so I explained that I was unable to confirm that anyone heard my radio transitions and there wasn't enough time to send a runner to their position. Without any way to communicate with the assault element, I did the only thing I could, to ensure the truck didn't make it past the kill zone.

Once the rest of the squad showed up and all of our sensitive items were accounted for, the cadre began his very loud critique of our ambush. He asked the group out loud, "Who initiated the ambush?" I raised my hand. He asked the assault team why they hadn't initiated the ambush, and no one gave a response. He called out the entire assault element for falling asleep. He said that he, or the other cadre there, had personally touched every single person on that line to confirm that they had all fallen asleep. He was absolutely irate about this. He told us, if we had let that vehicle make it through that kill zone, we would have hated our lives even more than we already did. The cadre wasn't happy that I had taken the shot because it was not in our Standard Operating Procedure (SOP), and I didn't have a clear line of sight on the vehicle. He told us that normally he would punish me for a blatant breach of SOPs, but since that shot woke the assault element up and the mission was a success, he wouldn't crush us… as badly.

Later on in the evening, once we reached our patrol base, I remember telling everyone and anyone who would listen, that I had been hallucinating and had seen the angel of death. I didn't have any biblical knowledge at that time, nor any other information, that could've helped me put a name to what I saw. The words just came out of my mouth, as I explained what I had seen to my teammates. I called it the angel of death, only because those were the first and only words I could think of to explain what I saw. Everyone was exhausted and at least a few others admitted to hallucinating as well, but none of them ever told me about such vivid experiences like this one.

Retrospective

"I have been on frequent journeys, in dangers
from rivers, dangers from robbers, dangers from
my countrymen, dangers from the Gentiles, dangers in the city, dangers in the wilderness, dangers on the sea, dangers among false brethren; I
have been in labor and hardship, through many
sleepless nights, in hunger and thirst, often without food, in cold and exposure."
                                        —2 Corinthians 11:26–27

SUT is hands-down the hardest military training I have ever done,
and I wasn't even done yet. Even when I think back to those days, I
cringe, knowing what I had to endure to get through it all. In this
first phase, I was physically broken down, mentally exhausted, and
filled with doubt every step of the way. The weight on my shoulders
from my rucksack alone was so great that each time I had to carry
the captain I mentioned, or his rucksack, it began to eat at me more
and more. I wasn't the strongest guy, so the cadre never killed me off.
I was one of the smaller guys on the team, and my weight wouldn't
have worn everyone down as quickly. The cadre meticulously made
our lives miserable throughout this entire phase of training.

When I look back on this training, I don't see Jesus walking with
me: He was walking for me. Jesus Christ had to carry me, for me to
be able to get through SUT. I reinjured my ankle before this phase
of training, and it never got better. It was easy to become depressed
and angry at each other, after being tested so harshly by our cadre.
Now, after spending time on an ODA, I can understand what the
cadre were doing; I know that the cadre did me a favor by being as

harsh as they were. I didn't have an infantry background, and even though I had deployment experience with a scout platoon, I had *so* much to learn. That is what SUT was for, to turn people like me into infantrymen.

I was under physical duress, and my mental state was constantly being ravaged with doubt. Throughout the entire squad-level portion of SUT our cadre was evaluating and rating us. Every single time my cadre pulled me aside to give me one my evaluations, he told me the same thing: I had failed to meet the standard expected, and he was recommending a NO-GO for me for that event. I would ask what I could do to improve, and he would direct me to ask my peers. Keep in mind, many other SUT students quit throughout SUT. Second chances aren't given for quitting. I was looking at failing SUT, based on every recommended NO-GO from my cadre, and my only hope was making it until the end and being granted a recycle for this phase of training. I would still have to finish the remaining platoon level training, and honestly I was struggling with the thought of having to do all of SUT all over again.

Ever since the day I almost drowned in a hole in a creek bed, I have had a different perspective toward any Special Operations personnel. It sounds weird, but there is something powerful about almost drowning and having your brothers pull you back to life—and to do all of it without saying a word. This is also how I see Jesus helping me now. When it feels like I am drowning, it feels as though Jesus grabs my hand, pulls me out of the mess I am in, and puts my feet back on solid ground, without having to say a word.

As for what I saw during that specific ambush, there are a few things I can say with absolute certainty: I was on the verge of falling asleep, everyone else had evidently fallen asleep, I saw what I described at that time as the angel of death, because of what I saw I could not fall asleep, and because I was not able to fall asleep the mission did not fail. I don't wish to fill in all the blanks, because truthfully I can't say anything else for certain. What I believe, now that I have done some research on angels and have a lot more biblical knowledge, is that God sent an angel that night to keep me awake. Regardless, I can't take any credit for not falling asleep. I am so thankful that whatever I saw kept me alert, when I couldn't have done it on my own.

> "For this very night an angel of the God to whom I belong and whom I serve stood before me." (Acts 27:23)
>
> "For He will give His angels charge concerning you, To guard you in all your ways." (Psalm 91:11)
>
> "Are they not all ministering spirits, sent out to render service for the sake of those who will inherit salvation?" (Hebrews 1:14)

Small-Unit Tactics—
Platoon-Level Training

Remember when I said SUT is broken down into phases? Well, after the squad-level training phase was over (the phase I just completed), platoon-level training was going to begin. It's well known in the Q-Course history that the cadre always toned it down for platoon-level training. By this point, most of the weak men had already quit or been injured. I could write for days about how hard that squad-level training was for me, but if you had told me that platoon training would be worse while out in the field, I'd have laughed in your face. Nothing could be worse than that, or so I thought.

We were getting some much-needed showers and hot chow after completing squad phase. Our team was less than half the size it was when we started, and the men remaining were solid dudes. We were taking a short break to do our laundry, go to religious services, and to clean our weapons, to prepare for the next phase of training that started the following day. We always relished the time we had inside the bays; anytime we had indoors we cherished, because we knew what being outside for weeks at a time was like. We were strictly eating MREs, unless we were back at base where there was a DFAC. Just like every other military school, when given the chance to eat in the DFAC, we all took food out of the DFAC with us. Of course, we were told not to take any food out of the DFAC.

Ask anyone who has lived on MREs for more than a day and they will tell you that food becomes currency. There simply weren't enough calories in the MREs to sustain the level of calories being burned, and the food in the MREs tasted terrible. When we were leaving the DFAC we would stuff our pockets with honey buns, cereal, pieces of fruit, and anything else that was edible and not tied down. It sounds really funny, looking back on it, because it just sounds silly that people would need to think about stashing food for later; but it highlights just how hungry we were. Anyone who has ever truly known hunger knows the primal urge men get when their survival needs aren't being met. We would constantly look out for each other and would share our stashes with anyone needing an energy boost or those that missed out on chow time for whatever reason. I can't say that I think what we did was wrong morally, but ethically it was wrong. We all knew that taking food out of the DFAC was wrong (because they had made a rule against it during this phase of training), but we weren't thinking about what the consequences would be.

We all woke up that Monday morning refreshed. The decreased stress from the cadre was already tangible. They were no longer trying to break us and were noticeably more cordial. We formed up after breakfast and started our morning patrol. We were only going a few kilometers away and the cadre were allowing us to walk tactically on the road to save time, highlighting that this was an "administrative" movement…meaning, no enemy. Stress levels were equalized throughout the platoon, and people were starting to look and feel more confident that the hard part was behind them.

When we all got to the link-up site, the cadre told us to drop our rucks, to pull out the equipment needed for that day's training, and to await further instruction. We are all pulling the items needed out of our rucks, when all of a sudden, I heard a loud voice say, "What in the fuck is this?"

I looked over, and twenty feet away a cadre was standing above a rucksack trying to pull something out that I couldn't quite see. As the cadre ripped hard one last time, a SAW (squad automatic weapon/ M249) spare barrel came flying out of the ruck, along with a poncho and two honey buns.

The spare SAW barrels are generally carried so the operator can swap barrels, when it gets too hot after successive fire, and be able to continue firing. The barrel is usually a dark metallic color, but the barrel the cadre was holding was a copper-brown color: almost making the barrel unrecognizable. Then it clicked in my head: that barrel should never reach a point where it is completely covered in rust. The person carrying it had taken the shortcut and assumed he wouldn't need it. Therefore, he didn't clean it and oil it like he should have. If this was in a real-world scenario, he could have just cost us our lives; those machine guns are often all that stop an enemy from advancing their attacks.

The cadre was looking at the rusted barrel and for the guy who that rucksack belonged to. The responsible student was chatting with one of his buddies when he heard the yell. He ran over, taking responsibility for the barrel and watched in horror as the cadre threw the spare barrel into a thick tangled mess of vines and dense vegetation. The student ran into the wooded area to retrieve the barrel. That was when that same cadre picked up the honey buns off the ground. We all knew it was coming, long before the cadre told us to dump our rucks. I had a honey bun in my rucksack, along with every other NCO and officer in the group. We often gave our food to the guys who were ill or injured to assist in their recovery and used these honey buns as pick-me-ups. But I won't lie, I was also sneaking them for extra calories for myself.

The cadre all began tearing through our rucksacks, pulling out items from every nook and cranny, looking for more contraband. They realized quickly that more people had honey buns than didn't; this wasn't an isolated incident. It was a blatant disregard of the rules that were told to us the day we arrived at Camp Mackall. Our cadre told us to pack our rucks and to start heading back to base. We learned soon after we got back to base that training was effectively cancelled.

The cadre put all of us in one giant formation outside the bays we slept in, when not in the field, and called one bay in at a time. Our bay was the second one called. We ran over toward the bay and could hear the cadre yelling loudly, "You have thirty seconds to get all contraband out of your lockers. This is the only amnesty period you will get."

I remember opening my locker; right there in the front, in plain sight, was a small cereal box with Cheerios in it. I used to snack on those Cheerios, when I was on fireguard at night. Now, I was shamefully carrying that small cereal box past the cadre to throw in a large trash can (already filled with the first bay's contraband). I remember feeling so guilty for "stealing" food from the DFAC. I remember thinking to myself how ashamed I would feel going home saying I failed because of an integrity violation…hiding honey buns and Cheerios. We got caught with our hands in the cookie jar and rightfully deserved any punishment the cadre deemed appropriate.

Once our bay was done, we left to join the mass formation outside, and the next bay was called in to take advantage of their amnesty period. This went on until all contraband was removed from the bays. Then the cadre went back to the first bay and began tearing it apart. We watched as articles of clothing, chairs, personal hygiene products, boots, and anything else not nailed to the floor were thrown about the room. On certain occasions, items were thrown right outside the bay door and off the second-floor balcony. Nothing was left untouched. It was always a horrible feeling, seeing that happen to your stuff, because you knew you had to go through and start sorting through the items strewn about the bay to get your shit together again. It never even crossed my mind that some guys were still willing to try and hide contraband. I was amazed at how much food was found after the amnesty period was over. The bay before ours had half a trash bag full of food, and this was after the amnesty… I couldn't understand it, then or now.

Our bay got trashed like the first one did, but we didn't have one single item of contraband in our room. Our squad had the talk before we went in for our amnesty period. We unanimously agreed that we did not want to be sent home over extra calories, and we meant it. We cleared out everything that could have been considered contraband. When the inspection was over, the cadre simply told us to clean up the mess and return to formation. Because of the unique layout of the building, doors inside the rooms connected all the bays; so someone could walk from one end of the building to the other, without stepping outside the bays. This was very useful during training, but what we heard come out the next room made my heart sink.

Not only were the cadre finding more food, I heard one start yelling extremely loud expletives at one individual in particular.

It took awhile to learn what all transpired. The main gist was that the cadre found a GPS rolled up in a pair of military socks and stashed at the bottom of his rucksack. None of that looked good, and none of us believed the guy when he began pleading with the cadre that he forgot it was there. We all knew it was a lie, but we were curious about how the cadre were going to handle the situation. That team had been recognized formally in training for having the fastest movement times and most accurate land navigation techniques in the entire class. Now we thought we knew why. The cadre violently ripped apart the remaining bays, searching everything and everywhere they could think to look. When it was all over, we stood there in one giant formation as it poured rain on us. The cadre had the student with the GPS standing in front of the mass formation facing the rest of us. They asked him publicly why he had the GPS, and he kept up with the story that he had forgotten all about it. I knew he was lying, immediately… and so did they.

The cadre told us to go gather all our equipment, to empty our lockers, and to bring all of it out to formation with us. Once we were all outside, they opened up our ranks and told us to dump our belongings onto the wet ground. Every dry article of clothing I had was now wet, not just damp, but soaked. I was unfortunate enough to have been standing near a puddle. So, when the cadre grabbed my duffel bag and dumped it out, the contents landed right in the puddle. The cadre again went through every article of clothing. They unrolled every sock and pulled every pocket inside out, before throwing each article of clothing back on the ground. We were all soaking wet; we were freezing cold in the February/March weather; and we had no idea what would happen next.

We found out when the senior-ranking cadre came out with a couple pieces of paper that the student not only used the GPS but that he had used the GPS since his pre-selection training days. He had somehow snuck a GPS in and had used it while the rest of us were using maps and compasses. I suffered a lot physically, enduring those land navigation courses, and the fact that this guy got accolades for being fast but was actually cheating the entire time just irked me.

They called this guy out for his lack of integrity, and I don't remember seeing him again.

Even though his time at SUT was at an end, ours wasn't, and we still had almost three weeks left. We knew the stress levels were going to get ratcheted up again after this incident. What we didn't expect was the cadre coming out to the formation, telling us to ground our gear, and to go GI party the barracks.

For those that don't know what a GI party is, it is when soldiers collectively clean areas utilized for training or quartering soldiers. I'm not sure where the term was coined, but I do know they are never fun. We worked well into the early-morning hours, not finishing the GI party until about three in the morning. Once the bays were spotless the cadre inspected them. Then they took the keys and locked all the bays. We returned to formation, and they let us stand there until sunrise. That's when the Special Warfare Center and School (SWCS) Command Sergeant Major (CSM) arrived. I had seen pictures of him hanging on some of the walls on Fort Bragg, but I had never heard him speak before. He told us how disappointed he was in us and that he was considering recycling the entire class for failing to correct this integrity violation.

I didn't think I had it in me to go through this course again, and the seed of doubt really planted itself in my mind. Instead, he said that he would leave it up to the cadre to determine who would pass this phase of training at the end of the course and walked away. I'm sure he was more involved than that behind closed doors, but he successfully put the fear of failure in all of our minds. The cadre came out of their office and told us that we would conduct training as planned that day, and that's just what we did. We marched and trained just like we did since we arrived. It wasn't until after we got back to base that first night that we realized we didn't know what the sleeping arrangements were. The cadre told us that, since we couldn't be trusted to follow direction without direct supervision, the CSM told them not to allow us back into the bays. This meant that we would be sleeping outside, for the next three weeks.

We were to conduct patrol base activities in and around the "Nasty Nick" obstacle course and its surrounding terrain, making sure to fill in our foxholes before moving out every morning. Platoon-level SUT was going to look very different for us. We would be spending every waking moment in some type of training environment or pulling security with noise and light discipline. It took us a few days to get into the new routine but we eventually did. It generally consisted of starting the day off with our early-morning tactical movement to the training area, training at the training area, moving tactically back to base, and then we went right into digging foxholes for patrol base activities. We were required to have a fully established patrol base, complete with foxholes and all the little details, before the cadre would have us fill the holes in, move to another area that same night, and do it all over again. Anyone who hasn't conducted patrol base activities can't truly appreciate how exhausting and time-consuming those activities can be. After the first few days, we finally started getting about three hours of sleep a night per person. This was how the remainder of our time would go in SUT. We were only allowed to use the latrine on base for going to the latrine: no personal hygiene was to be done with warm or running water.

We were normally close enough to a building that we could smell the food from the DFAC and could see the other students make their way to the showers before starting their day. I have rarely been drawn to envy like I was at that point in my life. We even asked our cadre to keep us out in the woods, just so we wouldn't have to smell the bacon that we couldn't eat; our requests were denied. I wanted so badly to stop eating MREs and to just get warm. We were all chilled down to our bones, never getting the chance to thaw out, except when on a movement when our blood would get flowing.

It was the first time in my life I remember seeing grown men snuggle up next to each other in their foxholes to conserve heat and to try and stay as warm as possible. It was in these hard conditions that I met some of the best men I have ever known. Captains, NCOs, and soldiers—we were all brothers working together and accepting the demands the cadre put us in with our heads held high. This miserable situation in many ways helped us bond together, even more so than we had during the first few months. This lifestyle of ours, living out in the woods, digging foxholes every night, living tactically for weeks at a time…we started to call it the "Honey Bun Hotel," in honor of one of the reasons we were out there in the first place. This was the routine for us for the last three weeks, minus a few days at the end for equipment cleaning and counseling from the cadre informing us if we passed or not.

One morning, about five days prior to the end of training, we woke up cold and wet, ate our breakfast MREs, and started moving out to the training site. Today was different than most days for me. I volunteered to carry the Pig (M240B machine gun), which is substantially heavier than my rifle was: easily adding thirty pounds to what I was used to carrying. I took the responsibility with happiness in my heart. I knew physically I was weaker than most of the guys here, but I also knew they noticed my effort.

Selfishly, however, if I could go back in time, I might not have volunteered to carry that machine gun. I had no clue they were going to make us run six miles, in full gear, to the training area. "No walking allowed" was the rule of the day. Maintaining noise and light discipline, we all just started running. We weren't even a mile into the movement before I began falling behind. Since our squad started in the front of the formation, it took awhile for me to reach the end of the line. Men stronger than me were passing me by, never breaking their stride. Eventually the only thing behind me was the pickup truck driven by the cadre assigned the medical role: for those that got injured or fell out.

I'm sure my feet were shuffling long before I ended up behind all my peers, but I hadn't realized that I wasn't really picking my feet up off the ground; I was just kind of sliding them forward. I was mentally and physically drained already. Now, with an additional thirty pounds, I literally couldn't lift my legs off the ground. My muscles were failing, and the cadre in the pickup truck saw it happening. He pulled up alongside me and started off real polite, saying, "SGT Calhoun, it's okay if this isn't for you. You know you aren't going to catch up to the guys, so why are you still here?"

I remember hearing those words, almost feeling them enter my brain and toying with my emotions. I remember thinking about the warmth of my wife, about my daughter's laugh, which I'd not heard in almost three months, and then about how I told myself I'd never quit. I would never be able to live with myself if I lay down next to my wife as less of a man than I wanted to be. Quitting wasn't in my vocabulary, and I told the cadre I was going to be just fine. About a minute later, I remember taking a step with my left foot, not lifting the toe off the ground from exhaustion, and stepping on a stone about the size of a marble. It didn't take but a second before the ankle gave way and I fell face-first into the asphalt road. I heard a loud popping sound come from my left knee.

I think I blacked out, because I don't really remember hitting the ground with my face, but I do remember standing up with blood coming out of my nose. My fingers were burning as they had been on the receiving end of my body weight, and the machine gun dragged them along the concrete. I stood up, if that's what you would call it, to assess the damage done to my body. I hadn't fully processed the excruciating pain coming from my left knee until I took my first step on that leg. My knee immediately collapsed under the weight and I went down again… hard. I didn't need to do much assessing after hitting the ground that second time. I hadn't expected my knee to be unable to support my weight, but now I was acutely aware of the predicament I was in. I had a long way to go still; none of my platoon was in sight; and I was in excruciating pain.

This entire incident probably lasted about two minutes, but it felt much longer. The cadre was steadily unleashing verbal assaults on me, telling me I was a "fucking quitter" and "too weak" to be here and to give up. I told myself at that time not to look at or acknowledge that cadre again until the movement was complete. I knew he was playing a mental game that I wouldn't win if I engaged. Even before this, I had become accustomed to seeing people get injured and watching them push through the pain and into mission success; but I never felt pain like that before and was questioning my physical ability to finish the Q-Course. It's a funny thing how fear and failure can play tricks on the mind when things get hard. Every man in the course will tell you they thought about taking the easy road and quitting when things got tough. The difference between the ones that quit and the ones that didn't…well, the ones that didn't quit have worn the Green Beret.

With all these thoughts of failure and physical pain, I wasn't even paying attention to the fact that I was still moving forward. I wasn't able to put a lot of weight on my left leg; I surely wasn't able to run or jog anymore; but I never stopped the forward progress. Before I realized it, I had hobbled more than two additional miles and was nearing the point where I would leave the paved road and start moving on a dirt trail filled with soft sand. My destination was about a mile and half from the point where the paved road met the dirt trail. I knew I was getting closer, but I was trying not to focus on how much further I'd have to carry this heavy-ass rucksack and machine gun. I needed to focus on putting one foot in front of the other.

I don't remember the cadre saying anything to me once we left the paved road. He followed me for the last mile and a half in his pickup truck. I came up to a hill, and at the top of that hill I could see the rest of my platoon enjoying their much-deserved break after that heavy six-mile run. I ascended the hill and found my squad. They were about to send a team to come look for me and for the machine gun I was carrying. As they took the gun from me, I did a "rucksack flop" (falling violently to the ground, landing on the rucksack). I started drinking some water and filling my team in on my knee. Up to this point, when guys got hurt, we tried to cover down for them because we all knew it could be us next time that needed help. My squad began tearing through my rucksack, taking items like ammo and food out of it, to lighten the load for me, and one of the captains in my squad took the machine gun from me and gave me his rifle.

As I was lying there on the ground, watching my team prepare to carry me through the rest of that day's training, I began to realize how bad my knee was throbbing. I heard one of the cadre tell the platoon to get up and to get ready to move out. As I stood, I put all my weight on my right leg, hesitant to put any weight on my left leg. I had no choice, though. I took my first step with my left leg, and slowly began putting weight on it. My knee gave out under the weight, sending a wave of fresh pain up throughout my body, before I fell down again and grasped my knee in pain. I was done. There was no possible way to push through this one. This wasn't an ankle in land navigation where I could use a rifle as a crutch and hide in the woods when the cadre passed by. The same captain who had taken the machine gun from me went to get the same cadre medic that was verbally insulting me earlier in the pickup truck, to tell him I wasn't able to continue training.

The cadre walked up to me, demeanor completely different than it was in the truck, and began assessing the injury. I lay on the ground, and the cadre took my left foot into his hands and began pushing my left leg into a bent position to test the flexibility. After he realized I couldn't bend my leg, he noticed that the uniform surrounding my knee was skintight. My knee was swollen to the point that the uniform, normally loose and baggy, had become tight and stretched. I remember this whole event distinctly, because of the compassion the cadre had for me. I always wondered if he felt compassion because of his medical calling or if it was guilt that he felt: for degrading me and calling me a weak failure before realizing my injury was substantial. Either way, he wasn't yelling at me now. Instead he pointed to two of the guys in my squad, told them to secure my gear, and he hoisted me over his shoulders in the fireman-carry position to carry me down the hill I had just climbed up. He helped me get into the pickup truck for a quick ride to the medical center.

The guys at the medical center on Mackall were awesome, in all respects. These guys were battle-tested medics who were keeping guys like me in the pipeline, and they are good at what they do. They made sure all my gear was secure and all my sensitive items were turned in then put me in a van to drive me to the hospital on Fort Bragg. I had some X-rays taken, and a doctor took a look at my knee. The doctor told me it looked like a sprain and it would take a few weeks before I could train on it again. *Devastated* doesn't begin to describe the emotions I was feeling. I remember asking the doctor if there was anything I could do that could miraculously make this go away by tomorrow morning, and he laughed at me in a compassionate doctor-like way. He told me I probably wouldn't be able to put any real weight on it for a while, let alone train with other Green Beret students.

I sat in a state of depression the entire forty-five minute ride back to Camp Mackall. All I could think about were the foxholes I'd dug every night for weeks and the below-freezing weather we slept in following torrential downpours with lightning storms galore. We sweat all day and froze all night, but we did it together. I had never been more proud than to have suffered alongside these men and to have seen many of them do things I would have thought physically impossible. Finishing this part of the training pipeline was significant because it had, at that time, the highest attrition rate than any other part of the course. Now, I was certain I would not be finishing, let alone passing. I was still receiving NO-GOs from my cadre during *every* evaluation, so passing was uncertain even before the injury.

I have always known people that have said they could man up and do things when it counted, myself included; but until SUT, I had no clue what my body could or couldn't take. I learned I could go over three days without one minute of sleep: patrolling and moving in a tactical manner the entire time without once breaking noise or light discipline. I put every ounce of brotherhood, physical power, and will power that I had into that course. I left it all on the field. Now, I was going back to get my gear just to turn back around and have to do it all over again after my knee healed. I tried fighting off the thoughts of quitting, but this book is about me being honest, and I never wanted to quit the Q-Course more than I did at this time. I just didn't think I had it in me to come back out in a month (a generous estimate, as most serious sprains take six to eight weeks to heal) to do this all over again, adding yet another three-month period away from my wife and daughter.

We pulled into the medical center, and I hobbled out of the van with my crutches. I was catering a now-wrapped knee and gimped my way back to the cadre office to tell the cadre what the doctor said. Temptation to sin was creeping in, because I thought about lying to the cadre that night. I wanted to tell them that the doctor said I was okay. It's funny because I was on crutches and I knew they had the paperwork; so, at the very least, they would most certainly know I had lied when I wasn't able to walk the next day. It still amazes me how those kinds of thoughts will come through a man's mind when things get tough, because they do. Quitting has tempted the best of the men I know, but the best of them never do. I remember knocking on the cadre's door. I took a step back and waited for them to open the door. The door swung open, and one of the cadre invited me to sit down until my squad's cadre arrived.

When my cadre showed up, I told him the truth about what the doctor said. I gave him the medical forms he needed, and then he told me wait outside until he came out with further instruction. I stepped outside and walked around the corner of the building, because I was worried I might cry. I had never worked so hard for something and not been able to achieve it; that thought alone was breaking my will and spirit. I was second-guessing everything at that point: thinking about how weak I was for not being able to push through this. I'm not really sure how long I was out there standing, but I know I never heard my cadre walk up to me. I just turned around, and there he was. He asked me how I was doing, and I told him I was pretty bummed about what happened but that I would be back next class to do it again if permitted. I didn't even really mean those words when they came out of my mouth, but I felt like that's what he would have wanted to hear. So that's what I said.

He looked straight through me and said with a little smirk on his face, "Not everything is bad, hang in there." He turned around and walked away before I could ask him any follow-up questions about what that meant.

It's important to remember here that this cadre I'm interacting with treated me like shit for the previous three months. He put my peers and me through the grinder. We weren't allowed to talk to the cadre unless we were in leadership positions. Even then, it was only for mission-oriented training tasks: never in a personal manner like this. It's also important to understand that the Q-Course is a meat grinder in regards to its students. There are so many more people that get injured, get recycled, simply quit, or get peered out, than those that graduate the entire SFQC pipeline and earn the Green Beret. The course doesn't care about an individual or their injuries; they want people that can get through it, no matter what. They aren't there to cater to anyone's personal needs or desires; they were simply there to train us to be the best soldiers we could possibly be.

So I knew what to expect when the cadre called me back into the office and told me to sit down. My cadre, the same man who made me carry that weak captain over three kilometers, all while being arty-simmed (simulated artillery), that same guy was telling me that he had decided to give me a go for the SUT phase of training. I sat there with what must have looked like a blank expression on my face, because he asked me if I understood what that meant. I told him I really didn't, because I knew I had a few days left of training. In the last few days of the course, there were at least two GO/NO-GO events that were requirements to pass the SUT phase. I knew I hadn't completed those tasks yet. At best, I was hoping they would recycle me into the next class and let me start at platoon phase. So I wouldn't have to go through the really shitty parts of training again, but I *never* expected, or even hoped for, this. I was told later on by a senior-ranking Green Beret (now a SGM actively leading his troops in one of the Special Forces groups) that no student to his knowledge had ever been given the leniency of getting a go, injury or not, without completing the entire phase of training. I hadn't heard of a student getting any leniency either, hence the dread and depression I was feeling earlier when I thought I'd have to redo the training.

At that time, I thought it was luck, but now I know that it was God's hand in my life. These types of things don't happen in this community, because there are people out there that would fake an injury if there were even a chance of still passing the course.

The next day, before I went home, I saw my cadre about to leave on his motorcycle. I hobbled over to him on my crutches to thank him for vouching for me. He told me I didn't need to thank him. He said he had been watching me, and noticed that I was always in the middle of everything that was happening. I wasn't one of the major players, but I was always there to give/do what I could. He told me that I had the right attitude and mentality, even and especially after continuously being told I was receiving NO-GOs. He commented on the fact that my level of effort and my attitude didn't change after each negative evaluation that he gave me. Once he brought it up, I asked him if I had really failed everything. He told me that I had not failed and I was a great student. He was testing me psychologically to see if I would quit if I thought I was going to fail anyway.

The cadre had told me that by default, in the event that a student can't finish, they recycle that student, because it made the decision clear-cut every time: harsh but fair. My cadre had gone out of his way to tell his peers that he witnessed me giving everything I had during that training. He noticed how I tried to carry the collective weight every chance I got and that I cared about the welfare of my peers more than my own. Those were qualities that I had never given a lot of thought to, because it just felt natural. I like sleeping well at night knowing I gave everything I had. That is one of the things the cadre look for in training: those people who may not be the biggest or strongest but that remain formidable because they choose not to get run over. We had to choose to face challenges, not to just confront them, but to run them over completely. These are the types of men that the Special Forces Qualification Course wants on an ODA.

Retrospective

"My flesh and my heart may fail, but God is the strength of my heart and my portion forever."
—Psalm 73:26

I learned a lot about integrity during this phase of training. Sneaking food from the DFAC was the first and only time I ever blatantly disregarded the rules during the Q-Course. The course was designed very meticulously, and not consuming calories was part of the training. Our stealing honey buns took away from the effectiveness of the training. In the real world, there may not be a DFAC to steal from, what then? I look at *James 2:10*, where he writes, *"For whoever keeps the whole law and yet stumbles in one point, he has become guilty of all."* This verse gave me such great understanding after reading it. I was fortunate in my SUT class to have been rightly punished for breaking the rules, because I feel like it was a good learning point for me. We paid dearly for our actions but built character in the process.

> "All discipline for the moment seems not to be joyful, but sorrowful; yet to those who have been trained by it, afterwards it yields the peaceful fruit of righteousness." (Hebrews 12:11)

There are times when we are fed well, have a nice bed to sleep in, and clothes to wear, but how many of us volunteer to give those things up just to serve our nation? Great men and women volunteer to give up all those things everyday because they understand there has to be a transfer of identity, when we serve our country. We must learn that our lives are no longer about us as individuals; our lives are now dedicated to our country. We are willing to give up everything, including our lives, to protect and serve our great nation. How much more has Jesus done and provided for us than our nation has? How much more should we be willing to sacrifice to follow our great Lord, Jesus, our Savior, who died for our sins so that we may have eternal life with him?

> "Whoever does not carry his own cross and come
> after Me cannot be my disciple." (Luke 14:27)

Most of the time, we don't even remember the times that we were well fed and warm, but we never forget the times we go without. That person/soldier you see walking down the street, you have no idea what he/she has gone through or the individual sacrifice and challenge that he/she face daily. Many Christians around the world are also enduring suffering and persecution, for a greater purpose, for the name of Jesus.

> "And not only this, but we also exult in our trib-
> ulations, knowing that tribulation brings about
> perseverance; and perseverance, proven charac-
> ter; and proven character, hope; and hope does
> not disappoint, because the love of God has been
> poured out within our hearts through the Holy
> Spirit who was given to us." (Romans 5:3–5)

When I face-planted the concrete and sprained my knee, I was literally hitting rock-bottom. I was already barely able to make it day by day, and when I realized the extent of my injury, I felt defeated. I remember thinking to myself on the drive to Fort Bragg that I wasn't good enough to pass the course. That injury could have been my ticket to another intelligence unit, where I knew I would thrive, but something deep down kept telling me to be quiet and keep walking. When I told myself not to look at the cadre in the truck while he was trying like hell to get me to quit, I know now that little voice inside was the Holy Spirit. The Holy Spirit was with me on that walk, numbing my mind, enabling my swollen knee to keep walking, and the Holy Spirit was with me on the ride to and from the hospital on Fort Bragg.

This SUT course is just one of the many reasons that I have a powerful testimony: one that no one will ever be able to take away from me. I could not and did not get through this course on my own. One-hundred percent of what I had to offer was not enough. I gave more than one-hundred percent, but everything beyond the one-hundred percent threshold... that was all Jesus. Jesus lives in the one-hundred-and-one percent and higher. To see Jesus carrying us, we must first be willing to give all we have and then keep going. Just as the medic had let me continue to struggle, as long as I had the strength and will power to continue; I believe Jesus lets us give everything we have. Thankfully, He never leaves us. Just like that same medic did when I finished that movement, Jesus will throw us on his shoulders and carry us the rest of the way and take care of us.

> "No temptation has overtaken you but such as is common to man; and God is faithful, who will not allow you to be tempted beyond what you are able, but with the temptation will provide the way of escape also, so that you will be able to endure it." (1 Corinthians 10:13)

Even in the midst of the Honey Bun Hotel, I never stopped smiling. I always volunteered to dig first, to take the first guard shift, to do the shitty details that nobody else liked. Praise be to God, my cadre was watching me the entire time. If that cadre hadn't have given me a go, I more than likely wouldn't be writing this book. While I was standing outside the cadre's office waiting on a verdict, I could not fathom repeating SUT. I remember, while waiting for the cadre's instruction, asking the God I ignored to give me the strength to endure SUT again. God answered my prayer request in a way that I could never have hoped for. I am ashamed to say it wasn't until years later that I even gave God the credit for how everything transpired.

I remember getting home and telling my wife everything that had happened. It was all such a whirlwind of emotion, but I will never forget how I felt that day. Looking back on it, I know that God had waited until I had nothing left to offer before swooping down and finishing the race for me.

To top it all off, my knee recovered enough for me to train in only three weeks, twice as fast as the doctor had anticipated. I would be able to go out to SERE, Survival Evasion Resistance and Escape, with my same SUT class, if I could get medically cleared to go. Knee sprains don't generally just go away. After two separate days of imaging, X-rays and an MRI, and getting two different opinions on my knee: I was cleared to train. God was so good to me, and I never once even thought about him after my pity prayer. It is only because of God's love that I was granted new hope and new mercy. You can do anything you want and be anyone you want to be, with God. It may hurt, bad things may happen along the way, and you may get set back over and over; but if God loved me that much as I ignored Him, how much more so will He love us for submitting to His will and authority? To God be the glory for all of my success.

> "Heal me, O Lord, and I will be healed; Save me and I will be saved, for You are my praise." (Jeremiah 17:14)
>
> "After you have suffered for a little while, the God of all grace, who called you to His eternal glory in Christ, will Himself perfect, confirm, strengthen and establish you." (1 Peter 5:10)

SERE School with Retrospective

The next phase of training was SERE school: survival, evasion, resistance, and escape. I wish I could write down and tell you all about SERE and what it entails. It is easily the most important training I have ever received. The course's main purpose is to enable soldiers who could end up detained or beyond enemy borders to be able to survive and get back to safety. Unfortunately for you, I am not able to talk about the training that goes on there past some obvious observations. I will give the stories some context, but if you find yourself wondering what goes on in SERE, there is only one way to know, and that is to go.

SERE is where I found my passion for wilderness survival and bush craft. I am very thankful for the knowledge that I gained there. We learned how to live in and off the land. Living off the land is just such a natural and humbling experience. Other than a scarce meal here and there, after the first week of training, we were not going to be given any food. If we wanted to eat, we had to catch the food. If we wanted shelter, we had to make it. If we wanted water, we had to find it.

I personally killed and prepared two snakes for my small group, throughout a two-week period; those two snakes were the only things we caught to eat during SERE. Each of those snakes was split between six people. The two snakes didn't do anything to curb our hunger. I learned during this time what it felt like to lose every ounce of fat. I lost weight so rapidly that I could smell the distinct odor of muscle degradation as my body began consuming itself. I will note that a cadre of ours brought a three-day-old road-killed rabbit one day for us to eat. That road-kill rabbit was a welcome gift. Never before in my life have I looked at road-kill and thought that adding it to my menu would be a delight, but it was. The sight of rotting meat, infested with maggots, normally would have made me sick to my stomach; but after having gone nearly two weeks without food, I was thankful for any kind of food. He could have brought us hamburgers, or even some clean water; but he brought us what we needed, not what we wanted.

I have struggled with fasting for God, because I have known hunger, and I don't ever want to experience it again. I have learned to appreciate every single bite of food and drink of water since SERE school. To this day, I am grateful for the food I have. I know the migraines that come with malnutrition. I know the physical pain and cramping that muscles endure, as they begin to process themselves and break down after all fat reserves have been depleted. I now look at homeless people with hungry signs in a completely different light. I have felt more compassion toward them and their situation ever since SERE. It's amazing to me, even now, how something as simple as being hungry can have such a lasting impact on us.

Eventually in SERE the students are detained. During the time we spent in simulated captivity, everyone faced a variety of threats and fears. The surprising element was how each person dealt with these tests and trials. All forms of comfort can be stripped from us, and to many that may be a form of suffering. It is a totally different situation, when the things you are lacking are the very things needed for survival.

Mighty men can cower from small things, given the right circumstances. Seemingly weaker men can also stand up and refuse to cower, no matter how overwhelming the threat. I speculate that perhaps the mightier men are less accustomed to facing things that can crush them, and weaker men may have had to face things that can and have crushed them throughout their lives. When I think about the threats and fears we faced down throughout SERE school, I think about the story of David and Goliath. We were being taught how to face a Giant armed with a sword, using only a slingshot and a pebble.

When I think about the seemingly weaker men, who never give up and never back down, I think about Christians. When you have been walking with Jesus for any length of time, you have faced down things that could or should have crushed you. Instead of being crushed, you have a testimony to share with the world about how God saw you through each trial or difficult time. The longer you live a victorious life with Jesus, the more peace you have in the midst of the storms.

> And David said, "The Lord who delivered me from the paw of the lion and from the paw of the bear, He will deliver me from the hand of this Philistine." And Saul said to David, "Go, and may the Lord be with you." Then Saul clothed David with his garments and put a bronze helmet on his head, and he clothed him with armor.
> —1 Samuel 17:37–38

In SERE we were also being trained to never give up hope. We learned how to search for and maximize on every opportunity that presented itself. Praying that there was someone, somewhere, losing sleep in their efforts to find us: if we were in the hands of our enemies. We would celebrate any and every small victories that we could get.

We should all keep that same mentality, especially if we are Christians. When we live for Jesus, we know we will come under attack from the enemy. We may lose things, or we may face threats that make us want to cower. We need to learn to never give up hope. Thankfully, as long as we have Jesus, we will always have hope. We should find strength and encouragement from our fellow believers. We should search for and maximize on every opportunity that God gives us, no matter the circumstances that we are facing. Even small victories are victories, and those victories can increase the collective morale when we fight the good fight with each other.

> So he answered, "Do not fear, for those who are with us are more than those who are with them."
> (2 Kings 6:16)

Communications Training

After SERE school I was admittedly a different person than I was before graduating from SERE. I was more mature in a way. I felt like the possibility of me making it through the Q-Course was actually starting to look good. After SUT and SERE, the next phase of training was for occupational specialty training. For me this meant it was time to learn about radios. I was trying to become a communications sergeant, and on an ODA, the duties delegated to the commo guys are overwhelming.

In all, we spent about three months in this part of the course. Other than the final two-week field problem, this was physically the easiest phase of training yet. We were going home every day after training, eating regular food (not MREs), and getting plenty of sleep, so I couldn't complain. The course material itself was very challenging for me because I have never been a technological kind of guy. I was learning how to do things that my team would rely on me to know in the future. This was always on the forefront of our minds as we studied for hours every night, in preparations for the daily quizzes we had. We learned the basic ins and outs of computer hardware and software. We studied radio wave propagation theory. We learned how to use over ten different Army radios with all of their components that go along with them for secure use.

The final two-week field problem required us to move tactically into an unknown environment. We would be dropped off at a designated point, then we would ruck march twelve miles to our objective. Each student was required to send a certain number of radio calls using different devices at various times throughout the day. That meant we would have to set up a patrol base and would live for two weeks out of our foxholes. We only moved when the mission required. We had limited battery supplies; so we needed to charge our batteries manually, using a device that is similar to the pedals on a bicycle. Manually charging one of these batteries can take up to three hours, if we could continuously charge the battery and the weather cooperated. It's exhausting. Which is the norm with all patrol base activities.

Sleeping and eating was on the bottom of the priority list again. The cadre would visit us daily to check on our medical statuses and to give us the mission for the day, which mostly consisted of small reconnaissance missions. Occasionally we would attack enemy vehicles and personnel in ambush postures. We were being tested on how we could manage ourselves on multiple levels, big-boy rules applied. Not only did we have our radio call requirements, but we also had to live as though we were in a denied territory. We were pulling continuous guard and never allowing ourselves to be lulled into a false sense of security.

After about three days, we had worked through most of the kinks in how we were running operations and had transitioned to a rather smooth flow of operations. It was around this same time when the medical concerns began to spike. I will point out that this was early summertime in the North Carolina backwoods. The temperature with humidity was over one hundred degrees, every single day we were out there. Our mission success depended on limited supplies. So the first thing that went into our rucksacks was the mission essential gear. After that we could try to fit our food, clothes, or extra boots. Our rucksacks were at least a hundred pounds with all the equipment, ammo, batteries, and food. We didn't have the space or physical capacity to carry clean clothes out or to bring out vast amounts of soap to bathe.

Due to our lack of hygiene supplies, we were unable to clean ourselves or conduct proper hygiene. The guys began to get prickly heat: where the skin feels as if it's being continuously injected with needles, similar to a tattoo gun (not as harsh). Our inability to bathe really began to become an issue when we started getting the reports of guys with serious poison ivy and poison oak rashes. I had never seen a person covered from head to toe with poison ivy sores until then. One poor guy's butt crack had blisters and rashes from crawling and laying in poison ivy. At first, only three or four guys (out of approximately thirty) had poison ivy or oak. By the beginning of the second week, there were only a handful people remaining who didn't have poison ivy rashes—myself being one of them. Most of my team was incapacitated in their medical conditions. As soon as I was moved into a leadership position, I radioed the cadre and had him come out to our site. When he arrived, I gave him a legitimate, mission-capabilities brief. I told him that we were mission ineffective and requested that the guys with the most severe rashes be taken to a medical facility. The cadre told me that the course didn't have any wiggle room for success. We either had to figure out how to make the mission work, or we would all be recycled for failure to meet our objectives.

Sleeping on the ground in North Carolina, with less than desirable weather conditions, can take a toll on anyone. But the men on my team were training to be Green Berets, and we loved being out in the field honing our skills. So when I say that over two-thirds of these men were physically unable to conduct their mission, it should give you some idea of how terrible the conditions and rashes were. The guys looked as if they had contracted some lethal disease that was spreading throughout the team. The pain associated with having poison ivy in the genitalia, near the eyes, and in other sensitive areas was so extreme that a few of the guys had to stay naked, while we tried to disinfect their clothes with the few supplies we had in an attempt to make their lives more bearable.

The few of us fortunate enough to not have rashes had to conduct over six reconnaissance missions, while simultaneously providing first aid and comfort to our teammates. At that time, I hated life because of how tired I was. We were running twenty-four-hour operations with a skeleton crew, and we were getting burnt out. Looking back on it, I am appreciative of all the knowledge I received because of the position I was in. I was able to get vast amounts of instruction from the cadre and managed to learn things that I doubt I would have learned if the cadre had to teach thirty of us instead of four.

Once we were finally all done with the communications exercise, we were ecstatic. We had just endured yet another two-week period of prickly heat, crappy sleep, little food, and somehow we were all still smiling. I was only ever focused on getting to the next gate. I never looked past the next challenge, because I knew from experience that a simple injury could change everything.

Retrospective

"Give thanks to the Lord, for He is good, For His lovingkindness is everlasting. Give thanks to the God of gods, For His lovingkindness is everlasting."

—Psalm 136:1–2

The biggest lesson I learned during this training was to be grateful for the things I had going for me. At the time, I felt stressed out because of the responsibility required of me with such limited manpower. When the thoughts used to cross my mind of envy—that my battle buddies weren't being forced to go on recon mission after recon mission, crawling through the same poison ivy and oak that had so quickly affected our peers—I would think about how grateful I was to be able to sleep at night without having the poison ivy itching me like crazy. I would watch my friends take baby wipe after baby wipe and try to bathe as best as possible. I would also see them flinch while cleansing the open sores.

By the end of the final field exercise, I was so tired and yet so grateful that I came out relatively unscathed. Though I never gave the glory to whom it rightly belongs. Thank you, Father, for protecting me and giving me the endurance to push forward in my times of weakness. It is only by recognizing Your works in our lives that Your name can be properly glorified.

Robin Sage

The next phase of training was the final culminating exercise of the Special Forces Qualification Course called "Robin Sage." Again, for training and security purposes, I can't delve into too much detail here, but I can give an overview.

So Robin Sage is about a month-long exercise where the students join together after their respective occupational training and prepare for a "deployment" into a training environment in "enemy territory." We were divided into teams and began operational preparation once we had our planning bay set up. The whole idea was that we are going into a country where there weren't any conventional forces to support us; in other words, we were on our own. There are a lot of aspects to mission planning that I had never thought of prior to this course, and believe me when I tell you, a good officer can be a night-and-day difference-maker when planning a mission.

When the officer is on point, the planning goes smoothly and tasks are delegated and executed immediately. Officers should know exactly what needs to get done and be decisive in their decisions. Not only were we responsible for our personal security, but we had to figure out how to find food, water, ammo, and various other things that most people don't think about. This training is designed to simulate Special Forces missions—such as direct action, foreign internal defense, counterterrorism, special reconnaissance, and the fan favorite…unconventional warfare. The simulation takes each team through various areas, time periods, and mission priorities to ensure we all had a firm understanding of what our job is and how to get it done.

It was that simple, except, just like any other military training, things never go according to plan, and being an operator is all about adjusting on the fly. I consider myself to be extremely lucky because of the team I was put on. We all became fast friends and easily relied on each other to accomplish our respective tasks. We had the communication guys (like me), the weapons sergeants, the engineers, and the medics—all conducting individual tasks that collectively allow an ODA to function properly.

The officer is the leader, the face of the team, and ultimately is responsible for mission success and the welfare of the men under his command. Generally, the team won't operate effectively if the leader hasn't earned the respect of his NCOs; this is a critical lesson for any new officer to remember. The NCOs are there to ensure the tasks delegated by the commander or team leader are completed to standard with no additional supervision. The team sergeant is the senior enlisted NCO on the team and is akin to a 1SG role for a military company. His job is to ensure the team members are individually cared for, accounted for, disciplined, fed, paid, and so on. My opinion is that the single most important job on an ODA is the team sergeant role. I have seen amazing teams function with shitty officers and great NCOs; but even with a great officer, if a shitty NCO is running the team, nothing operates well.

So you can imagine how I felt after spending almost two weeks preparing for our training deployment as a communications sergeant and then being told two hours prior to infiltration that I would be the team sergeant until told otherwise. I was confident in my abilities to be the commo guy; that was a role I had been prepared for. But being a team sergeant, that was a whole different ball game. Quite frankly, that was not a role that I felt I could be overly successful in. I can look back on it now and see that the cadre did the role swap precisely because they knew how I would feel and wanted to see if I could make it happen.

While the responsibility can be daunting, I can't say enough how glad I am that I had the team I did. My predecessor (a sergeant first class) had helped the captain put our infill plan together and it was a solid plan. I knew what my role was and how to do everything I needed to do, but there is just a surreal feeling when put in a situation that could make or break your career. I almost felt like I was in cruise control. With the training we endured, and the extensive planning and rehearsals we had conducted: we knew what we had to do. This was a critical lesson that I often reflected on throughout the rest of my career, being thrust into a leadership role as a relatively junior NCO. I had spent the time required to study our plans, and we had rehearsed, over and over and over again, working through the kinks. Now it was just my body going through the motions while my brain worked the team sergeant duties.

Without going into much more detail, I will say that we utilized four means of transportation to infill into our country, one of those ways was walking. Our rucksacks were all over 130 pounds, the weather was hot, the air was humid, and we were exhausted. Because of the method of infill, there was a point where we had to break down our rifles and hide them in our bags to pass certain security checkpoints—which was all well and good, unless someone lost a piece to their weapon.

As the team sergeant, I was responsible for telling my commander the status of the men, their equipment, their ammo, and their water. As our team departed the previous method of transportation, we moved tactically into the wood line far enough for us to take a knee so I could put hands on my team's sensitive items. I learned the hard way not to take people at their word while in a leadership position. When lives depended on it, it was important to know we hadn't lost any equipment. This is pretty standard procedure for any military unit. When under duress, extreme physical weight, and a time hack that never seemed to work in our favor, it is hard to explain how hard of a task this is to do. It was pitch-black, with very little illumination from the moon, so all we had were our night vision goggles to guide us. No flashlights could be used because we were in denied territory. Our mission, as well as the mission of our adjacent teams, would be compromised if we were discovered. I got accountability of everyone's gear, and we headed out toward a point already plotted on our maps, moving silently and slowly through the forest.

We were waiting to assemble our rifles until we reached a certain location because of information we had gathered prior to our mission infill. We were approximately a kilometer away from that location, when I saw one of my teammates throw his hand up in the HALT hand signal. And then I saw him use the respective hand signal to say he needed to speak with me and the captain. The captain worked his way to the middle of the formation where the signal was given, and I worked my way up from the rear of the formation. All three of us knelt down, and my buddy told me that he was almost positive he heard something metallic fall out of his ruck onto the ground but that he couldn't find whatever it was. Let me tell you, even turning around was a chore when you have a 130 pounds on your back. So for me to ask my guys to ground their rucks so we could do an equipment check pained me, but that was what I had to do.

We grounded our rucks; I put guys into a security posture; and I joined the captain in his search for anything on the forest floor, using only night vision goggles. The teammate of mine who had heard the sound was checking his rifle for parts. He came to the horrible realization that his firing pin had come out. I'd be lying if I didn't say my first thought was that I was going to get recycled because I failed to get the team successfully through the infiltration. I immediately informed the captain, and we began scouring the forest floor with our hands, hoping to stumble across the pin. The sinking feeling I had was so overwhelming, because I had seen situations like this before. These situations never end well for the guys in charge.

As these thoughts of negativity flushed through my mind, the same guy who had lost the firing pin walked up to me and put the firing pin in my hand. He found it. I was ecstatic. Since the cadre following us was starting to get pissed that we weren't moving, it felt great to tell him we were just doing an equipment check and instead of having to report that we lost a firing pin. I felt so grateful in that moment that my luck—God's hand—had come through once again. I look back on this moment with significance because it was yet another "small" thing could have kept me from my graduation ceremony.

There was another instance where almost everyone on the entire team had finished the last of their water; there was only one canteen left between a dozen of us. Something training related happened that was going to end up splitting our team. As the team sergeant, I told the guy with the full canteen of water to give it to the guys that were going out on the mission. We were staying behind, so we could deal with the water problem while they were gone on their mission. While I just assumed that this guy was going to give up the water, because that's what I would have done; I was completely wrong. He not only wouldn't share the water freely; he nearly got physical with me when I took it from him by force and gave it to the guys leaving. I was completely shocked at that guy's attitude. When the rest of the guys went on their way, one of the other senior NCOs and I pulled him into our security position to talk to him about his actions. He simply didn't care that his peers had consumed all their water or that a mission just popped up out of the blue. He wasn't willing to sacrifice for the team.

The rest of the Robin Sage exercise was among the best of experiences I have ever had. I met some amazing people, some of whom would end up walking the same hallways I did later on in my Special Forces career. I worked my ass off to accomplish the mission. I will never forget the feeling I had when that exercise was officially ended and we all began cheering. We were finally done. The only thing left was graduation, and then we would be off to fight the good fight. We spent the last two days of Robin Sage at Camp Mackall, cleaning weapons, equipment, facilities, and so on. Then we headed back to Fort Bragg on the typical Blue Bird buses. The ride back was surprisingly quiet. I know I was just tired. It felt good to be done, but it was still surreal that I had completed the course.

Retrospective

"Whoever exalts himself shall be humbled; and whoever humbles himself shall be exalted."
— Matthew 23:12

Robin Sage was the culmination of over a year's worth of training, where we would be tested on how much information we retained and if we could properly apply it. I view Robin Sage as an example of what our lives are all like. We may spend our entire lives learning, training, and preparing for whatever we are trying or hoping to accomplish. We as Christians can go to church, read the Bible, and pray often, to build a relationship with God and learn how to walk with Jesus. We can't forget that there is a purpose behind our preparations. At some point, we should be able to apply what we have learned. Being tested helps us to identify what we have retained and what we still need to work on. Sometimes what is asked of us is not what we were expecting or hoping for; much like when I was thrust into the team sergeant role, and I was only preparing to act as the communications sergeant. As Christians, when we are being tested, we will have witnesses. Depending on how we handle ourselves in each situation, we may draw our witnesses closer to Jesus or we may repel our witnesses away from Christ.

Throughout the entire course, I always felt like the other shoe would drop at some point and the prospect of my graduating would be crushed. But it didn't. I wasn't overly confident that I could do everything on my own, but I wasn't on my own. I was walking through those woods with men who had already bore the responsibility I was now carrying. I was surrounded by men who had the knowledge and wisdom that I could learn from. Sometimes being a leader means owning up to the fact that you can't achieve a solution alone. Asking for help and admitting my faults gave the senior guys on my team the ability to give me their guidance. I told them where I was lacking, and instead of sleeping, they would teach me out of old Army manuals while the others were sleeping. Asking our Lord for help and humbling ourselves before Him makes room for Him to lift us up and strengthens us to overcome every struggle. In every situation Jesus is also walking with us and has the knowledge and wisdom that we need. We just need to learn how to seek His guidance in every situation.

> "Listen to counsel and accept discipline, That you may be wise the rest of your days. Many plans are in a man's heart, But the counsel of the Lord will stand." (Proverbs 19:20-21)

The day one of our teammates was putting himself before the welfare of the team was a really bittersweet day for me. On one hand I felt so honored to be working with the guys I was with, but on the other hand, I was wondering how someone like this had managed to make it all the way through the course. All the people I saw with attitudes like that had been peered out or had quit already. We had multiple conflicts with that same guy over this entire training period. He made my life much more difficult than it needed to be during that time, but I learned a lot because of him.

That man is a good reminder to me that there will always be people who are more concerned with their own interests than in the interests of the collective group. I also learned that you can't assume anything about someone's character, based solely on their position, title, accomplishments, and so on. We have to evaluate each individual based on their individual actions and decisions. Jesus even warned us that there will be wolves in sheep's clothing, among those who claim to believe in God. So even at the completion of the Q-Course, I shouldn't have assumed that there weren't any selfish men remaining among our ranks. We are fully capable, though, of not allowing those individuals to bring down the group. Stand in righteousness, because if you don't stand up for what is right in God's eyes, then you may lose the right to stand.

> Do not withhold good from those to whom it is due, when it is in your power to do it. Do not say to your neighbor, "Go, and come back, and tomorrow I will give it," when you have it with you. (Proverbs 3:27–35)
>
> "If your brother sins, go and show him his fault in private; if he listens to you, you have won your brother. But if he does not listen to you, take one or two more with you, so that by the mouth of two or three witnesses every fact may be confirmed." (Matthew 18:15–16)
>
> "Beware of the false prophets, who come to you in sheep's clothing, but inwardly are ravenous wolves. You will know them by their fruits. Grapes are not gathered from thorn bushes nor figs from thistles, are they? So every good tree bears good fruit, but the bad tree bears bad fruit. A good tree cannot produce bad fruit, nor can a bad tree produce good fruit. Every tree that does not bear good fruit is cut down and thrown into the fire. So then, you will know them by their fruits." (Matthew 7:15-20)

Graduation and Language Training

I remember getting off the buses at Bragg, excited to get in our privately owned vehicles (POV) and going home to shower and to see our wives and kids. We were smiling wearily when the cadre told us to form up so he could put out further guidance. We formed up. The cadre congratulated us for completing the final phase of training and began putting out our next formation time, which was fortunately over four days away. This meant some serious family and food time while I let this accomplishment sink in. The cadre was just about to release us before he realized he forgot to put out one more piece of information. He began calling a roster of seemingly random names. He called approximately thirty people or so. Without any known link between the names being called, we all started to become more and more curious.

As the cadre neared the end of the list, I heard my name, "Calhoun, Kirby." After a few more names, the cadre then looked up from his list and thanked us for being a part of the new pilot language program that would extend our tours at Fort Bragg for another nine months. My hand immediately shot into the air. "Sergeant," I said, "did I understand you correctly in that every name you just called is going to be stuck here for nine additional months, for more language training? And did I hear my name?"

The cadre hadn't stuttered though, I knew I heard my name. I felt the balloon I had rode in on deflate immediately, as I thought about enduring nine more months learning a language I didn't see myself actually using. I got home and waited until after the celebration had subsided, before telling my wife the news. I was devastated because I wanted to go to war again; it was time. I didn't join the Army to speak Pashtu in a classroom. I already proved I could pass a basic language test. What more could they want from me? I was the worst Pashtu student in my previous Pashtu class. So I couldn't see why they would want me in there, but alas, that was where I went.

I did get to enjoy the graduation before embarking on the next phase of training.

September 29, 2011, was the day I stood in formation and donned my Green Beret: becoming a new member of the Special Forces community. It is a humbling experience to stand in a formation where great men have stood before. The feeling of humility and reverence was palpable in the building where we were conducting the graduation ceremony. We marched out of a hallway into the auditorium, moving in sync with a bagpipe player who led our formation through smoke from a machine. Many of our families and friends were there, in the stands, to see us graduate. As we finished our movement to our seats, we all stood and said out loud the Special Forces Creed:

> I am an American Special Forces Soldier!
> I will do all that my nation requires of me.
> I am a volunteer, knowing well the hazards of my profession.
> I serve with the memory of those who have gone before me.
> I pledge to uphold the honor and integrity of their legacy
> in all that I am—in all that I do.
> I am a warrior.
> I will teach and fight whenever and wherever my nation
> requires.
> I will strive always to excel in every art and artifice of war.
> I know that I will be called upon to perform tasks and isolation, far from familiar faces and voices.
> With the help and guidance of my faith, I will conquer my
> fears and succeed.
> I will keep my mind and body clean, alert and strong.
> I will maintain my arms and equipment in an immaculate state

befitting a Special Forces Soldier,
for this is my debt to those who depend on me.
I will not fail those with whom I serve.
I will not bring shame upon myself or Special Forces.
I will never leave a fallen comrade.
I will never surrender though I am the last.
If I am taken, I pray that I have the strength to defy my enemy.
I am a member of my Nation's chosen soldiery,
I serve quietly, not seeking recognition or accolades.
My goal is to succeed in my mission—
and live to succeed again.
—De Oppresso Liber

As you can see, the creed is very heartfelt. I got goose bumps reciting the creed on my graduation day, something that rarely happens. Something about the gravity of the accomplishment really struck home for me. Throughout the Q-Course, the main focus was just to pass the current phase of training, and not to worry about the next phase until the current phase was completed. Now I stood in a formation with some of America's most intellectual and formidable soldiers. We were now qualified to join an ODA and to deploy into the far-reaching corners of the world. I had seen a lot of people come and go throughout the Q-Course. A majority of the men I began the course with didn't make it all the way through, which is the norm for most classes. There were Silver Star recipients in my graduating class, which should help you to understand the types of men in this formation. Even the ones that didn't have any real combat experience had been so rigorously tested that even without a deployment they were able to meet any and all requirements asked of them. This moment was hands-down the brightest moment of my military career. I was high on life. My dad, whom I hadn't seen since before I left Germany as a child, even came to the graduation.

While I would love to say at that time I gave all the glory to God, in reality, I didn't. I had endured so much pain and never really saw that maybe God wanted me to graduate that course more than I wanted to graduate it. As I have said, I always claimed Catholicism, but I never practiced Christianity, and never once truly understood that I wasn't the one who graduated this course; Jesus did. He merely used me to do so. For my lack of faith earlier, I want to take a moment here and take the time to give credit where credit is due.

> Heavenly father, Lord of all, my King, and Savior, Jesus Christ thank you for pouring out Your Grace on me. You were crucified, died, and rose on the third day to pay for my sins, so that I may know YOU in heaven. Even 2000 years later, You took time to nurture me and give my body the strength it needed to pass a course that I wouldn't have passed on my own. I give You all the glory Lord, and am graciously humbled that You would look upon Your servant with the love and forgiveness that I do not deserve. I humbly ask that You would open my eyes so that I may use the tools You have given me to do YOUR work. In Jesus's holy name. Amen.

The bitterness quickly came back to me after graduation, when I said goodbye to a lot of my friends as they all left for their respective duty stations to fight the good fight.

I, like a select few of my peers, had been chosen for the additional language course after graduation, and the time had come to start it. Just like a majority of my previous six-month training period learning how to speak Pashtu, I felt grossly overwhelmed and always felt like I would never get a full grasp of how to speak the language. I spent nine months, eight hours a day, five days a week, doing nothing but consuming Middle East news written in Pashtu, and conducting telephone interviews. We would rehearse certain scenarios applicable to a deployed environment, such as: searching a detainee or vehicle, exclusively in Pashtu, using terminology we had spent weeks learning. I learned to have a great respect for people with great minds that easily handle foreign languages, because I am not one of them. I did however learn a lot more than I did in the original course, because of the baseline I had developed during that training phase. The entire time I was in this course, all I could think about was getting to my duty station. I was ready to get out of the training environment and get my hands dirty again.

All I wanted was to deploy. I never once considered that maybe God's plan wasn't the same plan as mine. I would learn down the road that the Pashtu language I had learned might very well have saved my life on multiple occasions, once I got to Afghanistan.

Retrospective

"But the Scripture has shut up everyone under sin, so that the promise by faith in Jesus Christ might be given to those who believe."

—Galatians 3:22

When I graduated from the Special Forces Qualification Course, I was elated. This journey and achievement seemed like an impossible feat, every step of the way. I felt so proud and honored to have finally achieved something so few have.

At the beginning of the ceremony, as a class we said the Special Forces Creed, which you saw in the previous chapter. As I sat down and started to think about writing this book, I happened to stumble upon the program from my graduation that contained the creed. As I read it, I noticed a small phrase that I had not paid any attention to before. "With the help and guidance of my faith, I will conquer my fears and succeed." I never noticed the word *faith* in there, even after I read it dozens of times.

We all have a measure of faith, according to scripture; the question is where we are placing our faith. The creed didn't specify what "my faith" was in, and at that time I don't know if I could have pinpointed where I had placed my faith; but when I was in difficult situations, my desperate pleas/prayers were only aimed in one direction. My focus, throughout this course, was on not letting my peers down. During certain phases of training, when someone would quit, it was just one less person who could help carry the machine gun or who could take a guard shift. During patrol base activities, less people meant it took longer to finish the work and less rest time in-between tasks. I could have more easily walked away, if I were the only one I would be letting down. Even if the other men wouldn't have noticed my absence, it still would have felt like I was letting them down. I also didn't want to give up the opportunity to work with and be surrounded by men who make the difference. These men are incredible national assets, and inspired me to give my best for the opportunity to stay in their ranks.

I don't know how every man, who donned the Green Beret, got through this course. I can only speak for myself. I can only say that it was an uphill struggle the entire way. I can only say that I was ill equipped to handle that hill. For a long time, I wondered how I did it. I think many of us have a story about something we did that we didn't think we could do. Eventually, after many years, I understood. I now know, beyond a shadow of a doubt, that without the intervention of Jesus on my behalf, I would not have graduated. No matter what, even when the chips are stacked against you, never lose faith. *Faith* by definition means to trust completely, regardless of circumstance.

"I can do all things through Him who strengthens me." (Philippians 4:13)

"For by grace you have been saved through faith; and that not of yourselves, it is the gift of God; not as a result of works, so that no one may boast. For we are His workmanship, created in Christ Jesus for good works, which God prepared beforehand so that we would walk in them." (Ephesians 2:8-10)

"For through the grace given to me I say to everyone among you not to think more highly of himself than he ought to think; but to think so as to have sound judgment, as God has allotted to each a measure of faith." (Romans 12:3)

"For You formed my inward parts; You wove me in my mother's womb. I will give thanks to You, for I am fearfully and wonderfully made; Wonderful are Your works, And my soul knows it very well. My frame was not hidden from You, When I was made in secret, And skillfully wrought in the depths of the earth; Your eyes have seen my unformed substance; And in Your book were all written The days that were ordained for me, When as yet there was not one of them." (Psalm 139: 13-16)

First Impressions

Seventh Special Forces Group is located on Eglin AFB, and that's where I was headed next to start my career as a United States Army Special Forces Communications Sergeant. I had never lived in Florida, but when we crossed into the Sunshine State, I couldn't have been happier. I just finished one of the hardest courses the United States Army has to offer and an advanced language course. I felt ready to report to my unit and start my new job, but I still had to get my family moved into our first house. I had moved plenty of times by now and knew the drill: always take the full amount of leave when allowed, because you never knew when you would get leave again… So that's what I did. Here's how that choice affected my life.

A few of the guys from my language class had also been assigned to Seventh Group, and one of my good friends was even attached to the same company. Unlike me, he wasn't married with kids at the time. So he did what I chose not to do and reported in early to the company, taking the last slot on an ODA for communication sergeants. The only slot left belonged to the operational detachment bravo (ODB), which to a new recruit just isn't as exciting. The ODB serves two main functions within a company and is generally filled with senior NCOs because of the managerial type work that is required. The first function is to act as a support mechanism for the teams, or in other words, to serve as a company level staff for the teams. The second is to ensure dissemination of information from the commander to the teams using the B team channels. The B team is considered (generally) to be higher in the command chain than the teams because of its close proximity to the command team, but the main priority is ensuring the teams can operate, in a nutshell.

What I didn't know when I found all this out was that the operations sergeant (senior NCO on a B team) had a reputation for crushing new Green Berets. Jon had a reputation of being an asshole, plain and simple. It is hard to put into words the austere conditions I was forced to work under when working for Jon. I was admittedly in a sour mood already, having watched a good friend of mine take a slot that his team sergeant, MSG McKenna, told me was originally mine, but since my buddy was there first, he got scooped up. That's how things worked now; the days of regular Army were officially over. The first lesson I learned was that by not taking the initiative, and choosing my family over my work, it had cost me time on an ODA. This wasn't a new concept to me, as my wife will gladly attest to, but I came to resent the choice I made because of the work environment I ended up in. I often fought back envy when I saw my friend having a good time on an ODA; while I was stuck at work until 9:00 p.m. every night, because Jon was a perfectionist with a B team full of new guys who hadn't learned to perfect anything yet.

The tasks we were given, and the things we were asked to do, were things that we hadn't yet learned. Our occupational training only covered so much, and there was so much more to learn. Everything Jon asked of us, we should absolutely be expected to learn and know how to do. The problem was that he wouldn't teach us or train us on how things needed to be done on a B team. The team was full of brand new operators, and we didn't have seniors to learn from. Normally there are senior and junior team members on a team, especially on a B team. Jon wouldn't tell us what his expectations were in a reasonable manner. He would just walk into the office at 1600, for example, give us a monumental task to complete, which we had never done before, without any guidance, and tell us he wanted it done when he got back to the office at 0530 the next morning. To give his leadership style an analogy, it would be like teaching children how to swim by taking them a few miles off shore, in the ocean, by boat, and then throwing them overboard and telling them to meet you back at the beach: without first teaching them the techniques necessary to swim, without testing them in a pool with still water, and without any explanation of rip currents or hazardous marine life. What could go wrong?

We all thought we were being taken advantage of, and to be honest, it pissed all of us off. But this was the Army, and nobody gave a crap about our feelings. I can recall multiple times having to work through the night to get tasks done on an unrealistic timeline. I had never done inventories on such a large scale before, especially without any guidance from someone more knowledgeable than myself. I would call my wife and tell her I wasn't coming home. This meant she would have to change plans last minute, again, to coordinate day care and make sure the dogs were taken care of. I know it sounds menial, but after years, it is very stressful on a spouse to not be able to rely on their husband. Now there are times when we needed to be away from home and times when we needed to stay at work to finish something time-sensitive. The times when operators aren't gearing up for, or gone on, a deployment or some kind of training is few and far between. Those glimpses of what would be a small reprieve… that's what we didn't experience on Jon's team. There wouldn't be any reprieve. My wife handled the bills, the kids, the extracurricular activities; she was going to a university full-time, working full-time, and wasn't even able to rely on me to come home to let the dogs out. I just happened to have a leader who cared more about results than his troops.

In just a few months I spent multiple nights at work. I was going to ranges, taking care of a company-sized element's worth of communication coordination, inspections of over $500,000 worth of equipment that I was personally signed for, and learning how to operate clerically on a B team. I hit a low point in my life the first few months I got to Seventh Group. I hated every aspect of my job and felt my leadership was letting me down by allowing this guy to run us into the ground. I became depressed, angry, and emotionally distant from anyone except my peers who were dealing with the same stress. I never let my emotions affect my work ethic, but I struggled every single day with rage.

After a month or two of my arrival, another new communications sergeant showed up and got sucked into the whirlwind of anger emanating from our team room as well. I had the honor of working with my now great friend Erik for some time. We got into a rhythm of helping each other out whenever we could. We endured the long hours, working through lunch with no food, the overnight workdays, and the bipolar-type attitude that our team sergeant displayed toward us, together. You can only imagine how we felt when we found out we were going to JRTC in Fort Polk, Louisiana, together as a B team, in preparation for a deployment to Central/South America.

As a communications sergeant, my primary job on a B team level was twofold. First, it was to ensure the communications equipment for the company commander, company sergeant major, the executive officer, and the senior warrant officer, along with a few others, were working and operational. The second was to make sure that the B team itself was operational—meaning that we needed to establish an operations center, and that the tactical communications within the B team itself were all working. The tactical communications was easy because we had spent months learning the equipment in the Q-Course, and it was easy to train on radios and other devices while back in the team room; which I did frequently. Setting up an operations center, though, that required setting up special devices that are highly technical and enable an ODA or ODB to get unclassified and classified computer access.

To set up a device with a satellite dish like that requires knowledge of computer hardware, software, and all aspects of security: similar to knowledge associated with the CompTIA Security+, Network+ Certifications, with the use of some military-grade security devices. I didn't have the slightest clue how to set one of these dishes up, because I didn't receive any training on how to set one up. After we arrived at Fort Polk, Louisiana, I learned that Erik wasn't going to be joining us at the location I expected. This change in plans meant I was going to have to figure out how to set one of these things up on my own.

Fortunately for me, I had the number to the customer service line and assumed I had time to set up the equipment within a few days' time period. The scenario for our training hadn't started yet. That was where my assumption was very wrong. My team sergeant came over to me and said, "Calhoun, you don't go to sleep until this device is up and running," then walked away. It was going to be a long night. As I pulled out the instruction manual and began to read,

I started slowly assembling the hardware. The hardware came in over thirty large black cases/boxes. I had no idea what I was doing. I was new, so I didn't know any of the other guys that could possibly know how to work this device. I was hungry and tired. It wasn't until I started putting the hardware together that I realized a critical element to the device hadn't been packed: the power supply. Erik had attended the training for this device and assured me he had double-checked all the boxes to make sure all the equipment was there. So now I had another problem on my hands. Fortunately, I found some very nice commo guys from another team who let me borrow the piece I was missing (until our power supply got there). Then I continued learning how to get the machine up and running. My team sergeant let me sit there and work for three and a half days without sleeping one wink and did not let me leave to get food. I was stuck eating spoonfuls of that Goober peanut butter–and–jelly combo that comes together in one jar (it was the only thing I purchased at a gas station while driving to Louisiana).

In those three days, I lost almost seven pounds. I was so tired that, apparently, at some point, I had a conversation with the company commander that made him assume I was under the influence of something because of how intoxicated I appeared to be. I had been sleep-deprived and not fed before, in training, but I didn't understand the reason for it in this setting. I expected some hazing; it's part of the tradition between senior and junior members on a team. No matter what type or amount of experience anyone has before joining the Special Forces community, it is nearly impossible for most new Green Berets to understand how the community works well enough to hit the ground running. I was the only commo guy on my team, but after the first day, one of the senior communications sergeants (also named Eric) from one of the ODAs collocated with us, came over to me, and asked me how things were going. I told him exactly how things were going, and he told me all about my team sergeant and all the things he was notorious for. Every chance this senior commo sergeant was able to sneak away, to give me hand, he would. I became greatly indebted to him and over time became great friends with him.

I had just finished my third all-nighter. I finally had all the computers up and running—Internet access to them all, the printer was working—and I even had fresh coffee brewed. My team sergeant walked in the room where I had set up, looked at all the computers, asked me if everything was functioning, and said, "Took you long enough."

He then started tasking me for that day, before the company commander walked up to me and asked me when I had last slept. I told him I hadn't since we had arrived but would love to anytime now. He told my team sergeant then and there not to mess with me for at least eight hours, so I could get some rack time.

Things leveled out for a few days after that, but then he began to start treating everyone around him like shit again. One day he yelled across the room to me, while sitting at his desk in the operations center, "Hey! Calhoun, my fucking computer isn't working again. Why can't you do your fucking job?"

I didn't even turn around, but out of frustration, I did something that has always gotten me in trouble, and I asked him very sarcastically, "Is it fucking plugged in?"

He looked down by his feet where the charging cord had, in fact, been disconnected from the charging block. His computer battery had died. As I glanced over my shoulder to see that it was working again, and I said to myself, "Fucking crayon eater."

I thought it had been under my breath, but over seven people heard it throughout the room and started laughing. I immediately regretted saying it. This guy already made my life miserable, and I being the dummy that I am just had to go poke the bear by slinging an insult at him. To this day he denies ever hearing me say it, and I'm sure he would tell you he would have kicked my ass if he had; but now that bygones are bygones, this was my first real jab back at him, and at the time it felt great.

The feeling didn't last long, however. The next day, I don't remember the exact reason he got upset with me, but he did, and he was really angry this time. He told me to go to the room (conveniently far out of earshot of my peers) where I had my rucksack and sleeping bag, and he followed me in the room and shut the door behind him.

He looked me square in my eyes and said to me, "You have no idea who I am and what I've done. I'm not the guy you want to piss off."

Not breaking eye contact, I started taking off my ACU top and said to him, "If this is how you have to handle your business, then I am right here. I am not afraid, and while I don't choose violence, I am not afraid to become violent if provoked. I've had my ass kicked before, and that is the absolute worst-case scenario here for me."

He looked at me, turned around, and walked out of the room. Looking back on it, I think he expected me to cower, but when another man steps in your face and wishes to do you harm, any ideas of peace are no longer viable options.

He never wanted to fight, and I don't think he even meant to say the things he did in the way that he did. But that wouldn't stop me from standing my ground. I am glad I did, because after that he actually mellowed out quite a bit. He still worked me and my teammates into the ground; but we were becoming a highly functional unit, and were all successfully doing the jobs of senior-enlisted non-commissioned officers.

Before we left for JRTC, the first time I had the opportunity to speak with the battalion command sergeant major, he pulled me aside to ask me what my language was. I told him it was Pashtu, and he asked me if I wanted to go to Afghanistan with the rest of our battalion. In no uncertain terms, I expressed that I absolutely wanted to deploy and use my language training.

As we were nearing the end of our JRTC rotation, with about a week or so to go, we were starting to talk about going home. My team sergeant, Jon, pulled me aside and asked me if I still wanted to go to Afghanistan. I told him I did. Jon then told me that I would be deploying, two weeks before Christmas, and that meant I would be switching to a different company within the battalion. I was elated. I would finally be getting a shot to prove my worth as a Green Beret, in a combat zone. I watched most of the battalion deploy to Afghanistan, without me, just a few months prior, and I had just accepted my fate that I wouldn't need my Pashtu anytime soon. My team sergeant, who normally talked down to my teammates and me, showed real concern for the first time since I'd known him. As a junior Green Beret, there was still a lot that I hadn't learned yet, and he didn't want me deploying without the knowledge I needed.

I struggled with my personal feelings with Jon because he treated me worse than anyone I had ever seen in a work environment. He made the drill sergeants at Basic Training seem like friendly people. I hated feeling so angry and negative all the time. On the flip side, even though I think Jon struggled with his own anger issues, he wanted nothing but the best for me and my teammates. He worked us like dogs because he wanted to look good in front of the company leadership, and because he had a team of newbies who needed to learn faster than we had ever been forced to up to that point. Jon understood what Green Berets did in a combat zone, and he cared about our safety and well-being (even if he didn't show it well). He altered the training for the remainder of our time at JRTC just for my benefit, to help prepare me for the deployment. He began running us through first aid training scenarios; I was pretty much giving IVs to anyone who had the misfortune of walking in front of me, at one point. We did refresher training on other communication skills that I hadn't needed yet. We discussed tactics and techniques that I had already learned but hadn't rehearsed in a while.

We had trained for four of the remaining seven days left in our JRTC rotation, when I got a phone call from my wife. Her grandmother had passed away, and understandably so, she wasn't handling the information very well. With how most of the interactions went with Jon in the past, I was unsure as to what to expect from him when I told him I needed to go home to console my wife. I half expected him to tell me that he didn't care who died, I wasn't leaving, or just ignore me all together. Instead, he earned my respect that night. I watched him work tirelessly for hours (regardless of working twenty-hour days for the past four days), trying to find a faster way to get me home than a ten-hour drive. He stepped out of "work mode" and became human in my eyes for the first time, because he showed compassion. That was when I recognized Jon for the person he was—not just the senior NCO, who had to be a leader instead of a friend. I eventually got cleared to rent a car and drive home to be with my family. I had mixed emotions. I was happy JRTC was over, but sad that my wife was hurting, and guilty about feeling happy about leaving JRTC. I got home and spent some much-needed time with my family, as I prepared to deploy to Afghanistan less than three weeks later.

Retrospective

"But I say to you who hear, love your enemies, do good to those who hate you, bless those who curse you, pray for those who mistreat you."
—Luke 6:27–28

I wasn't shocked when I arrived to Seventh Group and got attached to a guy like Jon, considering the luck I'd had up to that point. Even in conventional units there are overbearing leaders, but I always had a feeling that I was meant to be there, to learn from this leader in particular. It doesn't make much sense to me either, but even though I hated being treated like crap, I knew he was very experienced and good at what he did. There are a lot of things I could say that would single him out to anyone who doesn't know me, or my story, but because he is still serving his country, I won't. Even though I think I pissed him off in every way possible, he still had an underlying tone of sincerely caring when it came to me and the other guys on my team. He didn't show it well, but that's not what the Army was paying him for.

After having spent some time on the B team and ODAs afterward, I know now how daunting the task was in front of him when he took on a B team full of rookie Green Berets. None of the guys on our team were new to the Army. We all had previous jobs before going SF. So he knew that we knew enough to follow the rules. We knew where to find Army regulations to plan training and to properly conduct operations. He turned a very young and eager group of men into efficient operators within a very limited amount of time. While we still disagree about his methods of instruction, I can't deny the efficiency or effectiveness of his ideas and planning abilities.

I truly believe there are people in this world that God puts in our lives for some unknown greater purpose. I was confident when I first met Jon that he was someone that could rise to great ranks if he so desired. He has already surpassed a majority of his peers and has plenty of time left in his contract to go even higher in rank; if he decides to serve his country past his twenty-year commitment. Jon is one of those people that will grab your attention right away, whether for good or bad. He is always at the front, tackling everything head-on as if it were the most important mission he's ever had. It gives me great comfort knowing it is people like this that lead our nation's most elite soldiers. During this time in my story, though, Jon was nothing but a bad memory for me as I focused solely on the deployment to Afghanistan.

Afghanistan

Getting to Afghanistan was much different than my deployment to Iraq, where we had been herded like cattle from one place to the next to keep accountability of personnel and equipment. This time I was traveling in a group of seven men, including me. I was, by far, the lowest-ranking individual in the group (the only NCO) and the only one in the group without a Special Forces combat rotation. So I kept my mouth shut unless spoken to and listened intently to everything these guys were saying. I was going to soak up as much knowledge as possible, in my last-minute efforts to overcome the feeling of being underprepared. Even though I had been deployed before and had experience doing a lot of the things that would be required of me, there was still a sense of inadequacy back in the recesses of my mind. One of the greatest fears I have had throughout my entire military career was the thought of not being strong enough or smart enough and it costing my comrades their lives. Now, I was on my way to Afghanistan where I knew fighting had far from subsided.

The worst part about this trip was the lack of information I had regarding which team I would get assigned to. I knew I'd be spending some time with the B team in country, until they moved their temporary headquarters out of the Kandahar area and into the Panjaway District Center. The Panjaway District was one of the most IED prone areas in Afghanistan, at that time, with a fierce insurgent population. The Panjaway District is often considered the spiritual home of the insurgency in Afghanistan; there are certain areas within it that are certainly "off-limits" to law-abiding local citizens and American soldiers.

While still at the American compound just outside of Kandahar, I was introduced to the new command team, my senior communications sergeant, as well as a majority of the B team support guys as well. I never felt more at home than when I arrived. My senior, Josh, was one of the nicest guys I had met in the SF community, yet. He was an excellent communications sergeant. He became my first true mentor and remains to this day a good friend of mine. He showed me the ropes of the day-to-day activities. He told me what was required of me daily, weekly, before mounted and dismounted patrols, and many other things required to maintain the highest level of operational awareness.

They soon grew to appreciate my work ethic because I am a workhorse, and when treated with respect, I will work myself into the ground for my leadership. They couldn't truly understand my joy for working with them, but everyone there had heard of Jon and knew of the personality he had.

I didn't want the first few months of my SF career to change the way I viewed Special Forces, so I tried to mentally reset my brain for this new normal. I worked my ass off every single day. I wanted the people I worked for to know I was an asset and that I belonged there. I had never been the fastest, strongest, or smartest guy in any group for certain, but I can say that my work ethic was impeccable when it came to the military. I maintained that standard, or I would always know I wasn't living up to my full potential.

While I was on the B team I was staying on a compound that was about a fifteen-minute drive, through a secure area, away from the Kandahar Air Field (KAF) proper. Because of the work we did, we often drove through the local Afghanistan military checkpoints while traveling from our base to KAF. Many times, I would get out of our truck to talk with the Afghan military in Pashtu. They found it absolutely fascinating that an American took the time to learn their native language. I am sure I sounded like a third grader; but I was able to talk about current events, the status of their military equipment, military procedures, and ask about the welfare of their families. I found these dialogues very interesting and felt a sense of accomplishment for successfully learning enough Pashtu to converse with them. It was quite exhausting deciphering and translating everything in my head to be able to carry on a conversation, but I practiced every chance I got.

After being in Afghanistan for a week or so, it was time to leave the comfort of KAF: where air support and manpower was almost unlimited. We drove for over two hours to the Panjaway District Center on the other side of the Kandahar District. When we got to the remote outpost, I realized the state of security there was very different than it had been in Iraq. In Iraq, we broadcasted that we were Americans. We were there for the world to see. Here, I'd have driven right past the large complex if my buddy hadn't mentioned the entrance as we approached it. The complex was tucked away under the shadow of a mountain, with no American military in sight. As we slowed down and pulled onto the small road leading up to some large metal gates attached to a walled-off compound, the gates slowly swung open. We pulled in, and I saw Oakley sunglasses and American M-4 rifles greeting us.

There were three main sections of this compound. The first was the SF side where I would be staying with the B team. One or sometimes two ODAs collocated there. Another side held a conventional Army unit that was pretty much just extra guns if things got nasty. Lastly was the Afghan district center, which served as a town hall of sorts. This was the area designated by local authorities as being safe and secure enough to hold high-level meetings with local authority figures and Americans. We used this site for many different things in the short time I was there; the most exciting of them was creating a brand-new process for locals to volunteer to serve their country as military or police. This was for the locals who wanted to be trained to fight the terror in their own backyards. That enrollment period only lasted about a week, but I got to hear a lot of stories of what radical ideologies do to the average person in countries like Afghanistan.

I remember one young man in particular, because of the scarring he had on both his feet. From his feet to just below his kneecaps looked like the skin from Freddie Kruger, as though his legs had been scalded in a fire. He walked with a severe limp, which I knew would disqualify him from getting recruited. Then he told me his story, and I had to let him sign up to at least ask our physician if he could make it. He told me, right after the war kicked off in Afghanistan, the Taliban began running rampant through the area in Afghanistan where he lived at that the time (I apologize for not remembering the precise location or year). The Taliban was threatening everyone if they were caught helping the Americans who had just gotten firmly established at that time. The punishment for helping Americans would be the death of the individuals and their families. According to the young man, the Taliban showed up at their house one night because of rumors that his father had helped Americans somehow. This was denied, obviously; but in retaliation for even being accused, the Taliban poured boiling hot oil all over the lower half of the man's son, who was now applying for military service. My job was only to help get them enrolled. I wasn't calling any shots, but I would be lying if I said that story didn't affect me. Sadly, this young man wasn't the only one with a story like this or worse.

For days, all I could think about was my daughter. What if it were her? If the terrorists in Afghanistan had their way, that was just the tip of the iceberg for what they would do to American children if they had the chance. That was the consequence for an Afghan child, because of a mere accusation of his father. There wasn't a fair trial by jurors. Afghan laws didn't work because they couldn't be enforced. This was a different world completely. Here I was talking to a man who had been tortured as a child as a means to punish the father. The craziest aspect was how little the past mattered to him, outside of the fact that his wounds would keep him from service. He said he didn't live in fear because his father showed him how to be brave. All he wanted now was to bring the fight back to the kind of men that still did things like that.

After we arrived at the Panjaway District Center, it took us about two weeks to get everything set up perfectly, but once we had things up and running, the communications and IT section ran very smoothly. There were only a few of us there that could work technical issues. We all worked hard and helped each other out every chance we could, to make our lives altogether much more enjoyable.

One of the reasons communications sergeants tend to have the best work ethics on an ODA (my humble opinion) is because their job is never over. When the phones go down, the Internet stops working, or the radios aren't working: we have work to do. Losing comms was not an option. Special Forces compounds are often remote with limited manpower, so comms are the best defense to avoid being overrun by any organized attack.

One little compound, approximately a forty-five-minute drive from the Panjaway District Center, held ODA 7123. The closest friendly element to ODA 7123 was ODA 7125 and they were located three-to-five kilometers away in a small village called Talukan. ODA 7123 was the only ODA on that little compound, with a small support element and some Afghan military. They lived their lives every day as if they could be forced to leave anytime; they were prepared to leave in a hurry if it ever came to that. One day, the mail came to us at the B team level and it was time to drive out to the teams. We would deliver their mail as well as other necessities. Our first stop would be at this little compound where ODA 7123 was holed up.

I didn't find this particularly alarming when I first heard it, because I wasn't aware at that moment in time where exactly this location was and its significance. Looking back on it, I understand why the stress level ratcheted up in everyone else who was going on this mission. The roads were naturally narrow, but the large number of IED strikes on the road leading to ODA 7123 had quite literally blown chunks of the road out of existence: that road was even harder to drive on. I remember this mission particularly well because the entire drive was silent. The only sounds came from the engine of the vehicle, the radio chatter, and the occasional voice of the senior-ranking person in the vehicle calling in their checkpoints on the radio.

I was the gunner in the rear vehicle on the movement. My main priority was to ensure that nobody came up behind our convoy to try altering our direction of travel—meaning, we didn't want someone dictating where we had to turn: that's how people get blown up or stuck in shitty situations.

As we neared the compound, our rate of travel slowed to a creep due to the narrow roads. Less than two hundred meters from the compound entrance was a slight S-bend in the road that unbeknownst to me had been a prime location for IEDs. As the first vehicle took the turn left on the S-shape and began to turn the wheels back toward the right, the road gave way and the lead MRAP slid down off the road and into a little irrigation canal. The MRAP wasn't able to self-recover. When the order to dismount was given, so that we could attach our winch to the first truck and help recover the vehicle, my adrenaline began pumping.

Since I was gunner, I wouldn't be getting out of the truck, but it was my job to protect the men who were. We were in a narrow section of the road. There was a two-story house less than twenty feet to our left, and the outer perimeter wall of the friendly compound was less than ten feet to the right of the irrigation canal the front truck was stuck in. The only good news was that because the wall to my right was friendly territory, I only had to focus on the rear and my left; the bad news was that military-aged males started popping their heads out like gophers to see what was going on. I can only imagine them asking themselves if anyone had set an IED there because they hadn't heard the explosion. Us getting stuck there caught them unaware. We didn't waste any time rectifying the situation, so we were already in recovery mode by the time they thought about attacking us. I had a .50-caliber machine gun pointed at their faces at that moment. I assume out of fear for their lives, they didn't move one inch once they realized we saw them. They froze in place, fearing we were about to bring American pain down upon them, but that wasn't our mission. We were just the mail guys this time. We just wanted to drive on our safe and merry way, which we did shortly thereafter.

When we pulled into the compound, the first thing I found quite alarming was that we didn't just park our trucks like we normally did in a staging area until it was time to leave. The ODA at the compound immediately implemented our trucks into their base defense plan to give some relief to their guys who had to vigilantly man their posts twenty-four hours a day, seven days a week. Once we got situated, we gladly took turns pulling security while the leadership dropped off the mail and met with the ODA leadership there. It is hard to explain, but there is nothing like welcoming Green Berets onto your compound. Every time you see any friendly American face, the brotherhood bond increases even more, but I learned quickly that this place was a powder keg of violence. So the few men living on this compound were always happy to have friendly company and to get resupplied. While Josh and

I were pulling guard, he told me where we were and why the tension felt palpable on the drive in and in the atmosphere.

He told me a story that I had heard about before but never directly correlated it to the geographical location, until now. Less than a year prior, on March 11, 2012, a SSG Robert Bales had walked off of this very same compound into the village directly outside of the village gates and slaughtered sixteen civilians, women and children included. This was all over the news. I couldn't believe this was where all the blood had been shed. I looked right out the front gate from where I was sitting. I envisioned SSG Bales just walking out of those wrought iron gates, into the village we passed coming in, and murdering sleeping women and children. Some categorize this location as the home of the insurgent revival. Insurgents exploited the deaths caused by a deranged American to recruit new zealots longing to meet Allah in their fight for jihad.

Less than twenty minutes after this realization, I heard the first shots of gunfire. I had just come off guard rotation and went to the roof of the nearby building where another operator was returning fire. He was aiming right next to the spot we had stopped previously to help recover our MRAP. I joined him on the roof and, not knowing the full situation, asked him what he needed. He put me in a pre-established fighting position on the roof that had sandbags for walls. He told me there were at least two MAMs (military-aged males) hiding behind a small compound wall across the street from where we were. There was approximately 150 to 200 yards between us and the two MAMs. The guy I was with needed me to make sure they didn't maneuver from the wall they were currently behind to one across from them, where they would be able to utilize better cover and concealment. While I was locking that spot down with a slow rate of fire, the guy who'd just given me direction was maneuvering to a different location on the roof to provide better cover. Then, I heard a call on my radio. We had an element that was about to leave the compound to maneuver on the village, where we were taking contact from, to provide more cover fire.

I had never been here before, so I wasn't sure where all the locations were that were being talked about on the radio. I took all commands from the other Green Beret on the roof who was more or less the eyes in the sky for the ground element. My task remained the same: make sure nobody was allowed to cross the field to gain a better vantage point. What we didn't expect was to have two insurgents shoot at us from behind the wall we were trying to prevent the other known targets from reaching. If they already had sights on us from that position, they would have sights on the front gate. As I came to that realization, they took a few more shots at my position, with one or two rounds hitting the sandbag in front of me. As I returned fire, another guy came out from behind the same location and started to run for his life across the field to the further location. That guy even ditched his gun in the process. They seemed to know we were sending people out and they were trying to leave quickly.

After those last few shots the gunshots ended. I sat on the roof, scanning my sector in case they tried to reengage our positions. I didn't believe they were prepared to fight us at that time because of the guy ditching his gun. It just didn't feel right; he looked scared. I believe he was probably a new recruit and, more than likely, realized he bit off more than he could chew when shit got real. Thanks to one of the extremely talented Special Forces engineer sergeants and his Afghan counterparts, two large IEDs were found emplaced in the road where our MRAP was recently stuck. When that call came over the radio, we all knew what happened. They sent the inexperienced fighters out to shoot at us as a distraction, to give the IED expert more time to emplace the bombs. It was a tactical maneuver. They wanted to ambush us later on. They called in reinforcements, after we recovered our vehicle. Fortunately for us, God was with us that day. Our engineer pulled both bombs out of the road; either IED could have single-handedly disabled one of our vehicles or even killed someone.

Once the IEDs were discovered, the dismounted patrol's orders were changed from advancing on the enemy to recovering the IEDs and returning to base. When the patrol made it back in the gates, the other guy on the roof told me I could head back downstairs. Shortly afterwards, the guy from the roof came down and when he saw me he told me to grab some joe (coffee) and asked me if we had brought mail. That's how it went, I guess—shooting one second and the next talking about the mail you just got and having a coffee. I knew I was in the right place; this was what war was supposed to be like in a Special Forces unit. Work hard, play hard, live hard; life isn't guaranteed.

When we left the compound about an hour later, we took an alternate route to avoid the hornet's nest. We got back on route and finished the rest of the day without incident. I remember laying in bed that night thinking about the incident that happened there. Any good that America accomplished in Afghanistan up to March 11, 2011 was erased when SSG Bales murdered those innocent people. Any chance of recovering the trust of the local population in that particular area could only come with divine intervention.

A few days later, back at the Panjaway District Center, one of the weapons sergeants from the B team was running a range. We were doing transition drills: shooting with our rifles first then switching to pistol in one fluid motion to continue shooting. The idea is that if in the middle of a firefight, should your gun ever jam, grabbing your 9mm (which is always loaded with the safety off) will get the job done without letting your opponent gain fire superiority. To reach the point where this becomes muscle memory, it takes hundreds of repetitions and putting rounds into targets. There were approximately six of us out there, but we were putting a lot of rounds down range and it wasn't even lunchtime yet. We regrouped after a few hours of shooting to load magazines and put up some new targets. After we had everything set up and ready to roll, we started with more transition drills, each of us having rotated to a different target and lane. The way we had the targets set up, there was a steel target on the left and about a meter to the right of that one was a paper target. The idea here was to shoot at the paper targets with the rifle and at the steel targets with the 9mm. That's important to note because if you are shooting at steel targets within 100m with a rifle you run the risk of catching a ricochet. Those little bullets will bounce right off of metal and come flying right back at you.

While I was walking toward my target, I remember shooting three rounds of my rifle into the paper target, and as I was transitioning to pistol, I felt a rock hit me right in the collarbone—at least that was my first thought. It sucked the breath right out of me, similar to falling off a ladder and having the wind knocked out of you. I called for a cease-fire. Once everyone had stopped firing, I asked who had thrown a rock at me. I looked around for a rock and didn't see anything; my buddies were all looking at me like I was crazy. I did a quick self-assessment and decided I was fine. I did, however, stop doing transition drills and switched to stationary target shooting. I wasn't going to tell anyone how bad my neck was hurting. It was extremely tender. After three or four more hours on the range, I was completely wiped. Just as I was about to call it a day at the range, one of the senior weapons sergeants that was on the ODA collocated with us popped up on the roof of the building adjacent to the range and asked us in a loud voice, "You guys aren't shooting steel with those rifles on my range, are you?"

That's when it hit me. I had caught a ricochet in my collarbone; it wasn't a rock. I stood there for a moment feeling like a jackass for having stopped the range to ask if anyone had thrown a rock at me, but at least now I knew what happened. After hearing him ask that, I remember going to my room where I grounded all my gear, took off my mulitcam top, and looked in the mirror—to my surprise, I saw just a flash of metal gleaming out of a nice little hole in my skin. At first, I tried to get it out myself with a multi-tool. All I will say about that is I won't ever try that again.

It had been hours since I had taken the ricochet, but I still had a laundry list of stuff that needed to get done so that operations could function as normal. Commo guys have the job that requires them to constantly be changing or updating something. It was such a pain in the ass, but I am so thankful for the experience that I had doing it. I decided, since I was able to finish at the range, I could manage without seeing a medic until after I had completed my list. The pain was definitely tolerable. It wasn't until more than eight hours after taking my gear off that I finally had a chance to speak with my newest team sergeant, Sam, who also happened to be a medic, about what had happened.

He took me over to the med shed. Once he had some gloves on and the lights turned on, he took a look at my collarbone and smiled, saying, "Holy shit, there's metal in there, all right!" He numbed the skin around the bullet hole with some Lidocane. He then made a small incision to open up the wound, so that he could grab the bullet fragment and clean out the wound. The entire time, I kept asking myself who could have shot the steel target next to me. I didn't think I missed my paper targets with my rifle, so I assumed maybe someone else hit the wrong target on accident.

We cleaned up afterward and he gave me some antibiotics. We started to walk back to our operations center when he said to me, "You know, an inch to your left, and that fragment would have gone straight through your trachea. Could have had an entirely different outcome, fuckin' righteous man!" He then told me good night and walked to his room. I stood there, outside the operations center, wondering how many bullets he had taken out of people that seeing one like this was worthy of being righteous.

It wasn't long after the ricochet incident that I got the best news yet. I was finally going to get put on an ODA. I remember the company CSM calling me into his office and asking me, "Kirby, are you fast? And can you swim?"

I responded, "Sergeant Major, I can be as fast as you need me to be, and I wouldn't place any bets on me winning any Olympic swim events, but I haven't drowned yet, and that's saying something."

"You are going to fill a spot on my dive team, can you handle that?" he asked.

I had no clue what I was in for, but I would rather die trying to be a badass Green Beret on a dive team than live and never know if I had what it took. The CSM stuck out his hand as he stood, signaling to me that the meeting was over and the decision was final. I grasped his hand, gave a firm shake, and less than forty-eight hours later I was deep in the Panjaway District Taliban territory, at Command Observation Post (COP) Talukan, on ODA 7125.

If you don't remember, I mentioned Talukan as being very close in proximity to the other village, where SSG Bales lost his mind and murdered innocent people. So this was a very high-risk area that had seen frequent combat the weeks prior. When I first arrived, I introduced myself to everyone on ODA 7125, starting with the team sergeant and team leader. They all shook my hand, but that was about it. I was new. I'm sure they could tell right away, not only that I was new, but also that I wasn't a diver which was at the heart of this team.

My senior communications sergeant, however, is still one of the coolest guys I've ever met. Jeff embraced me like someone would when they know they will finally get some relief from their job. Like I said before, being a communications sergeant is like being the IT guy, the radio guy, the Armed Forces Network Satellite dish installer, and so on, all at once. I knew how things were and knew that it was a lot of work for even the most experienced person. If we forgot to do something that was part of our job, it could cause all operations to cease. I knew I was new to the SF thing, and I wasn't a diver, but here in Afghanistan, when it came to guns and radios, I could do my job extremely well. I won't say I was perfect, because I wasn't. As the junior commo guy, my job was to do the heavy lifting, to allow my senior the availability to help do other things or to free up his time so he could plan future training for me on our downtime.

When I knew we were going on a patrol at 0600 in the morning, Jeff was always out there an hour early to make sure everything got up and running in the trucks with enough time to troubleshoot any issues that may arise. I knew that getting up an hour early wasn't necessary, but Jeff invested that time for a reason. Witnessing his dedication drove me to start waking up thirty minutes earlier than he normally did. I wanted to have the trucks up and running, with radio checks completed, before Jeff even came outside. I made mistakes sometimes and Jeff corrected me. It was exactly how I pictured an ODA operating. I heard the stories that these guys were telling, and I was damn proud to even be a blip on the 7125 radar.

After almost two weeks of me pretty much not talking to anyone and doing the things expected of the new guys, the team finally started to warm up to me. I think they wanted to make sure I understood where I stood in the pecking order, and it was right where I wanted to be: at the bottom and in the best position to learn. I did what I was told and mimicked the veterans of this lifestyle. I got to know most of the guys pretty well. Of course, it wouldn't be a good day if I weren't reminded that I wasn't a diver. But other than the occasional ribbing, I have zero complaints about that team. The team sergeant, Val, is among the most tactically proficient and physically fit men I have ever met. I could tell just by looking him in the eyes when he spoke that he was a man all about taking care of business. The team leader position was filled with one of the most humble captains I have ever met. He was one hell of a great leader with a reputation that preceded him. The entire ODA had a respected reputation.

During one of our morning briefs, Val told us that we would be going into a little village compound, less than three kilometers away, to speak with the village elders. We were going to provide them with a well-building contract, so that the town could afford to build a well. That contract would be putting money into the local population. For me to get permission to go on this patrol, I first had to pass the well-constructed IED lane that was built by the resident engineer sergeant. I'd have to get through this IED lane without allowing one IED to escape my eyesight. I found this very interesting because I hadn't seen or heard of anything like this before.

This particular area was a hotbed for antipersonnel IEDs. Vehicles weren't targeted a lot because the vehicles simply couldn't travel down into these remote villages; the roads and threat level just wouldn't allow it. There was a particular group of insurgents that started knocking entire steps out of staircases and replacing those steps with exact replicas that were made with explosives. There was also a particularly nasty tactic being used at the time by the Taliban fighters; they would emplace IEDs with small pressure plate triggers that were nearly invisible to see and would trigger with even the slightest increase or decrease of pressure. If we stepped on them, we were blown up. If the dirt on top of them was removed to the point where the weight distribution was altered, it would trigger the bomb, killing anyone nearby. These IEDs were literally everywhere. ODA 7125 rarely conducted a patrol without finding an IED or two, some of which were extremely well hidden.

Less than a week before my arrival to COP Talukan, ODA 7125 had been on a patrol, and a very senior and delicately trained Afghan IED specialist had both legs blown off right before the entire team took contact. The man survived, but as you can imagine, he doesn't sleep well at night. The team had a requirement that everyone had to pass the IED lane before being allowed to patrol, no exceptions (and after hearing that story, I knew why). It took me roughly twenty minutes to find the IEDs in the lane. I believe it was only because of the extra time Jeff spent training me up to his ODA's standards that I was able to so quickly find the training IEDs. He left no stone unturned and made sure I was on my A game.

Shortly after getting my GO, we were kitted up and ready to go on patrol. I was carrying one of the SATCOM (satellite) radios in my ruck. My job for this particular mission was to make sure we had SATCOM with higher elements, in case things went south. I was to stick close to the team leader if we took contact and keep comms operational. I also helped coordinate with our Afghan Army counterparts who were always along for the ride.

We were heading out around nine in the morning. The weather that day was beautiful and clear. The movement out to the village took about an hour, because of how slow we were walking and how carefully we were trying to walk in each other's footsteps. If we stepped in the same spots as the guy in front of us, we knew that step was cleared. When we finally got to the village, only three men came out to greet us—all elders—and none of them were happy to see us. Our team leader walked up to the front of our formation to meet with the elders, while we all assumed security postures and waited for Val to place everyone where he wanted us.

I took a knee next to a very small, run-down, mud hut that was right next to the village mosque. I watched as the Afghan Army guys just sat down in the middle of the road, none of them pulling security or even attempting to scan for threats. I got up from my spot at the corner of that mosque and walked over to where the Afghan machine gunner was taking a nice break from the long movement. He was stretching his legs out on the ground in front of him and looking skyward. I walked over, kicked the bottom of his boot, and told him to move less than a hundred meters away to the other side of the building where he could pull security overlooking a large field. Right after I said that to him, in Pashtu, we heard the first loud crack of a gunshot that nearly hit Jeff. Jeff was on the mosque roof spotting for our sniper. There were enemies nearby, and our indigenous help had gotten lazy. I don't remember the exact terminology used to express that the target had been eliminated, but that was what came over the radio after we heard our sniper take his first shot.

All of a sudden our sniper position came under precise machine gun fire, peppering the backside of the roof where our sniper team were taking cover. There was a four-man element with at least one PKM (Russian-made machine gun) or similar weapon within two hundred meters of our position. They were rapidly maneuvering in a canal to a flanking position for a better shot at our sniper team. My senior was up on that roof, and I remember his radio call calling for our element to open fire before they got shot. Right after Jeff came on the radio, I heard all our guns open up on the enemy position. I will tell you now, there is no feeling like the one you get when you achieve fire superiority, and it didn't take long before our guns were talking to each other (shooting in rhythm) to keep the bad guys from moving freely.

I made my way next to the team leader who had taken cover and was working on setting up his personal radio to get comms with higher for air support. I handed him my radio mic with higher HQ already on the line. Then I told our local interpreter to pull out his radio and see if we could hear iCom chatter (locals using unencrypted handheld radios). No sooner had the radio been flipped on than we could hear the talking between the men shooting at us. They were discussing how they were going to get out of the field and wanted to lure us out after them into an area that hadn't been cleared of IEDs yet. Shortly after that, the air support that we called in arrived. With a fierce vengeance, two Apaches flew in low and fast, in a terrifying show of force, and fired at the enemy in the field.

I can honestly say, I feel blessed for that mission because I only fired one or two shots that entire mission; but I got to witness the best ODA in Seventh Group (my opinion) tactically destroy a bunch of terrorist thugs and walk away unscathed. Even though it wasn't my first mission that could have gotten me a Combat Infantry Badge, Val put me in for one like the stand-up team sergeant he was. If not for him, I doubt I would have ever gotten one. It wasn't about awards to me, but Val knew the importance of having these things documented. I am most grateful for his wisdom and guidance. During my Iraq deployment, when I went out with the scout platoon, we took contact often. I remember at the end of that deployment, the scout platoon offered to write up my awards, if my home/parent unit (3ID) wasn't going to. My 3ID leadership said they were going to take care of everyone and write up the awards; I foolishly took them at their word and received the same standard award that was given to everyone else who never left the base. I mention this just to highlight one of the many ways that Val stood out for me, from all my previous leadership. This was the last mission I ever went on where we came under fire, and the first/only time it was ever acknowledged on paper.

We only went out a few more times after that, before we got official word to tear down COP Talukan. Americans were drawing out of Afghanistan, and COP Talukan was one of the many little bases that were destroyed as we pulled out of it. We left absolutely nothing for the insurgents to get their hands on, burning everything we couldn't take with us. I hadn't spent a lot of time there, but I could tell from the feel of the place that people had struggled there, and it was a little sad having to tear it down. I think a piece of us stays over there when we go overseas to fight for our country. It becomes a piece of who we are; we don't let it define us, but we never forget about it. As soon as we were done tearing the temporary lodging down, Val came up to me and told me I would be flying back home on the first bird. I was the only one on the team who wasn't dive-qualified. Since I admitted to them I wasn't great in the water, they wanted to give me extra time to prepare for dive school.

I will briefly mention that right before I left for this deployment, my wife and I tried to make another baby. If we could time the pregnancy right, I would be home for the birth. Within a few short weeks of arriving in country, my wife gave me the good news that she was pregnant and we were now expecting our second child.

Retrospective

> And He said, "I will make all My goodness pass
> before you, and will proclaim the name of the
> Lord before you; and I will be gracious to whom
> I will be gracious, and will show compassion on
> whom I will show compassion."
>
> —Exodus 33:19

I learned a lot in Afghanistan about Special Forces and how an ODA was supposed to work. But more importantly, I learned how much I loved America, when I sat down and talked with the Afghan recruit whose legs had been badly burned with oil. I felt such pity for him, and yet he was smiling just to have the opportunity to be trained and given a weapon. He didn't have any misconceptions about being the first Afghan Rambo. He simply wanted to do his little part to help with the big problem in his home country. I remember the pity I felt, but I remember even more the great pride I took in being an American. I knew that these things didn't happen in my great country, because many American soldiers made the ultimate sacrifice, in multiple global conflicts, to preserve our way of life. When I look back on that day from a spiritual perspective, I can see that God wanted me to see that man. That Afghan man was used as an instrument of God, to give me compassion for a people that I had been hardened against because of the war in Afghanistan and Iraq.

> "For they cannot sleep unless they do evil; and
> they are robbed of sleep unless they make some-
> one stumble." (Psalm 4:16)

Ever since the day I stopped at the little compound where ODA 7123 was holed up, and saw the village where SSG Robert Bales murdered those innocent people in their sleep, I have had a different idea of what evil is. In war, bad things can happen, but the devil used an American soldier that day to stir up a hatred for America that isn't likely to be diluted. Afghanistan is a very old country with a history more gruesome than most of us would care to admit. I know now that SSG Bales allowed something, not of God, to influence his actions and emotions.

> "Do not be overcome by evil, but overcome evil with good." (Romans 12:21)

Many of my brothers have come under attack because of the hatred he stirred up that day, and I pray that God forgives me for the hate I held deep inside toward SSG Bales for the longest time. I also want to take a moment to ask the Lord to heal and grant His peace to the Panjaway District. If it be Your will, Lord. Heal the world in the places that have been cut the deepest, so that the people may feel and know of Your love and forgiveness. I rebuke the devil and his works and pray that God sends angels to protect the Americans fighting for the oppressed, in Jesus's holy name. Amen.

> "For from within, out of the heart of men, proceed the evil thoughts, fornications, thefts, murders, adulteries, deeds of coveting and wickedness, as well as deceit, sensuality, envy, slander, pride and foolishness. All these evil things proceed from within and defile the man." (Mark 7:21–23)

Even in the worst of times, God is able to show that He is with us always. I stand firm in my faith that God's will was done that day that we came under fire. I believe God protected me and every other member of my team, that day and every other day. There were IEDs everywhere, and so many men walked by many of them unharmed.

In the past I had difficulty finding the proper terminology to explain how I viewed ODA 7125. But since then I have found the right description: *anointed*.

> "Have I not commanded you? Be strong and courageous! Do not tremble or be dismayed, for the LORD your God is with you wherever you go." (Joshua 1:19)

When I watched ODA 7125 work together under enemy fire, it was more impressive than watching a Hollywood action movie in slow motion. These guys worked so well together; I knew even then that they were special. God calls many to become warriors and to fight for justice, and ODA 7125 was a force for good in an otherwise lawless land. The feeling I got back then can easily be explained now as my ability to discern the anointing of God on that ODA. I am so blessed and honored to have served alongside the men of ODA 7125, in Afghanistan. Even though it was only for a few months, I was able to see what the cream of the crop looked like in action. Now that I am looking for God in the places of my life when I thought I was alone, I can see that He was there with me all along. God bless the men on ODA 7125 then, now, and forevermore, for being—in my humble opinion—the best ODA in the regiment.

> "Then the king was very pleased and gave orders for Daniel to be taken up out of the den. So Daniel was taken up out of the den and no injury whatever was found on him, because he had trusted in his God." (Daniel 6:23)

Our country owes men like Val, Jeff, and Josh as well as countless others, a special type of gratitude. When this country calls up the best men they have to fight for them, its men like Val, Jeff, and Josh who answer that call.

Josh was my first senior communications sergeant. He set a tone of professionalism that was very impressive to me. Josh taught me many things that were critical for my success, before I reported to ODA 7125. I am so grateful for his wisdom and mentorship.

When I arrived on ODA 7125, I felt a sense of amazement unlike anything I'd felt in the past. I spent my entire career reading stories about military heroes, and now I felt like I was sitting among the types of men I had only read about. I had been in the presence of a lot of great military men throughout my military career, but I can say I felt a tangible difference when I was in a room with these warriors. I was on the same team as men that I considered to be far superior to me in every way, and they treated me like a brother.

Jeff lived in and loved the small details. His presence commanded my attention, and I listened to every word that he said. He was teaching me how do my job the way I really needed to learn it. Even when he was correcting me, he never once treated me with disrespect. He taught me new things every single day. He challenged me in everything that I did. But most importantly, he trusted me to do my job. I can never repay a trust like that. All I can say Jeff, is thank you.

Not one of these men would boast or brag about a single thing they have done. They set the bar so high, in my eyes, that I never saw another team even come close to reaching it. These are just some of the men who have served our great nation. Just know that men like these have represented our country all over this world. While we enjoy the American way of life, these men go out for us all, to keep the fight far away from our borders. Fortunately, because they do their jobs so well, most Americans will never see the types of evil these men fight daily. Unfortunately, because they do their jobs so well, most Americans will never truly be able to appreciate their sacrifices.

Pre-Scuba

I flew back to Eglin Air Force Base with one of the other guys on the ODA, who was going to be training me to pass the dive school standard. People are known to have drowned during training events and the slowest person in the formation runs a mile no slower than five minutes flat. Of course, we had a little time off to spend with our families before we hit the pool, and I was ready for it. I only spent four to five months in Afghanistan, but I don't think I got more than three to four hours of sleep a night the entire time I was there. I worked long hours just as I had in Iraq to keep myself busy and make time go faster.

Now that I was back home, it was slowly starting to settle on my mind that I wasn't quite a part of this team yet. I never would be, unless I could get my bubble (award for passing the CDQC (Combat Diver Qualification Course)) and prove that I deserved a slot. When we made it out to the pool for the first time, I was very nervous. I heard stories about my teammate who was training me and what he could do to people in the water if they pissed him off. Before I left Afghanistan the team told me he never got tired and could hold his breath underwater for four minutes. I was fairly certain they were messing with me, but once it was just the two of us, I got nervous. I knew I was in for a very rude awakening in the pool.

Before I discuss my personal experience, I want to provide just a quick synopsis of how scuba school works for an ODA. There are teams like ODA 7125 that are considered a specialty team. They specialize in a particular means of infiltration—in this case SCUBA and military underwater operations. Anyone familiar with getting SCUBA-certified knows that there are a lot of intricate rules that must be followed, for safety reasons when dealing with oxygen, depth, and pressure. This school is designed to teach Green Berets and other Special Operations service members the ins and outs of SCUBA operations and the health risks associated with it. They also teach how to deal with wildlife—such as, sharks, jellyfish, or even barracuda—and are well versed in life-saving medical procedures should something happen. They do PT every day at this school, and from what I've been told, they run, far and fast, every day. I used to love running, but running five-minute miles consistently is no joke. Yet there are lots of guys doing it at CDQC. The attrition rate at this school is so high that it became too expensive to send people all the way down to Key West, where the Combat Diver Qualification Course (CDQC) is held, just to have them fail one of the first gates upon arrival. These gates include open-water swims in the ocean, a drown-proofing exercise, and other underwater activities that I will detail later on when I detail my experience. These are just a few of the easier tasks required to make it to the next steps and are also where a majority of people fail or quit. To prevent this loss of money, the individual Special Forces Groups started hosting what was commonly known as pre-scuba at their respective locations.

Pre-scuba was a two-week course when I went through it (around May 2013) that ran all students through a series of events that mimic the gates at the CDQC. The intent was to train prospective dive school students for the events and to weed out the people that don't have what it takes.

After a month or so of individually training with my teammate, I had made a lot of progress but was still below the standard in the water. However, it was time for my pre-scuba class to begin. Pre-scuba is a daily repetition of the gates followed by a swim in the Choctawhatchee Bay. Those swims were normally between three and ten kilometers each. Every day starts with a long run, and the last day of pre-scuba includes a timed ten-mile run with a "go/no-go" grade.

During pre-scuba, after a solid breakfast, we drove to the pool on Eglin AFB and would stretch out extremely well, before getting into the temperate water to prepare for the first event of the day: the subsurface fifty-meter swim. The concept is simple. At the starting line, the swimmer submerges completely, pushes off the wall, and swims fifty meters without coming up for air. If the pool is only twenty-five meters long, the swimmer will remain underwater at the turnaround and may push off the wall to head back to the starting point.

The first time I did this, before I started pre-scuba, I made it maybe six meters before I came up gasping for breath. My teammate, who was training me, looked at me with bewilderment in his eyes. He was in disbelief that I could only muster six meters. By the time pre-scuba started, I was making it consistently to twenty-five meters; but I kept freaking out when my body involuntarily started to convulse because I was denying it fresh oxygen.

The next event was called "clump retrieval" and begins with treading water. At the instructor's request, we would then dive to the bottom of the pool to grab a pool-friendly brick. Those bricks were always conveniently stored at the lowest part of the pool. We would have to calmly bring the brick back up to the surface, and demonstrate our ability to hold a heavy item and tread water. Once everyone retrieved their brick and surfaced, we would tread water and pass the bricks to each other, until the instructor told us to stop: normally lasting about five minutes.

The next event was a mini-series of events called "drown-proofing." This event was designed to show calmness under pressure, and all events were completed with the hands tied behind the back and feet tied together. It begins with a few minutes of bobbing: blowing out a controlled amount of air to allow the body to sink to the bottom then continuing to blow out the remaining amount of air on the ascent after a good push off the bottom. When our heads would break the surface, we would take a quick breath and start the process over again. I can't even pretend I was okay with this event. I frequently ripped open my restraints or slipped my hands out of the ropes. I was like a drowning animal that was straining to reach the surface for air. I often wouldn't complete even two consecutive bobs before freaking out. After bobbing came the swim, where all of us had to slowly swim in circles for five minutes without breaking restraints or stopping. As you can imagine, I didn't overachieve in this event either, but I can honestly say, it was the only part of the drown-proofing event that I was able to consistently pass. After the five-minute swim we started bobbing again, but this time we were required to do things like front flips, back flips, and mask retrievals while on the bottom of the pool (mid bob). Once all this was done and the mask had been successfully retrieved the event was over and the restraints were taken off.

Once drown-proofing was complete, the instructors would set up one long rope on the bottom of the pool. We would tread water with a smaller rope in our hands. When the instructor said to dive, we would swim to the bottom, tie the knot selected by an instructor (end-of-line bowline, square knot, clove hitch), calmly rise to the surface, and then ask for the knot to be inspected. I can now—and could then—tie all the required knots with great accuracy on land. The second my air supply was gone so were my critical-thinking skills. I was only ever able to tie a few of the knots, but never all of them consecutively and correctly. I was the only one in our class having issues with this event.

The last and final event in the pool was the weight belt swim. This particular swim is three separate periods of seven minutes each, where each swimmer wears an eight-pound weight belt and swims in the same circle we did during drown-proofing. Seemed pretty straightforward, and I didn't think I would have any issues with it. That was one of the more costly assumptions I have ever made. Even with a minute break in between time periods, I wasn't able to get my heart rate under control, because I was not relaxed in the water and was more or less starving my mind of oxygen. For a calm swimmer, the minute breaks were sufficient to keep them going.

Now, before I share my experience during the weight belt, it's important to understand that everything an operator can do to minimize risks is done. The Special Forces underwater community understands that better than most. They have designated medics standing by, anytime training is being conducted. The medics at pre-scuba were specialized diver-qualified emergency technicians who understand the intricate processes of oxygen expansion and how pressure and depth can affect a person. They have oxygen tanks, stretchers, and anything else you can think of at every single training event, to mitigate risks. People have died during freak accidents, and they take those life-and-death risks extremely seriously. They also make all students wear a vest that is strapped to the torso and contains two small air canisters inside of it. Attached to those air canisters is a pull string, which can be pulled to inflate the vest as a flotation device.

For guys like me who aren't naturally comfortable or gifted in the water, it was hard to catch my breath and slow my heart rate. My nerves affected my lung capacity and the amount of oxygen being used up. So starting with the fifty-meter subsurface swim, my heart rate was jacked up and never really slowed down throughout the day. By the time we got to the weight belt swim, I was exhausted, normally panting, and nervous. I could run for days, but for some reason, my cardiovascular system just refused to cooperate with me in the pool. When they said the command GO for our weight belt swim, on this particular day, I managed to sidestroke for the entire first seven-minute period. I was barely able to reach the surface from exhaustion, at the end of the seven minutes. I knew I wasn't going to be able to make the next two rounds, but for some reason that day, I decided quitting wasn't an option. I was tired of coming up for air, when everyone else wasn't. It was embarrassing for me to be that guy, and I wasn't willing to do it anymore. I made the decision that I wasn't coming up early that day. If I couldn't make the swim, I would drown trying. I don't think I actually started drowning until about two minutes into the second time period, but I vaguely remember the transition period from being conscious to being unconscious.

I had started at the surface of the water and slowly became less and less able to maintain my rhythm. Once I hit the point of knowing I was going to pass out, I just kept swimming, trying to make it to the surface. My vision started to rapidly deteriorate, as I drifted into unconsciousness. Suddenly, the next thing I know, I was sitting out of the pool with my safety vest off. There was an oxygen machine hooked up to me and a defibrillator lying on the ground next to me. I don't think he used it, but he was prepared to.

The first thing I remember hearing was the medic saying to me, "Holy shit, brother, good for you! Most people don't have the balls to go see the wizard, they normally quit first."

I had to go see a doctor to get cleared to train. To be honest, I never gave any thought to dying. My faith in the medical abilities of our medics far outweighed my faith in many private medical practices. This happened to me two more days in a row, before I finally managed to finish a weight belt swim. By the end I probably looked like a drowning cat, but somehow I made it.

There were only three days left until the end of pre-scuba, at which time the instructors would make a decision to either send a student to Key West to attend the CDQC or they would be denied the opportunity outright. I didn't have any illusions that I was ready to go to CDQC, but as long as I didn't quit, I was hopeful Jeff would be able to convince Val to keep me on the team. I would drown for the next three years straight, in pre-scuba, if that's what it took me to pass and earn a spot on this team.

I was especially keen to stay on this team after hearing my teammate tell me about the team sergeant from years ago on 7125. On a deployment, three ODAs (including 7125) had been assigned the task of inserting, via helicopter, into a mountainous region filled with Taliban. The only safe landing area for the aircraft was at least a kilometer away and below the target village. All three ODAs got off the birds, but only one ODA made it up the mountain into the village. The other two ODAs hit muscle failure and fatigue, before they could reach the village: because of the harsh environment and limited air supply at such high elevations. Members of ODA 7125 not only made it to the village but they cleared the entire village on their own. They killed a lot of bad guys, and did some heroic shit in the process. The team sergeant on ODA 7125, for that mission, had been the same senior enlisted adviser from back in the Q-Course who told me he never saw anyone get a GO without completing the entire SUT course. He had told us this very same story one early morning, before taking us on a seven-mile run at a six-minute-mile pace. I just failed to realize, up to that point, that I was on *that* team. Silver Stars were awarded to members of that ODA, and that was why I wanted to be on their team and nobody else's.

Three days before the end of pre-scuba, we were going to a different pool that was slightly shallower, and one that generally yielded better results because the student's confidence increased. I was told that morning that Val and my teammate who had been training me would be assisting with the training, which really meant I had to do well. I couldn't let Val see me doing the "kickin-chickin" underwater as I passed out. I was determined to pass my events that day, starting with the fifty-meter swim and in Val's grading lane. It was a twenty-five-meter pool. I was to push off the wall at the turnaround point and not stop swimming until touching the feet of the instructor standing at the finish line. By the finish line, I was convulsing, and my vision was narrowing to a near-blackout level, before I felt my hand brush his leg and he scooped me up out of the water. I had done it. I might have looked like a pansy, but I got it done.

The "brick retrieval" and "water treading" events I passed with flying colors that day. I made it all the way to mask retrievals, in drown-proofing, before swallowing too much water and choking. I immediately went subsurface again after catching my breath and completed the task correctly on my second attempt. I fumbled up my knots but did manage to tie most of them correctly before botching the square knot at the end of the event. The last thing I had to do was the weight belt swim. Even thought I didn't do great, I managed to squeak by just enough to where I would have given me a GO at that event.

I was so proud of myself for finally not failing as hard-core as normal during the events. I was ready to knock out the open-water swim. They took us out by boat to a point about five kilometers away from shore, dropped us in the water, and watched us swim toward the landmark we had been given. At some point during this swim, the water surface got choppy, and there were one- to three-foot swells smacking me in the face every other chance I had to take a breath. I accidentally breathed in a mouthful of seawater and a golf ball–sized, soft-tissue jellyfish. I had obliviously been swimming in a school of these jellyfish for some time. As the jellyfish went down my throat, I regurgitated it right back up and out into the water. I gasped for breath and a fresh swell immediately sent it right back down my throat, causing me to vomit again. I threw up a few more times in the water and switched sides so the swells would hit my back instead of my face. At this point in time, I was still easily a kilometer out. All I can remember thinking about was something that I had seen on *Shark Week* about sharks being attracted to vomit. I started swimming like there was a shark behind me. I have no idea where this irrational fear came from, but I can assure you, I swam faster that last kilometer than I had the previous four.

The following day we were back at the Eglin pool, and I had done okay on the fifty-meter subsurface swim, making it about forty-seven meters before almost blacking out. I felt it was progress because there was no wall to bounce off of in this pool.

"Brick retrieval," normally one of my easier events, was up next. When it was my turn to go down to the bottom of the pool and I reached the bottom, I felt an explosion of pain in the bridge of my nose and saw stars. I slowly made my way to the surface with a trail of blood behind me. It hurt like hell, like a bubble popping in my nasal cavity, and again I had to go back to the doctor to get cleared to continue training. The doctor told me that I had seriously strained and/or ruptured my sinus cavity and that further agitation could damage it permanently. Little did he know, the damage was permanent at that point. I haven't been able to go deeper than six feet without feeling excruciating pain in my nose ever since. I was told to sit out the rest of the day. The following morning, on the final day of pre-scuba, we did our ten-mile run. Afterwards, one of the scuba instructors came up to me and very politely told me that no matter what the decision was, he was proud of my progress and told me not to let it get me down. In other words, I wasn't going to get selected to attend the CDQC.

I almost felt bad for the guy sharing this information with me. I knew I wasn't ready, and he wasn't telling me anything I didn't already know. I thanked him for constantly bringing me back to life and told him I'd see him at the pool. I was grabbing some breakfast when Jeff called me, saying he needed to talk to me. I drove over to the team room, and he came outside to tell me I would be going back to my original company. My old team sergeant, Jon, had worked some deal to get me back. I told Jeff I didn't want to go and asked him if it had anything to do with my progress at pre-scuba. He assured me it didn't and told me that Val and even the company command sergeant major had both tried to keep me on the team. They liked me enough so far to try and keep me, but nothing would change Jon's mind. He wanted me back under his authority, and nothing could stop it from happening. Jeff apologized, and I could tell he felt terrible because he knew about the treatment I had received before. He told me that they even asked if I managed to pass CDQC as honor graduate, if that would carry any weight, and they were told no. I was stunned and felt like what was left of my confidence had just taken a shot to the genitals.

I didn't have much time to dwell on what to do because I had to go to the pool to train, but as I was walking to my car, I decided to do something I had never done before. I was going to drop out of pre-scuba. I went and talked to that very same cadre and told him I wasn't going to train today. I'm sure he thought it was because of what he said, but it wasn't. I had proven for days in a row I was willing to die before coming up for air, but now I was going to walk away because…what was the point? Even if I miraculously passed these events and went to CDQC and made honor graduate, I was still going to work with Jon again. I simply couldn't deal with that and failing to pass the standard at pre-scuba simultaneously. So I quit.

I called and told Jeff, and when I got back to the team room Val asked to speak with me outside. I remember having a hard time looking him in the eyes because I didn't want to see the disappointment in them with my quitting pre-scuba. He asked me what happened, and I told him the truth. I knew I wasn't going to pass but that it wasn't what fortified my decision. I simply couldn't justify the failure and then having to deal with being booted off the team. He told me then that he did everything in his power to keep me and that he liked me. He would have kept me on the team as long as I was willing to keep going back to pre-scuba until I passed it. I would have spent the next ten years of my life trying to stay on that team if they would have let me. However, that just wasn't the hand I was dealt. I was about to find out what the new deck had in store for me, at my new home, on ODA 7112.

Retrospective

"They passed through the Phrygian and Galatian region, having been forbidden by the Holy Spirit to speak the word in Asia; and after they came to Mysia, they were trying to go into Bithynia, and the Spirit of Jesus did not permit them."
—Acts 16:6–7

When I looked back on this chapter of my life and tried to see how my failure affected my life, I don't see failure at all. I tried as hard as I possibly could to pass this course. No matter how hard I tried, something kept happening that would stop me from making forward progress. I look at the scripture above, and I can see that there are, in fact, certain things and certain places that Jesus Christ doesn't want us to pursue. I had never failed at something so miserably before in my life, and my quitting on the last day has eaten me alive ever since. My personal desire would be to go back and finish the final day of training, regardless of passing or failing the test; but I rest easy in my belief that the Lord had different plans for me. The more I tried to force something that wasn't meant to be, the more He showed me it wasn't going to happen. Toward the end of pre-scuba I was starting to think I could eventually pass. Then it was as if every door and window was shut all at once. I don't believe that was by chance. For me to walk away from the prospect of being on 7125, I needed to have all hope removed.

Working for a man like Val was a special honor of mine. Val was my first ODA team sergeant and he set the standard in my eyes for my future leadership. Val is what I consider to be an Apex predator (top of the food chain). As far as Green Berets go, there are only a few that I have met that I can place in this category, and some of them are mentioned in this book: Val, McKenna, Vera, and Jon. All four of those men have served as a team sergeant on an ODA; I'd imagine only those at the top of the food chain have held that position. Thank you for your mentorship and guidance Val. I will always hold your ODA 7125 close to the chest and with the utmost respect for what you and your men sacrificed for our country.

I never expected Jon to be back in my life. If I'm being honest, I was extremely upset when I found out that I had to go back and work for him again. I did have a level of respect for his accomplishments and his rank, but I was not happy about getting pulled off of a team that I felt was far superior to any other team. I was being put back on a team that I expected to be miserable on. I wanted very badly to call ODA 7125 my home, but when the Lord makes a decision, he doesn't change it based on our feelings. Jon and I were destined to work together again, for better or for worse.

> "Be anxious for nothing, but in everything by prayer and supplication with thanksgiving let your requests be made known to God. And the peace of God, which surpasses all comprehension, will guard your hearts and your minds in Christ Jesus." (Philippians 4:6–7)

ODA 7112

ODA 7112 specialized in mountaineering. When I started on 7112, the team itself was transitioning as a whole; this is common when leadership changes happen and right after a deployment. The guys go off to schools, or to bigger and better assignments, or even move one or two doors down the hallway to a different ODA, where the grass perhaps is actually greener. From the day I walked in the door until the day I walked away from the team to become a civilian, Jon was the team sergeant. One of the weapon sergeants, engineer sergeants, and I were there from when Jon took over the team and were the only original three remaining when I left. I watched the team go through some amazing and some tumultuous times. As much as I was dreading working for Jon again because of his leadership style, I must admit that I always admired his work ethic.

One of the coolest and most down-to-earth people I've ever met, Forrest, was the team leader (the officer in charge of the team). He was a battle-tested, CDQC-qualified, brilliant officer—among the best I've ever met. His personality and leadership style counterbalanced Jon's micromanaging lifestyle, which had been shoved down our throats. Respect on a team starts at the top. If the team leader is poor a leader, the team can survive because the team sergeant can be a buffer between the officer and the troops. With Forrest, it was the exact opposite. He was often the advocate for team welfare, which we felt would have been neglected otherwise. All personality differences aside, Jon had a hell of a task ahead of him. He had a team that consisted of mostly new Green Berets; I was one of the more senior guys at one point in time.

Jon was tough on everybody, but he was particularly hard on new guys. They weren't allowed to even come upstairs into the team room unless invited by him, and he wouldn't invite them until they had shown they were reliable in the little things like showing up to work on time and always being in the right place, at the right time, in the right uniform. I always felt it was excessive, especially because our team of new guys ended up being one of the most productive ODAs in our company—thanks to the type of work ethic our leadership had. But at the end of the day, it wasn't my team. He had earned the right to run his team the way he wanted, which didn't stop us from hating him at times, but we always did what we were told.

I remember one instance of his over-productive mood in particular because it was Friday afternoon, around three o'clock, when someone knocked on our team room door with a few boxes in his hand. He told me they were specialized communication devices, which would allow leaders in combat situations to see the positions of their troops in real time. He also told me these devices were very complex so official training on them would be given to us at a later date. Instead of those devices going into the locked cage where they belonged, Jon told me, as he was getting ready to leave for the day, not to leave the office until I could give him an official class on the devices I had just received.

When I was ready to give the class, he would drive back onto the compound to receive said class. The devices weren't classified in nature, but we weren't allowed to take these things home to learn them. He was basically telling me I would be spending the weekend at the office, with zero help from anyone in the battalion. I literally went to talk to every other team in our company and one of our neighbor companies, I also reached out to our S-6 (communications) shop, and not one team had even opened the boxes that these devices were in. Everyone else had locked up these devices and were waiting for training. The more I reached out about one thing or another, the more I was told that they were only delivering the devices because they couldn't train us without us having them. The resources and information that I needed weren't even available yet.

I had only the small manual that came me in the box and had to learn the devices well enough to put them into action. I ended up staying at the office the entire weekend. Eventually, after calling dozens of numbers on a Friday night to try to find a customer service representative or someone who could answer some questions, I found a phone number for one of the guys who designed this technology. He said it was good timing because he happened to be driving on the interstate, and he ended up walking me through everything free of charge. He spent over six hours on the phone with me, walking me through the device intricacies. If that isn't a sign that God is good, I don't know what is. Jon came back out on Saturday for the class I gave him, then he told me to get everything ready because we would implement these devices into the training we would do on Monday. So I spent the duration of the weekend charging everything, and installing these devices in all of our military vehicles. In case you were wondering, the vehicle kits were also something we didn't have yet.

By Monday, the devices were working but we were very limited on the functionality we were able to use. Seventh Group hadn't been given the secure means to utilize the devices yet; without proper security, seventy-five percent of the device capabilities weren't usable. Maps also hadn't been created yet, for us to be able to download and use them. All in all, we were very premature in our efforts to utilize this technology at that time.

It was stuff like this that drove a wedge between Jon and I. There were times when I would tell support personnel that they could not leave, after they got done telling me there was nothing else they could do; instead they would need to have their leadership come down to where we were to explain to Jon what the support guys had tried to explain. Only then could we all leave for the day. Of course, this was absolutely ridiculous, but unless someone high ranking came down to explain that something wouldn't work the way Jon wanted, I would just be stuck there all night/weekend pretending like there was something more I could do. I am a hardworking guy, but treating me like shit has the opposite effect on my work ethic than just giving me purpose, direction, and motivation.

Jon's assumption that every "no" was an excuse or a short cut was a pain, but his intent wasn't wrong. He never wanted to waste resources. If we had equipment or supplies at our disposal (in our team room), he was determined to put them to use for our team. He didn't care if everyone had that same equipment for years and no one ever used it; if it was on our books and he could see it, we were going to maintain and utilize it. That mentality he had and that intent was respectable.

Shortly after I arrived on the team, all the slots were filled. I had a new senior communications sergeant and friend, SFC William (Wil) Cumbie. Wil was a very funny guy and he loved to have a good time. He was one of the first people I really came to lean on, when I was struggling with my job and working for Jon. Wil was right there next to me. Even though he didn't stay on the team very long, for the time he was there, he was a confidant and friend to me during a time when I felt I desperately needed one.

All of the men on this team became united very quickly, because we are all under the same intense pressure. Jon pushed every single one of us to our limits. The bond that developed between us is unlike anything that can be found outside of a special operations team room. I wish I could name all the men on this team here, to let them know publicly how much their hard work, dedication, and support meant to me. Most of them are still operators and still answering our nation's call so I can't. I can say that I couldn't have asked for better friends or teammates.

While Jon did many things that we might not have liked, he was also very good at doing things that highlighted our team in a positive light. One time, Forrest and Jon volunteered our team to help an Air Force veteran who had been blinded in combat. This Air Force veteran was getting ready to climb a mountain in Chile. We were teaching him some mountain-climbing physical fitness routines that would build up his endurance. We all took turns working out with him and loved every minute of it. We put him on a specially designed workout program, and watched him make significant gains in the gym. We spent one month training with this veteran, and it was a very humbling experience for me. One day, during one of the workout routines, I wore a blindfold so that I could feel what it was like to do things like deadlifts and tire flips without the gift of sight. I can honestly say I haven't taken my sight for granted since. I find it amazing how successful people can be in dealing with their situations. I don't remember ever seeing this blind man complain about his injury. He was all smiles and just happy to get some training before his endeavor. His testimony was powerful and it strengthened the resolve of our team.

In another instance, my wife approached me and asked if our team could do a first aid event for her Girl Scout troop (Troop 676). Part of the first aid badge work her troop was working on required them to interview a medical professional. I thought about how awesome it would be to have some Green Beret medics showing these young ladies some of their life-saving equipment and answering first-aid questions. I brought the idea up to Jon and he was thrilled to do it. He told me that it would be good publicity and an important thing that we could do for the community. Once the plan was approved by the commander, our two medics put together a small class that gave the girls scouts a chance to see and touch some medical equipment that doesn't come in standard first-aid kits. Both of these medics went from being steely-eyed killers to fathers and mentors to a group of kids in front of my eyes. It was simply fascinating. The girls in the troop were fascinated by all of the equipment and asked a lot of questions. I never heard of Green Berets helping scouts before this, and I was absolutely thrilled that my daughter was able to learn from our great medics.

Retrospective

> "Blessed is a man who perseveres under trial; for
> once he has been approved, he will receive the
> crown of life which the Lord has promised to
> those who love Him."
>
> —James 1:12

Struggling with leadership or management styles is not uncommon. Authority figures can easily be critiqued. I don't believe there has ever been a leader whom everyone has agreed with. I have had leaders who I would gladly follow to my grave, but perhaps everyone they have lead didn't feel that way. I have also had leaders who I would resist and begrudgingly follow only if I had to, but perhaps others they have lead followed them joyously. No matter what the scenario is, I don't believe the dissension is strictly caused by leaders or followers alone.

I mentioned some reasons that Jon drove me nuts. I also mentioned some of the ways Jon was doing good. I did that because I think we can look at anyone and approve of some of their actions and words while disapproving of some of their other actions and words. Only Jesus lived a pure and sinless life, and even He had critics. God is wonderful in His word; He directs and instructs us in all things. God knew we would have leaders appointed over us that we would not agree with, and He guides us toward unity even in those situations. I believe God knew that every person He appoints into leadership or authority would likely fail, as we all do, and He is telling us to stay the course and let Him be God in those situations.

> "Servants, be submissive to your masters with
> all respect, not only to those who are good and

gentle, but also to those who are unreasonable. For this finds favor, if for the sake of conscience toward God a person bares up under sorrows when suffering unjustly. For what credit is there if, when you sin and are harshly treated, you endure it with patience? But if when you do what is right and suffer for it you patiently endure it, this finds favor with God." (1 Peter 2:18-20)

"Remind them to be subject to rulers, to authorities, to be obedient, to be ready for every good deed, to malign no one, to be peaceable, gentle, showing every consideration for all men." (Titus 3:1-2)

God knew we would all face struggles in this world. I believe this is one of the many reasons we are instructed to fellowship. We aren't meant to face our struggles alone. Jesus is always with us, of course, but His help can look a lot like people who come into our lives to help us carry the weight we are under. My teammates on ODA 7112 were absolutely help to me, and I hope I was able to be help to them. We supported each other and lifted each other up, when we could. We had each other's backs in everything, and those men were my sole motivation at times.

Team Training

One of the many training events our team did took place at Camp Dawson, West Virginia, where we spent almost two weeks conducting military mountaineering tactical operations. We had trained for months on knot-tying, climbing walls at the gym, and rappelling from the tower on the Seventh group compound, but the training can't compare to the real deal.

One of my very good friends Raf is a mountaineer-certified expert. He taught us the intricacies of rappelling, anchoring, transporting casualties (lowering someone on a stretcher off the side of a mountain to a more secure location below), building cold-weather survival shelters, as well as other activities that keep ODAs with mountaineering specialties like ours current on our required skills.

When we went to Camp Dawson to test our abilities on actual mountains it was one of the coldest experiences of my life, but we loved every minute of it. To me, this was what SF was all about. Anyone could shoot, move, and communicate; but not everyone can do those things and also be able to operate, nearly invisibly, in extreme environments.

I remember the final day of this mountaineer training. We scaled to the top of one of the taller mountain peaks in the area. As we reached the top and started prepping the anchors to rappel back down, a blizzard hit that was unlike any snowstorm I've ever experienced, and I grew up in Germany and Wisconsin. We always anticipate poor weather, but when it snows so heavily that opening my eyes is painful because of the freezing snow hitting them, it makes a guy anxious about jumping off the side of a mountain on a wet rope. My nerves weren't shaken that much during a rappel since Air Assault School when I had to exit the rotary winged aircraft for the first time.

I wasn't able to see the rope I was holding, let alone the bottom of the cliff face, where I hoped to safely land. Similar to Air Assault and Airborne, this was another butt pucker moment for me. Thoughts of equipment failure were something I struggled with for every jump or rappel, but overcoming that fear and using it is what life is all about.

I opened my eyes to look off the cliff edge and slowly worked my way out into a good L-shape position, before jumping out into the snowy white abyss. I knew because of the climb I had at least seventy feet before I would hit the ground. So I zipped down the rope like it was a race to the bottom. As I was looking down, I saw the only other person that had already made it down waiting for me, which made me realize that the snow died down significantly once we below a certain elevation level. This is probably the most fun I've ever had doing military training. By the end of it, I remember thinking about the mountains I climbed in Afghanistan and thinking about the many hiding places the enemy will use in the mountains because of the fact they are hard to get to. Teams like ours could actively flush the terrorists out and kill them. In fact, anyone who knows how the war in Afghanistan started out knows it started in the mountains. (Check out the books *Jawbreaker* by Gary Berntsen and *The Only Thing Worth Dying For* by Eric Blehm.)

A short time after our trip to West Virginia and the day after our Christmas break in January of 2014, we were set to go to the swamp phase of Ranger School, held in Florida, and conduct an exercise never done before: working alongside the Ranger School students. Our ODA was going to be immersed into their scenario and would act as a reconnaissance element for them in a mission named "Operation Frozen Gator."

This is interesting because in most military schools, students are able to request intelligence on their target locations, but if the cadre didn't give it to them, it's because they didn't have it. It is rare to have active assets in a training environment because of the costs it would generate. This time, the students would be conducting their patrol requirements as per the Ranger School regulations and standards; the only difference was that this time the students were able to contact an actual recon team (us) that was already on the ground, on the radio, and they could use the information we gave them to better conduct their operation.

It sounds simple, but as anyone who has been to Ranger School or the SFQC can tell you, that is a valuable asset to have. A few weeks before we started this exercise, a new communications sergeant joined our ODA, who was senior in rank to me and moved to the senior communication sergeant slot.

Nate was about two hundred pounds of pure muscle and one of the fastest people I've ever met. Not only was he a physical beast, but his computer, radio, and weaponry skills rivaled the most skilled communication operators I knew. This was a blessing for me because it can take years to learn all the things he knew. This field exercise was the first time Nate and I would be working together in semi-austere conditions: eating MREs and sleeping outside in our patrol base (occasionally getting to sleep inside one of the rooms graciously lent to us by the Ranger cadre), but more or less spending two cold weeks outside. When we first arrived, Nate and I tested all our gear like we would for any other deployment. Once everything was good to go, he spent the next three hours teaching me how to build a high-quality jungle antenna, which can be used to expand the distance of a radio transmission and is nearly invisible if built properly. Together we built an antenna that far exceeded the requirements we had, but neither of us ever liked to do less than our best on anything we worked on.

I mention how awesome this antenna was because on one of the midnight missions, as our entire ODA lay on the ground near the Ranger students' target objective, getting rained on and shivering, a colonel literally walked into our antenna as he was observing the students move into their tactical positions. Officers observing is common practice in military schools because the high-level officers are the ones who make the big decisions about changes in course curriculum, among other things, and the good ones will always join the men in the field to get the true experience. This officer, he walked into our antenna, completely oblivious to it and the fact that he nearly stepped on Nate and me lying noiselessly under our poncho manning the radio.

When he stopped and finally realized he walked into something not natural, he asked out loud to no one in particular, "What the hell is this?"

When Nate and I removed the poncho, we thought the colonel was going to have a heart attack. We startled him so badly. But after our introduction, he admitted that he had been trying to find us for a while but wasn't able to; so he had decided to just focus on his students. Our team leader and the colonel went off to have a discussion about whatever it is officers talk about, and we continued mission, silently and slowly disappearing into the forest floor again.

About five days into the exercise, I had to get my wisdom teeth pulled because of pain I was having in my mouth. The only available appointment time in a three-month block happened to fall in the middle of this exercise. As you can imagine, my team sergeant was less than thrilled, but he couldn't tell me I couldn't go get my mouth taken care of. I went right from the field to my appointment. I showed up to the dentist office smelling like body odor and dirt, and less than two hours later, I had four less teeth in my mouth and was high on pain medication. I anticipated having a fairly standard forty-eight to seventy-two hours off because of the minor surgery. Instead Jon called and told me to report back out to the field the following morning. So instead of relaxing, I went shopping for ramen, pudding, things I wouldn't have to chew, so that I'd be able to eat while out in the field. I had the chipmunk look when I showed up the following morning and was in pain, because I couldn't drive while on the pain medications so I had to wait to take them.

On many occasions I have said or thought things like, "This is the worst possible situation I could be in," or something similar, but this is one of those times that takes the cake.

I spent the next week rucking with over seventy pounds on my back, sleeping outside, eating ramen cooked in my Jetboil, and popping pain meds like they were going out of style. I never felt pain like the kind of mouth pain I was having. I could feel the scabs in my mouth rupture under the pressure I was putting my body under. I wasn't able to heal properly and ended up with dry socket and had to go back to the dentist for an emergency medication refill. The look on the dentist's face when I told him I had spent the past few days in the field, instead of resting, prompted him to do a quick examination, showing that two of the four incisions had dry socket—a painful result of poor healing after removing a tooth. I appreciated the training but hated every single footstep I had to take because of the excruciating pain I was in. I can honestly say it took me a long time to forgive Jon for making me endure that pain, but I did. We ended up in the newspaper for this training event because of the high success it had. Looking back on it, I am very glad I endured the pain to be a part of something bigger than myself.

Retrospective

"I will lift up my eyes to the mountains; From where shall my help come? My help comes from the Lord, Who made heaven and earth. He will not allow your foot to slip; He who keeps you will not slumber."

—Psalm 121:1-3

By this time our team had worked together for quite some time and really had a good team rhythm. I never thought in my wildest dreams that I would be climbing a mountain, as a part of a twelve-man ODA, to train on how to kill bad guys. It was the kind of stuff I pretended to do as a kid, when I would climb trees and play Army with my friends. I found a love in the mountains that I lost at pre-scuba. Where my failure had consumed me for quite some time, it wasn't until I was on the mountains that I realized I could be just as good or better in a different calling, such as mountaineering. I'm far from an expert mountain climber, but I know enough to get around and handle my business because of the training I received.

As strange as it may sound, even as a Green Beret, I have always been terrified of heights. Obviously, it's something I was able to overcome time and again, but for those of you who share the fear of heights, you might understand how I felt when I looked out into the snowy abyss and wasn't able to see anything past my nose. I was terrified, but we had a mission to accomplish, and it was my turn to go next. I was carrying the radio that could talk through the mountain peaks, and I couldn't leave a teammate at the bottom of the mountain alone for long. A lot can happen on the side of a mountain, and working in pairs is one of the only ways to make sure everything goes according to plan. Just think about standing at the highest cliff face on a mountain, during a terrible blizzard, and holding a rope in your hand, knowing you are about to jump off the side of the mountain completely blind. No matter how many times you do it, it never stops taking faith.

> "And Jesus answered and said to them, 'truly I say to you, if you have faith and do not doubt, you will not only do what was done to the fig tree, but even if you say to this mountain, be taken up and cast into the sea, it will happen.'" (Matthew 21:21)
> "For the mountains may be removed and the hills may shake, But My lovingkindness will not be removed from you, And My covenant of peace will not be shaken, says the Lord who has compassion on you." (Isaiah 54:10)

I trusted my equipment to save my life in a blizzard on the top of a mountain and have an amazing experience to talk about now because of it. We learned and knew how to use our equipment, we did everything we were supposed to do to mitigate known risks, and then it was once again time to trust. This represents exactly how I envision learning how God operates and then walking with Jesus. We won't find scripture anywhere in the Word of God that states we won't ever face or have to overcome our greatest fears. God merely instructs us not to fear.

Once we start living that way, we have a different kind of amazing experience to talk about: our testimony. Just imagine the love Jesus has for us when are willing to make that leap of faith in His name and trusting in Him. I think about how many things could have gone wrong on that mountain, but my faith and commitment to my team still pushed me over that edge. The only problem would have been if I had let my fear of the unknown prevent me from trusting in my training and my equipment; then I wouldn't have a testimony of success to share.

Now I have faith in Jesus Christ. He is my anchor. He is my belay-man. The Holy Spirit is the feeling of courage that takes our hearts and guides it delicately through the fear or situation we face.

> "Come to Me, all who are weary and heavy-laden, and I will give you rest. Take My yoke upon you and learn from Me, for I am gentle and humble in heart, and you will find rest for your souls. For My yoke is easy and My burden is light." (Matthew 11:28-30)

Nate and I became very close friends after two weeks of being frozen solid. He is a Ranger-qualified Green Beret with tactical experience far beyond mine. I was so fortunate that Nate showed up when he did. The workload is overwhelming at times for the commo guys in tactical environments. So having a second pair of hands, and hands with even more experience than I had, was a welcome gift. Nate taught me more than any amount of book reading could. His natural ability to overcome obstacles and work through problems was a much-needed discipline in my life. I was hot-tempered and often angry with Jon for being such a jackass all the time. Most of us aren't great problem solvers when we are constantly angry and I wasn't an exception. Nate taught me how to do all the little things that were necessary to operate on an ODA. He took a lot of his personal time to make sure I was a better operator, and he was able to answer every single question I asked him during this entire phase of training.

> "Let all bitterness and wrath and anger and clamor and slander be put away from you, along with all malice. Be kind to one another, tender-hearted, forgiving each other, just as God in Christ also has forgiven you." (Ephesians 4:31-32)

Jon making me return to the field, after having my wisdom teeth pulled, really hurt the respect level I had for him. I had proven my work ethic many times over by that point and thought he should have cared more about my health and less about the training that we were doing. Now that it is in the past, I can see why Jon wanted me out there. It wasn't because I was needed for the operation or because he was trying to make me suffer. He made me return because he knew it would be a good experience for me to have. I can honestly say, I am proud of how I handled the situation. When the pain medication was working, I was able to walk around without too much pain, but when it started to wear off, every single step and every single breath were battles in themselves.

Long after this period of time, I came to admit how much I appreciated the training I received in those woods. Jon knew we had a deployment to Colombia looming over us, and he wanted to make sure I was as prepared to go as possible. I said the Lord's name in vain a lot during that exercise. Even though I wasn't giving God the attention He deserved, He never once left me alone. Nate was an answered prayer for me. My confidence increased substantially when I was still able to be an active member of my team, in spite of my pain. It was another one of those man-card moments where I had no choice but to work through the pain, because for every day I would have taken off, Nate would have been doing the job alone. I am so thankful that the Lord gave me enough strength to endure that training. That training stayed with me, and we reaped what we had sown when we deployed to Colombia.

Colombia

Not long after Operation Frozen Gator, our team had come up for a deployment to Colombia. We would be working with the Jungla, a Colombian counternarcotics and reconnaissance organization. Their primary mission was to find the FARC (revolutionary armed forces of Colombia) drug-making facilities and coca plant farms to destroy them, in an effort to stop polluting the public with narcotics as well as to diminish the power of the FARC by cutting off their revenue. We were only there in an advisory capacity, to help train the Jungla soldiers for mission success. Spanish was not my language; Pashtu was, so I didn't provide as much training as the Spanish speakers on my team did. One day that changed.

I was sitting in the operations center, drinking my morning coffee and doing the daily radio requirements, when Jon came in and said to me, "In two weeks you are giving a two-week course on rappelling and fast-roping to the Jungla. I recommend you learn Spanish," then he walked back out of the operations center like it was no big deal.

I knew rappelling and fast-roping like the back of my hand. Because we trained on both so fervently, subject matter knowledge wasn't an issue. I could teach a monkey how to rappel if you gave me enough time, but two weeks to learn enough Spanish to be able to provide a legitimate course is not an easy task. I spent every waking moment of the next two weeks studying key terms and phrases then writing them down on note cards and laying out all the equipment that I would need, to make sure everything went off without a hitch.

I was very fortunate that the Jungla students I was teaching were experienced rappel and fast-rope operators already. A good chunk of them knew some English. With their English, my terrible Spanish,

283

and a lot of pointing, we had a very successful two-week course. We started on a tower that was thirty feet tall and had four usable stations: two south facing stations, an east facing station, and a west facing station. The two southern stations were attached to a large wall and allowed for two students to rappel down simultaneously. The western wall had a fast-rope connection, and the eastern wall had a simulated aircraft platform that fit four people to simulate operations on an aircraft (which were different than those on a tower). We spent a week working with that tower. We practiced knots, different rappel and belay techniques, how to conduct proper equipment checks, and even had time to allow the Jungla teams an opportunity to practice their team internal standard operating procedure (SOP), which is what small teams are all about. The only way to get proficient is to rehearse, and to rehearse you have to take advantage of all the opportunities you have in front of you. These guys were taking advantage of every minute of it.

The second week's curriculum was very similar to the first week; the main difference was that we were now using an eighty-foot tower, instead of thirty-foot, to rappel and fast-rope down. The guys I was training were fantastic students and in retrospect probably taught me more than I did them. I must admit that watching them jump off the eighty-foot tower headfirst, showing off their machismo, was fun to watch; doing it myself for the first time was a real thrill as well. The very last day of our two-week course, they took me to a secure location near the peak of the highest mountain. It was one that only the local Jungla knew about, and we rappelled down the side of that mountain face and into a river until the sun began to set over ten hours later.

One of the times I was descending the mountain, I managed to land on a bush sticking out of the mountain face that had a hornet's nest in it. I got stung over forty times before I could finally get far enough away from the hornets. Just as I was finally out of the hornets range, my feet hit the wet ground next to the river. As I hit the ground, I slipped and fell onto a plant with prickers that felt like getting shot with bullets (not like normal thorns or prickers). It took a lot of coaxing to get me back up on the cliff face.

I learned a lot about the Jungla during those two weeks. I talked to those men about their personal lives and about the friends of theirs that had been killed recently by the FARC. Just traveling on motorcycles in a different part of the country got some of their friends killed by explosives. They told me about the things the FARC did. Almost every single one of them had a personal reason or story behind their pursuit of joining their elite police unit. They showed me pictures of their children and their wives, comparing them to famous American actresses (like J-Lo and Shakira) to show their knowledge of American culture. We talked about how much they missed their families. I told them I understood how hard it must be to be in the same country as their families but for safety reasons hardly ever being able to see them, but I couldn't really understand. These guys often hid their identity when conducting operations, because the FARC can almost always find someone willing to take a bribe and divulge someone's family information. It happens all the time, and these guys knew it.

They had recently just lost a comrade, only a few months prior. He lost his life removing coca plants from a field they had just raided. They noticed the look of confusion on my face when they said he died removing a plant. So they told me that the FARC would oftentimes booby-trap these plants just in case they were discovered, because they knew the Jungla would dig them up to burn them. A lot of brave men and women have given their lives to prevent cocaine from flooding the streets of Colombia, which also tends to spread into international waters: including the United States. Hearing their stories really made me think about how interconnected we all were as humans, in one way or another, and why the United States' intervention in South America is so important.

After the rappel training was complete, they took me to a few training sites where cocaine was being processed and developed for government study. They built sites identical to that of the FARC, so they could train tactically on the sites as well as learn the fundamentals of how cocaine is refined and processed. They trained to learn as much as possible about the drug that made their enemy wealthy, and I for one can tell you that they all despise the coca plant and all it stands for.

While I loved every minute I was able to get out and train with these guys, my job and specialty tended to keep me close to the operations center where the computers and radios were located. One of the many tedious jobs of any military unit is to inventory all the equipment, monthly, to ensure no items have been lost and that all paperwork associated with those items is in order. This is never fun, and the communication sergeants have a good chunk of the expensive gear, so there is always a lot to lay out, and it can take many hours.

One day while doing one of these layouts, Jon approached me and started laying into me about not being done with a different task that I'd just been given that morning. Instead of maintaining my composure, I shot off at the mouth, saying something along the lines of, "I'm fucking busy, now back off."

We both knew it wasn't my normal reaction, and I think it caught him off guard. Since at least half of my team was present at the time, I think he felt obligated to make sure everyone knew we weren't allowed to talk to him that way. He looked me in the eyes and said, "When you are done with that inventory, bring the gloves [boxing] to the operations center with you."

Now, I don't know how you would take this, but I felt like it was finally going to come to blows. I finished my inventory in record time, ready to get it over with, but I didn't bring the gloves with me. I walked in the operations center where he was waiting, and he didn't even turn around to face me before he asked, "What did I tell you to bring with you?"

I responded, "You told me to bring gloves with me. But I'm not going to do that until we have this talk first. First off, we both know violence isn't the right way to get results, but if you need to fight to feel good about yourself, we don't need gloves, I'm right here."

"Trust me, Kirby," he said, "you don't want to fight me."

I told him I didn't want to fight anybody, especially not my boss, but that we had to work something out because this hostile environment shit just wasn't going to fly anymore. I reminded him that just because I didn't like violence didn't mean I wouldn't resort to it, bringing back a memory from JRTC. I think it took a minute for us both to realize it was either going to get hot really quick, or it was going to cool down, but eventually he told me to go get the gloves and that his intent had never been to fight.

At the time I can't say that I believed him, but I left to go get one pair of gloves. I told him I didn't want him wearing any because I could take my hits and started putting my gloves on. Once they were on, he told me to get in the front lean and rest position. For two hours, he made me do push-ups and other cardiovascular events while wearing the gloves, which made my knuckles feel like cement by the time I was done. When it was all said and done, we sat down and talked about life for a while. I think he wanted to know what was going on that had caused me to spout off at the mouth. He was always in boss mode, so for him to be in a bad mood was normal; but for me to be an asshole, that wasn't normal behavior, and he knew it. I didn't really have any specific reason for acting out, but I really started thinking about it a lot the next couple of weeks.

I started thinking about why I was unhappy, while in the middle of one of the most beautiful countries in the world. My wife and I were going through some issues, and I came to find that unlike in my past, I was no longer able to work and put the family out of my mind. I couldn't stop thinking about my wife, my daughter, and my newborn son. I was thinking about how I was never home for them anymore. I really started noticing that there was a huge void in my life, and I assumed wrongly that it was family I needed to fill that void. Family is something I needed, but even when I was home, I was not a great dad or husband. I felt the void in my heart growing more and more, for years. I don't know if it was the whole boxing glove incident that tipped the scales, but I woke up one morning and it was like a light had gone on in my mind. I didn't have to let anyone talk down to me anymore. I was coming up on my contract end date and wouldn't be around for the next deployment if I didn't reenlist. It was a big pill to swallow because I was committed to retiring for a long time; but for some reason, it just felt right. Even though I had planned my entire life upon my military career up to that point, I decided to let go of the Army that morning.

I walked in to the operations center and told Jon that I wouldn't be joining him on his next trip to Afghanistan: he was shocked. I told him I had decided to prioritize my family after this contract was up, even though it went against all the plans we had discussed about my future in the past. I don't think he thought I would follow through with it, and after a day or two, he went back to acting the same way he had always acted.

A couple of weeks before redeployment back to the United States, Jon asked Nate and me to consolidate all the duplicate items. Jon wanted us to box up and lock up a good chunk of our sensitive items, to save time later on in the redeployment process. This is the last thing any good commo sergeant wants to do, because Murphy's Law states, "Anything that can go wrong will go wrong."

Perhaps Murphy was an 18E because that is the nightmare commo sergeants endure. Things always go wrong. One night while doing a routine radio check, one that normally takes five minutes because of the setup we had, the radio stopped working and started to overheat. We knew we had fried a radio. Normally this means we would just swap it out with a backup that was already programmed and ready to roll. This is the problem, when someone who doesn't fully understand commo micromanages commo guys and forces them to box up and send out all the spare radios. Jon assumed since the radios hadn't malfunctioned yet, why would they now? Well, Jon, being the kind of guy he is, decided to teach Nate and me a lesson. He walked us outside where the antenna was and told us that we could come inside and go to bed when the radio check was complete.

We had already spoken with our higher element using one of the many alternate means of communication and informed them of the issue. They blessed off on postponing the radio check until it could be fixed the following day. Jon didn't care; he made Nate and me sleep outside with a radio that didn't work until the next day when we were allowed to drive to a different location to unbox the spare radios that we hadn't wanted to box in the first place. All things considered, it was a small thing, making us sleep outside, but it reaffirmed in my mind that I would no longer allow myself to be subjected to someone with this irrational behavior. I knew it that following day, while driving back with the radio, that my days in the Army were coming to an end.

Just when I thought the shit show couldn't haven't gotten worse, I ended up getting dysentery or some type of parasite that kept me sticking close to the porcelain throne for the last two months of the deployment. It wasn't something I was unfamiliar with, as I had a lot of issues with dysentery in Iraq as well, but I can tell you firsthand that I can fully understand how people died so easily in the past from dysentery. The food from the local economy very rarely resembled something we eat here in the United States. Just like our ancestors before us, we are not immune to foreign disease and parasites. It did make going out on mission and conducting training very challenging and further reinforced my decision to let my contract end. I had never really sat down and thought about my health before. Now, I just wanted to go home and finally be with my family. No more sickness, no more overbearing bosses, just normal civilian life…whatever that was like.

Retrospective

"Behold, how good and how pleasant it is for
brothers to dwell together in unity!"
—Psalm 133:1

My experience working with the Colombian police and military
units was unlike the training I had done with the Afghan Army, on
many different levels. One that stands out the most now, and even
then, was that the Colombians were very religious people. Many of
the men I worked with in Columbia were Catholic. This deployment
was a lot different than my deployments to Iraq and Afghanistan,
but it was just as important for my personal and professional development. This wasn't a war zone like Iraq or Afghanistan. The men
fighting here had to hide their identities to protect their children. The
risks that these men take every day, just to take drugs off the street, is
an incredible sacrifice and one of the many sacrifices being made in
other countries that directly influences our country. God used that
group of brave Colombians to show me how interconnected we all
are as humans. The earth is so intricately interwoven and it's only
when we live in harmony together, working toward God's purpose,
that we can be truly be effective.

"Bear with each other and forgive one another if
any of you has a grievance against someone. Forgive
as the Lord forgave you." (Colossians 3:13–14)

I would love nothing more than to sit here and say it was Jon's
temper that drove me out of the Army, but it would be a lie. I don't
blame Jon for anything that I once hated him for. It took me a long

time to understand that Jon was never my problem; it was always something inside of me that was missing, making me feel not whole. The alcohol only numbed the pain for a while, but Jon knew something was going on before I even did. I ended up calling Jon a few years later and thanked him for all the things he put me through, good and bad. Because of Jon, my skills grew more each day.

His training provided me with such a wealth of knowledge for future application that I can't even begin to list them all. His continued friendship and mentorship is something I will value until the Lord takes me. I pray that the Lord guides Jon, and all those under his leadership, into prosperous times; that their hands and feet would remain swift for battle. I ask You, Jesus, to send Your angels to stand guard over them in times of war and peace. Give Jon the resilience to face adversity and continue forward on a path of victory. Lord, the last thing I ask in Jesus's name is to strike the fear of the God of Israel into the hearts of every enemy that Jon and his men may encounter, so that Your justice may be known in even the remotest holes of the world where enemies may hide.

Getting Out

A few months after we got home from Colombia, Jon approached me again about staying in the military. He asked me what I wanted for my future. I told him that even though I felt like staying in was what I wanted to do, it just didn't feel like the right thing anymore. We had gotten into more than a few verbal confrontations, and if I'm being honest, once I made the choice to get out, I stopped caring about what people thought about me, which was such a great feeling. None of my buddies from 7112 blamed me for getting out because they all had been a part of the same journey I had been on with Jon's leadership style. I just wasn't willing to reenlist so I could go back to Afghanistan, just to be stuck in an even more stressful environment than the last time. People shooting at me and trying to blow me up is enough stress for me, but having to deal with his temperament for another deployment, I just didn't see myself doing it.

I decided to leave the team. I finished out the rest of my time in the Army on the B team again. I managed to complete another JRTC rotation before my company shipped off to Afghanistan again. I felt ashamed in many ways, watching them all leave without me. I felt like I was betraying them in a way. I have never been one to let someone else do things I could do. It still eats away at my heart and soul that my brothers are still doing hero stuff while I'm at home being a family man now. I was blessed to have outstanding leadership for the last six months or so of my military career, while on the B team. Because of that leadership, I was able to spend a lot of time working on résumés and looking for jobs. I was also able to knock out two semesters worth of classes while still on active duty: putting me on a degree path well before getting out. I was able to help train and equip numerous newly assigned communication sergeants with all the gear and training they would be using in Afghanistan. I showed them the ins and outs of how things were done. I enjoyed being a mentor to others, knowing they would be using the skills I was helping them develop.

On October 8, 2015, less than three weeks before my official last day in the Army, I received a phone call in the middle of the night from my mom, and all I remember her saying is, "He's gone."

My grandfather had passed, after battling several different medical conditions, and she was just calling to let me know. She didn't want to talk and neither did I. I just lay back down in bed and cried myself back to sleep, knowing that heaven gained a very righteous man when he passed. Sometimes I wonder if it wasn't some kind of sign that my grandfather passed as my military career as a Green Beret came to an end. I don't doubt that my grandfather's prayers helped to keep me alive throughout all of my deployments, when I didn't yet know how to pray for myself.

Getting out the Army was one of the hardest choices I have ever made. For ten years the Army was my life. It consumed me physically, mentally, emotionally, and spiritually; so now that the time had come to get out, I didn't really know what to do with my life. I knew that pursuing an education was a no-brainer, because having a degree can often be the difference in getting a job or not, plus I had the Post 9/11 GI Bill: a benefit for soldiers providing them opportunities to go to college. But seeing as I got out in October of 2015, I had a few months before the next semester started at the University of West Florida.

During those few months, I applied for a job at a local Verizon wireless store in Pace, Florida. I was hired in the beginning of 2016. The job at Verizon was a great-paying job with an extremely professional atmosphere but it put my degree on the back burner again. At the time it was worth the money, and I dove into the wireless industry headfirst, again, finding reasons to put my family on the back burner. I worked my butt off for one of the most professional managers with Verizon Wireless, Lavon. He was an amazing boss to work for and was one heck of a leader. He was the one who unwittingly helped me acclimate into civilian society. I never told him how

293

hard I struggled every day, when I was forced to listen to people come in and complain about their cell phone problems like the world was ending.

Being around a lot of people is still something I don't like very much, but by working at Verizon with superior management, I was able to force myself into appearing normal, at least on most days. I'm sure my coworkers there would tell you I was crazy, but they put up with me and helped me out on a day-to-day basis, as I transitioned back into the "normal world." Even though I got out of active duty, I wasn't able to completely let go of the military life and remained in the National Guard. I enlisted right after getting out of active duty. I didn't really know what to expect, but I just felt it wasn't quite time to let the Army go completely. My unit was in Atlanta, Georgia, which is about a five-hour drive, each way, every month. I was required to travel up there for a weekend a month and two weeks in the summer. So while working for Verizon, I was also balancing the National Guard and my family life simultaneously. A lot of things started to happen that really sent my life into a whirlwind.

One of the first factors that affected me was my physical condition. While in active duty, my body had been battered and bruised more than once, but I had always felt good enough to work out with the guys. I was hitting the gym twice a day, throwing in cardio routines, to include ruck marching for years; even though I had aches and pains from previous injuries, they were never substantial enough to truly affect my life.

Once I got out of the military, I was no longer working out two or more times a day. My lower back went from the occasional back spasm or tightness to having back spasms every day: sometimes severe enough to inhibit safe driving. While I want to say it was a gradual process, it is actually quite scary to admit how fast I felt my back deteriorating. I started to seek the medical treatment that I didn't have time for while I was still serving. I started going to the VA and got my back imaged. I also pursued a civilian doctor for more tests and a more thorough workup. At the age of twenty-eight, my back looked like an elderly man who had spent his life doing hard labor. The back pain came at a critical point in my life because I was just trying to start enjoying the things I loved to do, outdoors, and was finding myself more limited with each passing day.

I ended up leaving Verizon, for a number of reasons, which is quite unfortunate, as I really enjoyed my time there. I got out of the military to be able to spend time with my family and to be more active in my kid's lives. Unfortunately, Verizon was a two-hour round trip from my house, and with the hours I was working I still wasn't seeing my family. I was trying to get my own company up and running. I was hoping to teach others the outdoor skill sets that I learned and enjoyed doing; I also wanted to set up some scout camps for Boy and Girl Scouts, to teach outdoor skills. This was the hope anyway, until my back really caught up to me.

With the reality of my physical limitations becoming more clear, I was having to let go of the post-military professional plans that I made; I was also having to let go of the physical activities that I loved to do and that brought me the only peace I was able to find. I sold my fishing kayak because it put a lot of pressure on my lower back, and kayak fishing was my favorite hobby. I was becoming very depressed and regretful of my decision to get out of the military. Yet I was glad that I was lucky enough to have made it as far as I did before having body issues.

Retrospective

> Concerning this I implored the Lord three times that it might leave me. And He has said to me, "My grace is sufficient for you, for power is perfected in weakness." Most gladly, therefore, I will rather boast about my weaknesses, so that the power of Christ may dwell in me. (2 Corinthians 12:8–9)

So much happened in such a small window of time. I hit new levels of low after getting out of the Army. When I started having back pains, it was just so inconvenient. I had so many new ideas and plans, and nothing was working out. Verizon was a great workplace, and I credit Lavon as being a key civilian mentor whose friendship I value very much. When he hired me, I felt like I needed a victory in my life, and he gave it to me when I was as far from God as I've ever been. My back has become such an issue that I have had to change my entire way of life. Until recently, I was very bitter because of it.

Sometimes God will allow us to struggle because He knows that it will bring us closer to Him. It took a long time for me to realize that God wasn't the one at fault for the way I felt or the emptiness inside of me. It can take a person's entire world changing to cause someone to come to God, or come back to God. I knew about God, but I didn't know where He was. I only ever noticed that I didn't see Him and never paid any attention to the people in my life that I know now were put there by God. In all my ways, I never once looked at myself as being the reason I couldn't see God. I was never really looking for Him.

> "You will seek Me and find Me when you search for me with all your heart." (Jeremiah 29:13)

It is important to me that I point out a major transformation that happened between when I got out of Active Duty and when I wrote this book. During that time, I have made it clear that I have come to know my Lord Jesus. He has opened my eyes as I have sought to know the truth. If you will reflect on my perspective of Jon during my time with 7th Group, we can all agree that I viewed him with respect for his rank and accomplishments, but mostly with contempt because of his leadership style. I truly had a hard time seeing anything positive in that situation.

Hindsight is almost always much clearer, and even more so when we are walking with Jesus. I can now look back on that time, and there was a lot of good that came out of those experiences. Good that I could not see, or chose not to see, during those times. My hatred overshadowed anything positive. This is not something that I think is uncommon for many of us. Sometimes our vision is so clouded that we fail to recognize the blessings God sends us. Those blessings may hurt, for a time, but God is allowing us to go through those hard times for a reason. I also believe that God can appoint relationships for us, and when those relationships have potential to bear good fruit, the devil can twist our emotions and perception to ruin those relationships.

Here is what I now know about Jon. Jon was, during my time in 7th Group, and remains today, a man that God is using for His purpose. Jon is supportive of me publishing these stories, though those stories did not paint him in a positive light. If I believed this book could help bring someone to Jesus, Jon wasn't concerned about how he looked. Today, I highly respect Jon not only for his accomplishments, but also for his character that I have finally come to know. His friendship, is something that I highly value. After the experiences we have had and the very honest conversations we have had, I am more than a little surprised that he still keeps in touch and genuinely cares if my family and I are doing well. Jon's friendship is something that I believe was appointed by God.

Throughout this book, without the retrospective pieces, you have seen Jon in a negative light. I had to meditate heavily before writing the chapters with Jon, because by the time I wrote this book,

Jon and I had become good friends. It was a challenge for me to revisit a time in my life when I was greatly overtaken by spiritual warfare. I told you some stories that greatly affected me, to explain why and how I felt the way I did during those times. Most of the stories that would adequately portray that time of my life, I left out.

All of the details surrounding my time working for Jon formed pieces of the puzzle. I could only see each situation for what it was. I never stepped back to see the whole picture: the completed puzzle. What good came out of Jon's leadership? The team. Our team was extremely close, even compared to other cohesive military units. I had friends who would sit beside me when I was stuck working, long after everyone was released. My teammates couldn't do any of the work for me, so that I could be finished earlier. They didn't sit next to me to contribute. They sat next to me, just so I had company and support. Our friendships grew to the extent it did, because of the stuff we had to endure together. Jon put our team under intense pressure, but we didn't get crushed, we came out as diamonds from the rough. Jon pushed all of us further than any one of us could handle on our own. We had to learn to rely on, and trust in, one another to help us when the pressure was too much.

Throughout the few years I worked for Jon, he took a team of fresh Green Berets, and in months, had us competing for missions with teams far more experienced than ours. It was only because of Jon, and how hard he pushed us, that we are able to say we did all the things that we did. Every single time we trained, he was the first one in and last one out. He almost always jumped out of the aircraft first, rappelled first, jumped into the water first, etc. He never once asked me to do anything that I had not already seen him do. He never asked us to do anything he wouldn't do, and he proved it time and time again.

It was important for me to portray Jon negatively so that you could see and feel how I felt when I was living through those tumultuous times. Likewise, it is just as important that you understand, Jon was never the problem. I was under heavy spiritual attack and because I wasn't following the Lord, I was completely unable to fight back appropriately. Jon may have had a leadership style that went against the grain, but I can honestly say I never would have been able to do what he did (especially with the same success rate).

God is using you, Jon, and I pray that you remain receptive to His calling so that we can see you do even greater things. Thank you sincerely for helping me to prepare for what God will ask of me in the future. Even when things got heated, you never stopped looking out for me or the guys. I am proud to have been on that team under your leadership. I am forever grateful and look forward to seeing how God will use you next.

We should be slow to burn bridges and cut off communication with people whom we may not like. God could have sent those individuals, for a purpose, either for us or for them. Through Jon, I learned my breaking point wasn't what I thought it was. Jon taught me that I could do more than I thought I could. Jon forced me to be reliant on others, because often the expectations set were unattainable for me alone. Each and every time I fell short, God sent someone along side me to assist or help me. Jon pulled out of me, more than I thought I had.

Turning Point

While all these things were going on in my life, I still had the National Guard responsibilities to ensure were being met. With my unit being a good five-hour drive away, I spent a lot of time alone in a car listening to music and thinking about things going on in my life. In early 2016, I was driving home from one of these National Guard drills at about 8:00 p.m. when something happened to me that changed my life.

I remember feeling what could best be explained as an ice-cold, yet somehow warm, bucket of slow moving oil being poured on my head and traveling down my entire body. Once my feet were immersed, a feeling that I can only describe as "electricity like in nature" started pulsing throughout my entire body. Liquid love is what I now think of when I reflect on how it felt. My body began to shake uncontrollably. I was driving on a highway just off of I-65, and now I was fearful that I might be experiencing some medical condition that I was unaware I had or perhaps something was wrong with the car. I don't remember pulling over, but I ended up parked on the side of the highway. As soon as my car was in park, the most supernatural thing to ever happen to me occurred.

One second I was on the side of a highway in Alabama, and the next I was in the Middle East. I was standing among rows of tents, just watching people walk past me, but no one appeared to notice me. One man walked right in front of me and I could smell his body odor. I don't know how long this vision was, but I don't believe it lasted very long. I know beyond a shadow of a doubt that I have never been to the place I was seeing. My focus was shifted as I felt the Lord say to me without words, "These are my people, love them and help them as if you would me."

As fast as the vision started, it ended, leaving me sitting in a car on the side of the road with my windows rolled down and the power turned off in the vehicle (neither of which I remember doing). The engine was running but all electronics and lights were off.

Almost as fast as I realized I was back in my car, I began shaking violently again. I was suddenly aware of the truth that I had denied my entire life. There was in fact a God and HE knew me. I sat there in my car and started talking to God.

I asked out loud, "Is this your purpose for me, Lord? Am I supposed to be helping these people somehow?" Once again, as if in response to my question, I felt that same liquid love flow down my body, from my head to my feet.

I became suddenly aware that Bible prophecies were being fulfilled. This last statement is critical in that it was a pebble that started an avalanche for me, because I went from not knowing the first thing about Bible prophecies to somehow knowing they were being fulfilled. I didn't know it at the time, but I believe I was filled with the Holy Spirit that night, and the Holy Spirit was warning me about the future. I don't know how long I was sitting in my car before I realized I was still parked: alone and in the darkness.

I tried to call my wife, but my cell phone not only wouldn't connect with my vehicle via Bluetooth, but my cell phone itself also wasn't working. My cell phone didn't work again, until after I had driven away from that spot.

I want to take a pause here and tell you why this event holds such meaning. Before this event, the single, only church services I had ever attended had been Catholic, and even since I was a kid, I hated church and everything in it. I guess I believed in God, but it was more because my mom always told me He was real than because I thought He was. I had never in my life thought about or cared about Bible prophecy. I hadn't read the Bible, and I didn't have any interest in doing so.

I was not living a Christian lifestyle. I was drinking, looking at pornography, yelling at my kids for no good reason, and waking up in nightly sweats thinking about the men whose lives were lost in Iraq because of my failures. On the surface I was a happy guy, but deep down, for years I was empty. I was only living my life by going through the motions.

The only times I had ever thought about God were during the times of pure desperation; when I was walking through the woods doing land navigation with two sprained ankles, or jumping out of an aircraft, or after driving over an IED in Iraq that was detonated by a vehicle behind me. These were the times I thought about God— when I feared for my life, not when I was driving home from drill. I don't know why the Lord spoke to me that night, but the series of events following that night altered my life and my family's lives forever. In John 8:32, Jesus says, "and you will know the truth, and the truth will make you free," and I became free, indeed.

I was thinking about this vision the entire drive home. At one point I remember thinking a thought that went against the grain for me. Prior to this incident, I was an extreme advocate for keeping people out of America from terrorist-laden countries. I knew what the radical ideology did to people. I had picked up body parts on more than one occasion after radicals "expressed" their beliefs. I knew what could happen if we opened up the floodgates and let wolves pour in with the sheep—which at the time, politically, was exactly what was being debated. The immigration policy of the United States of America has recently come under scrutiny by many people across the globe. I just wasn't okay with bringing the evil I had seen into our country and near our children, knowing that extremists hide among refugees.

When I started contemplating the vision I had and what it could mean, I realized that I had a heart of stone towards the people I wanted to keep out of my country. At that time, my first thought was that Jesus wanted me to help those refugees. It was as though a light switch had been turned on and my biased emotional walls came crumbling down. I couldn't hate anyone for wanting to leave their war-torn countries. I wanted to love them and understand their struggles.

It was also during this short drive home that two very significant realizations came to the front of my mind. The first was that after this vision, I knew as a matter of fact that Jesus Christ is coming soon, and that if He had already come, I wouldn't have gone with him. I believe this was specifically referencing the rapture of the church. The second realization was that Biblical prophecies were coming true and that we are living in prophetic times. I didn't understand either of these thoughts.

When I got home after finishing the last hour and a half of driving in silence, I told my wife everything that happened. I think she might have thought I was slightly nuts, but to her credit, she went and bought me a Bible the very next day, per my request. That day I started reading the Bible. I began pouring over the prophetic books in the Bible: Ezekiel, Jeremiah, and Daniel, just to name a few of the Old Testament books. I also read the four gospels, soaking in every single word our Lord Jesus Christ spoke during his ministry.

I spent about three months learning and studying Bible prophecies and reading materials published by people who spent their careers studying them. Perry Stone is a God-gifted man, and spoke truth many times directly into my heart and soul on his Manna-Fest program. He is filled with the Holy Spirit and has been a major influence in my pursuit of truth. The only time I have ever experienced such a carnal desire to learn, like I have now toward Bible prophecies, had been during AIT when I discovered my love of HUMINT. Believe me, my desire to learn all I could about Jesus far surpasses that desire.

It is hard to put into words the yearning I got, to learn everything I could about the Bible and Jesus, but to say it consumed me would be a major understatement. I learned that many biblical scholars were preaching that we are nearing the imminent return of Jesus Christ. The most alarming part about this whole experience for me was that because of the Army life, I was very much aware of the state of the world and the things happening in it. The more prophesies that I studied, the more it rang true to me that we were living in those times: because I felt as though my experiences pointed in the same direction.

The discernment of what was true and what wasn't became vividly clear to me. As I read about these prophecies, I just knew they were true. I really began to struggle internally with how to process the information I was consuming. I was reading about Jesus, but I sure didn't feel saved. It felt like a heavy weight on my chest, knowing that we were in the end of days and I didn't even know where I stood with the Lord.

Two months or so after my vision, I saw a large sign on the side of Highway 90 in Pace, Florida, for a church: Pace Assembly of God.

The pastor there, Joey Rogers, was holding a *Prophecy Files* event where biblical prophecies happening in current events would be discussed. To most people, seeing that sign could easily be a coincidence; but those people don't know the prayers that I was praying before seeing that sign. Many times I asked God to show me the truth and to help fix my life so that I could be saved. The thought of going to church never crossed my mind until seeing that sign. The same liquid love covered me again, as soon as I read the sign. Thoughts of going back to church, after having been raised in one and hating it, and then getting this supernatural feeling were both signs that were out of the norm for me. I put the date into our calendar and told my wife that I felt drawn to go to this *Prophecy Files* event two weeks later, and she told me to go.

My life was altered again that night. Pastor Rogers, a man whom I'd never met or even heard of before this, began talking to the people in the church about things that are happening in the world. Everything he said was accurate and correlated with the things I had just spent months studying. As a Human Intelligence Collector and a Special Forces operator, part of my job was to discern the truth from the lies, and I believe Pastor Rogers spoke the truth that night to me. He started talking about the Holy Spirit outpouring in the final days where in Joel 2:28 it says, "It will come about after this that I will pour out My Spirit on all mankind; and your sons and daughters will prophesy, your old men will dream dreams, your young men will see visions." I read this passage only hours before arriving that night, and when Pastor Rogers quoted those same verses, I felt the liquid love cover me again; only this time, that feeling didn't leave me the entire time I sat in that church that night. What are the chances that he would mention this one verse of the thousands to choose from?

Then he stopped speaking for a moment. In the middle of his message, he said into his microphone something along the lines of "If you are feeling the Holy Spirit fill your body right now, raise your hands." I suddenly became aware that the liquid love feeling was the Holy Spirit moving in my body, explaining why it happened at precise moments of revelation. I also became aware that Pastor Rogers was also filled with the Holy Spirit and that the Holy Spirit was talking directly to me through Pastor Rogers: when he said into his microphone that Jesus was the answer to the questions I had. I realized at that time my hand was in the air, without conscious thought, and that I had been called to this meeting.

That night I accepted Jesus as my Lord and Savior, alone; and on my drive home from the church, I officially denounced the devil. Since that day, I have been baptized and regularly attend church service at Pace Assembly, where I am constantly blown away by the revelations being unveiled there. My wife and I will pray together, to ask for an answer from God about a very specific question, and the next time we go to church, Pastor Rogers amazingly answers these questions in such a way that it is undeniably the Holy Spirit speaking to us through him. He does this on a weekly basis. I have come to learn that is what church is all about. It's not about the routine or the singing or the statues; it's about being among fellow believers in a place where the Holy Spirit can use a man of God to literally speak out loud the answers to our prayers. God can and does speak to us in many ways, through Holy Spirit filled pastors is just one way, but I want to hear from God anytime He has something to say to me. So we go out of our way to not miss services.

I had never seen people speak in tongues before attending this church. Outside of the book of Acts, I didn't really have much contextual insight as to what it was all about. But let me tell you what, seeing a gray-haired eighty-plus-year-old woman screaming unintelligible languages in the middle of a church service shocked me very much. While I don't fully understand most biblical intricacies quite yet, I know strange and supernatural when I see and hear it, and that's what this was. It pierced me to my bones, hearing an unfamiliar tongue come out of some country grandma near Pace, Florida. I'll never forget that first time, and I have been very fortunate to hear great men and women of God break into tongues many times since then. This is just another way God speaks to us.

Since I have accepted Jesus into my life, my marriage has improved, my relationship with my kids improved, and my overall mental and emotional health were restored. I have found something that I have been searching for my entire life: peace. I stopped drinking alcohol and will have my undergraduate degree around the same time this book publishes. While I am far from perfect, I continue to try and allow Jesus into more aspects of my life. I actively seek God's face, and He has blessed my life greatly.

When I thought the deployments and hardships had taught me to be thankful for what I had, finding Jesus truly hammered home the message. All aspects of my life are changing. I anxiously wait for the Lord to open the next door I was meant to walk through, only this time I won't be walking through it for me. This time, and forever on, I walk for my King...Jesus Christ.

Retrospective

"It will come about after this that I will pour
out My Spirit on all mankind; and your sons
and daughters will prophesy, your old men will
dream dreams, your young men will see visions."
—Joel 2:28

I have always believed there was something greater than us in the universe, but throughout my entire life and military career, I often doubted the existence of a loving Creator. After having spent over a decade in the military, I was mentally, physically, and emotionally exhausted. I never expected to find joy in teaching HUMINT to soldiers, while in the National Guard, who have not yet seen combat. Even more of a surprise was the revelation I received from God. When the Holy Spirit filled me in the car that night, I believe He did so for a few reasons. I believe God wanted to fill the void I had in my heart and life. Without the military in my life, my purpose was gone on a day-to-day basis. I also believe God wanted to replace my hardened heart with a heart that would reflect the love He had for all His children.

"Moreover, I will give you a new heart and put a
new spirit within you; and I will remove the heart
of stone from your flesh and give you a heart of
flesh." (Ezekiel 36:26)

I never realized how much I had been searching for Jesus, until He revealed himself to me in the car. To be filled with and to experience the love of Jesus Christ is a feeling that has no earthly comparison. I broke down crying in the car that night for feeling such hatred toward my fellow man. I had taught myself to be calloused and to hate people because of the evil I have seen and experienced. Now I know I can love everyone, even if I don't agree with his or her words or actions. Everything I had been built and designed for was to help other people and to protect the innocent from evil, but I allowed the devil to twist and influence my thoughts. Since I had not searched for God, the devil had deeply inserted himself into my heart. I was wrongly viewing people with anger that were being forced from their homes by terrorists. That night, I knew that God's people were hurting. I almost felt as if the Lord wanted me to feel what He feels toward his lost and hurting sheep. I had spent years of my life only worrying about American lives and the lives of those who helped Americans: never truly grasping the severity of life in Asia, the Middle East and Africa. God created everyone, and He will always move His people to help those in need.

I believe now, after prayer and studying God's Word, that God gave me the gift of discernment in Iraq. When I was ashamed and humbled by the feeling that I had failed to protect my fellow soldiers, the Holy Spirit intervened and helped me to discern, sometimes just by looking at someone, when someone was being truthful or not.

> "For the Word of God is living and active and sharper than any two-edged sword, and piercing as far as the division of soul and spirit, of both joints and marrow, and able to judge the thoughts and intentions of the heart." (Hebrews 4:12)

I have been able to relive moments of my life that have haunted me for years, and I can now see God everywhere I look. He gave me friends I didn't deserve; he gave me a family that I have far too often turned my back on; and he gave me a sense of patriotism and loyalty that matches that of my grandfather during World War II. God walked with me every step of my journey, always being nearby, even in my times of doubt. I never thought in my wildest dreams that I would end up going back to church, until the series of events transpired that you just read. I can understand skepticism of a story like mine, because I have been a skeptic. However, when God opens up your eyes, you are able to see things you weren't able to see before. It's like having a veil lifted, finally seeing life the way it was meant to be viewed: as God intended.

While I still struggle with sin and temptation, I am able to see the long game now. Our souls are meant to be free and joyful, forever worshipping our Lord and Savior. It was only after I confessed to God that I couldn't beat my alcohol or pornography addiction alone that he began to show me how to change my ways. Even though I am still far from perfect, I sleep well knowing God loves me in spite of my weaknesses.

The Lord spoke to my heart that night about the state of the world and the people on it. He told me without words that the end is near and it's time to pick up my cross and to follow him. I hadn't heard of or cared about any biblical prophecies before this instance. The Catholic services I have attended didn't spend much time teaching those lessons. I was terrified when I realized how close we are to the end, and that if the Lord had come for his people that night, I would not have gone with them, nor would my wife or children. I let my previous experiences in churches prevent me from finding a church with people who have genuine love for one another, and where I could be well taught about Jesus and His word. Honestly, I didn't realize I could experience something different in a different church; I didn't know that there are churches that aren't concerned with schedules or rituals but are more concerned with experiencing God's presence and God's glory.

I didn't have any desire to write this book, or to study Bible prophecy in the middle of taking college courses. I didn't want to start tithing 10 percent of our already-limited income. I didn't want any of that. I most certainly didn't want to relive and write down past experiences that have pained me to my core, but the Lord Jesus Christ is coming for His sheep, and He is coming soon. It's not up to me, or anyone else, whether Jesus comes or not. Jesus said in *Matthew 24:30* that *"the sign of the Son of Man will appear in the sky, and then all the tribes of the earth will mourn, and they will see the Son of Man coming on the clouds of the sky with power and great glory."* The only decision I have to make every day now is whether or not I am willing to stare down my temptations and pick up my cross, to follow Him. I look for the coming of the Lord, now more than ever; as I watch the world destroy itself and the devil seeks to deceive as many people as possible about the truth.

God loves each and every one of us as His children. I no longer view people as good or bad; instead, everyone is a tool to be used by either good or evil. We choose, with every action and every word, who we are allowing to influence us. I can now see that everything here on earth is a reflection of the spiritual battles happening above us. Instead of seeing terrorists, I see people who need Christ. Instead of seeing people as cowards for fleeing ISIS or groups like it: I feel sympathy for them. God is the only one who can undo years of hatred in a fleeting moment. God also led me to Pace Assembly of God so that I could learn from a true servant of God: Pastor Joey Rogers. God has called me, and I will give my life in service to Him.

Conclusion

"But I do not consider my life of any account as dear to myself, so that I may finish my course and the ministry which I received from the Lord Jesus, to testify solemnly of the gospel of the grace of God."

—Acts 20:24

We can't shy away from the hard questions; instead, we need to embrace them openly, and read our Bibles. Ignorance was not bliss, the moment I realized the Lord is coming soon and I was not prepared. It has been almost three years since the night I came to know God was absolutely real. Since then, I don't think I have gone even one day without reading the Bible, doing research on bible prophecy and current events, and researching archeological excavations and the evidence being found that supports biblical history. Every day that I read the Word of God, something new is revealed to me. The more I read the Bible the more layers of dirt are removed from my eyes that have blurred my vision all of these years.

The Bible is a collection of so many stories. Through all of these stories, I can see what God instructs and how God works in those situations; that way, when I face a similar situation, I know how to respond and I know what promises God has made that I can stand on. Reading these stories helps me to recognize how God works on our behalf. No matter what our situations look like, there are answers within the Word of God, we have only ever had to pick up the book and read with an open heart. I have read the entire Bible now. Many of the books within the Bible I have read dozens of times. Each time I re-read the same verses, I gain a deeper knowledge.

I can look back on my life now and see God at work everywhere, but what if I had the knowledge of God while I was walking through those difficult times? Perhaps, I wouldn't have been surprised to see God show up. I could have seen Him all along. I could have spent all of those years knowing of the promises God made to us. I could have saved myself so much heartache and potentially even physical pain, if I was able to effectively defend myself against every attack of the devil.

The flip side of not knowing God for all of those years, even though He was at work in my life the entire time: now that I can see and recognize the truth, I basically started my journey with thirty years of experience with God. No one will ever be able to convince me that God isn't real or doesn't care about me. I have years of evidence that proves otherwise. So for anyone in a situation similar to mine, once you start reading the Bible and looking for where God was all along, you will also have a lifetime worth of experience to stand on. That foundation isn't easily shaken, but it does take work to uncover. You can think of it as though you are excavating God's work in your life. The more you read the Bible and pray seeking God, the more you will be digging up and dusting off the evidence that was there the whole time.

> "Trust in the Lord with all your heart and do
> not lean on your own understanding. In all your
> ways acknowledge Him, and He will make your
> paths straight." (Proverbs 3:5–6)

Reading the Word of God is what feeds our spirits and our souls. While Jesus was in the wilderness and fasting for forty days, the devil was trying to tempt Him with the prospect of food. In Matthew 4:4, Jesus responded to the devil, "It is written, 'Man shall not live on bread alone, but on every word that proceeds out of the mouth of God.'"

I may have only recently started to walk my life with Jesus, but I know that I can trust in Him to always be there, because He always has been. Before I had any desire to look for or follow the Lord, He was there for me, never failing to pick me up and carry me when I had reached the end of myself. I believe Jesus shows off beyond the hundred percent thresholds; anytime I gave one-hundred-and-ten percent, the first hundred might have been me but the last ten was all Jesus. I don't have to guess what His character is. I don't have to guess whether or not I can trust in Him. I don't have to guess whether or not God is good. God has shown me exactly who He is to me, throughout my entire life; I just didn't see it before.

I can probably best explain it by talking about the trust I had in my fellow soldiers, after years of serving with them. I knew from going through difficult situations and unfavorable circumstances that I could rely on many of those I served along side. I learned who would keep a level head under extreme stress. I learned who was willing to give up sleep or food or comfort, just to help me or someone else out. I learned who worked hard and who could be trusted to get the work done. Over time, I learned whom I could rely on and trust in, because they had shown me their character and values. This is something many veterans say they don't usually experience outside of the military; the comradery is usually unmatched in the civilian world. Sometimes it isn't until we are in a life-or-death situation that our true convictions become known. The military breeds comradery because of the situations soldiers have to endure with one another.

The trust I had in a few soldiers after four weeks of SERE school, or after a four- to seventeen-month deployment, can't compare to the absolute trust I have in Jesus for Him never once leaving me or forsaking me. My fellow soldiers were willing to die for me, or any of our other teammates, but Jesus did die for all of us. His credibility is unmatched.

I don't know God's whole plan for me, but I am so joyful that He has opened my eyes to see Him. I don't deserve the love He has for me, but I know that I have never been more satisfied and filled with peace than I have been since I invited Jesus Christ into my life.

To every young man or young woman: I don't care what your life looks like or what choices you have made, God can turn everything around for you. If you are looking for a way to serve our great nation, American military service members are a force for good in

313

this world. Our military is not perfect and never will be, because it is filled with and run by fallible humans. God uses our great men and women in service, though, to bring hope and help to many areas around the world. We fight for values and principles worth fighting for. I started as a punk kid who was constantly in trouble with my school, the law, and my family. I ended up making something of myself, and that same opportunity that I had is available to so many.

To our existing military members: God bless all of you. Thank you for holding the line. So many have fought and died for our American way of life, and it is only because of the continuous sacrifices of our great military that we have preserved that way of life. If you are yearning for more, or believe you have reached your full potential with your current unit/military occupation, I encourage you to try out for one of our elite forces. My joining Special Forces was the best accomplishment of my military career and it wasn't because I earned a special award and beret. I was blessed to work along side some of the greatest warriors this country has ever produced. It was a great privilege of mine to work with and learn from the men who earned the Green Beret.

To all of our nations veterans: thank you for your service. I started to spiral, after I returned to civilian life. I struggled to live with the things I have seen and done. I don't know if you have struggled, but if you have not found peace yet, please know that you can. Your career may not have looked like mine. You may have seen or done much worse than I have. No matter what story you have, if you are struggling, Jesus is the answer. Jesus is the key to hope, peace, love, joy, forgiveness, healing, salvation, and anything else we have need of.

To everyone facing an obstacle or a situation that seems impossible to overcome: don't lose hope. Never give up. Give everything you have and then keep going. God already has a plan and a purpose for your life. God has made promises to us. We just need to not give up, before He has had the opportunity to deliver on His promises. If you haven't pushed yourself further than you thought possible, give it a try.

To anyone struggling with the will to live: Jesus is the answer. You are already so loved. God is real and cares about you specifically. If you haven't found the evidence of that yet, please seek the truth. If you don't believe anyone in your life cares for you, please find a church that is filled with the body of Christ; you will find people who would love nothing more than to come along side of you and walk with you, while you learn of the love, purpose, and plans Jesus has for you. If you can't find a church, you can stream the Pace Assembly of God services online. Pastor Joey Rogers is a great man of God and a humble shepherd. If you pray and have questions, God can use him to give you the answers.

God bless you on your personal journey. I pray that the Lord bestows the gift of discernment on you, so that you may see and hear the truth that is Jesus Christ. Thank you so very much for taking your precious and valuable time to read about my life's journey and how God has affected my life. I hope my story and struggle helps bring you, and those close to you, even closer to our Heavenly Father.

If I can just leave you with one question: if God has done all of this for me, what has God done for you? If you haven't done so already, I hope you seek and find the thread of God's work in your life.

"So faith comes from hearing, and hearing by the word of Christ." (Romans 10:17)

CPSIA information can be obtained
at www.ICGtesting.com
Printed in the USA
JSHW010256131119
2314JS00008BC/7